William Cowper, William Trego Webb

Selections From Letters

William Cowper, William Trego Webb

Selections From Letters

ISBN/EAN: 9783744710893

Printed in Europe, USA, Canada, Australia, Japan

Cover: Foto ©Thomas Meinert / pixelio.de

More available books at **www.hansebooks.com**

SELECTIONS FROM

COWPER'S LETTERS

EDITED
WITH INTRODUCTION AND NOTES

BY
W. T. WEBB, M.A.
LATE PROFESSOR OF ENGLISH LITERATURE, PRESIDENCY
COLLEGE, CALCUTTA

London
MACMILLAN AND CO.
AND NEW YORK
1895

PREFACE.

In making this selection of Cowper's letters I have kept two main objects in view: to set forth all the phases of his life and character, and to illustrate his greatest work, *The Task.* For students of Cowper the book may thus form a useful companion volume to my edition of that poem in this Series.

For much that is valuable in my Introduction my grateful acknowledgments are due to the Rev. H. T. Griffith's "Introduction" and "Life of Cowper" in Vols. I. and II. of *Cowper's Poems* in the Clarendon Press Series. And as regards both my Introduction and Notes, I have to express my indebtedness to the excellent *Life of William Cowper* by Mr. Thomas Wright, Principal of Cowper School, Olney.

W. T. W.

CONTENTS.

LETTERS FROM WESTON UNDERWOOD.

LETTERS FROM EARTHAM.

Letters from Weston Underwood.

Letters from Mundsley.

INTRODUCTION.

WILLIAM COWPER was born on the 15th of November (Old Style), 1731, at Great Berkhampstead, in Hertfordshire—a parish of which his father was rector. His mother was a Donne, of the same family as the poet of that name, and descended by several lines from Henry III. She died when Cowper was six years old, and he was sent to a boarding-school. In 1741 he was entered at Westminster School, which he left at eighteen. He was soon after articled to an attorney in London, in whose office Thurlow, the future Lord Chancellor, was his fellow-clerk. In 1752 he took chambers in the Temple, and in 1754 was called to the Bar. In the former year he was seized with his *first derangement*, and for change of scene visited Southampton in company with Mr. Thomas Hesketh and his party. During these years much of his time was spent at the house of his uncle, Ashley Cowper, with his daughters, Harriet (afterwards Lady Hesketh) and Theodora Jane, with whom he fell in love, and who is the "Delia" of his early love-poems. He gave his time to literature and the society of the wits of the "Nonsense Club" rather than to law, and renewed his connexion with his old Cowper's LIFE.

school-fellows, Churchill, Colman, Lloyd, and Thornton. In 1763 he received the nomination to the office of Clerk of the Journals of the House of Lords, but visions of opposition to the appointment, and fears of his own incapacity, so wrought upon a mind already weakened by an attack of melancholy arising from his lonely surroundings, that he went mad (his *second derangement*) and attempted suicide, his madness taking the form of religious despair. After eighteen months in Dr. Cotton's private asylum at St. Albans he recovered, and in 1765 was placed by his relatives at Huntingdon. Here he met the Unwin family, with whom he lived for the next two years. On the death of the Rev. Morley Unwin he accompanied his widow (the "Mary" of his *Letters* and poetry) to Olney, in Buckinghamshire, on the river Ouse, where he came under the influence of the Rev. John Newton, curate of the town. In 1773 his old malady again overtook him (his *third derangement*), and he again attempted self-destruction. After his recovery he diverted his mind with carpentering, with drawing, and with gardening—a favourite pursuit; and found amusement in keeping three tame hares. In 1780 a period of literary activity began, and at Mrs. Unwin's suggestion he produced his First Volume, comprising *The Progress of Error*, with the other Moral Satires, which was published in March, 1782. Mr. Newton wrote a preface to it, which was first prefixed to the fifth edition, 1790. Meanwhile, in 1781, Cowper formed the acquaintance of Lady Austen, widow of Sir Robert Austen, who subsequently came to live at Olney, and who inspired the *Task* as well as *John Gilpin*. These two poems, with *Tirocinium*, made up his Second Volume, which was published in July, 1785. The *Task* was commenced in the summer of 1783; and finished, revised, and transcribed in the autumn of 1784. Before its publication a rupture took place between Lady Austen and the poet, and in May, 1784, she finally left Olney. At this time he became intimate with the Throckmortons, and in the same year he began his translation of Homer, which was finished in September, 1790, and published in July, 1791. In June, 1786, Lady Hesketh paid him a visit, and by her care he and Mrs. Unwin were transferred at the close of the year to Weston Underwood, a neighbouring place—a removal which was closely followed by the death of William Unwin. In the following year occurred his *fourth derangement*, and in December, 1791, Mrs. Unwin's health began to fail. After writing a fragment of a projected poem, *The Four Ages*, he undertook an edition of Milton, which brought him into communication with Hayley, to whom in August, 1792, he paid a visit of six weeks at Eartham, near Chichester. In January, 1794, came the final breakdown, which necessitated the removal in July, 1795, of himself and the now helpless Mrs. Unwin to Mundesley, on the Norfolk coast. In October, 1796, they were taken to East Dereham, in Norfolk, where soon after Mrs. Unwin died. Mentally shattered, Cowper survived her three years and a half, and died very peacefully on April 25th, 1800, and was buried in Dereham Church.

Cowper lived in stirring times, the events of which **His Times.** he viewed with interest "through the loopholes of retreat" by means of that "map of busy life," the newspaper. When he was fourteen years of age occurred

The Young Pretender.

the invasion of the Young Pretender, in 1745, his victory over Sir John Cope at Prestonpans, and his final defeat at Culloden in 1746.

Wars with France, Spain, and America.

During the first fifty years of Cowper's life England was almost continually at war with France or Spain or both together. The War of the Austrian Succession led to hostilities with France in 1744, and, in 1759, the capture of Quebec by Wolfe made Canada a British possession. In 1762, in consequence of the Family Compact, war was declared against Spain, which was followed by the Peace of Paris in 1763. In 1775 the American war began—the result of an attempt to impose import duties on the British Colonies in North America. The battles of Lexington and Bunker's Hill in 1775 were followed by the American Declaration of Independence in 1776, and in the following year, under the Convention of Saratoga, General Burgoyne surrendered to the American General Gates. This was the turning-point of the war, and France, in 1778, and Spain, in 1779, entered into an alliance with the American States; while in 1780 England, in self-defence, declared war against Holland—a year that was marked by Rodney's famous victory over the Spanish fleet off Cape St. Vincent. The same year saw all the powers of Europe arrayed against Britain under the "Armed Neutrality" compact, which claimed that a neutral flag should protect all cargoes. From 1779 to 1782 Gibraltar, bravely defended by Elliot, was besieged in vain by the French and the Spanish. In 1781 Cornwallis's capitulation at York Town resulted in the acknowledgment of the independence of the United States in 1782; and in 1783 the Peace of Versailles was concluded with France and Spain.

In Cowper's life-time, too, occurred the commencement and consolidation of our Indian Empire. In 1751 Clive captured Arcot from the French, and in 1757 won the battle of Plassy. In 1765 by the Treaty of Allahabad the revenues of Bengal, Behar, and Orissa were ceded to the East India Company. Warren Hastings became Governor of Bengal in 1772, and in 1774 Governor-General of British India. In 1779 Sir Eyre Coote defeated Haidar Ali and his Mahratta hordes at Porto Novo, and again at Pollilore. The younger Pitt's East India Bill, erecting a Board of Control over the Company's administration, was passed in 1784; and in 1785 Hastings returned to England, was impeached in 1788 before the House of Lords, and at length acquitted in 1795.

Indian affairs.

Another stirring event of Cowper's day was the "No-Popery Riots." In 1778 a Bill was passed to relieve the Roman Catholics of the worst of their civil disabilities. Popular riots followed in Scotland, and in 1780 Lord George Gordon convened a monster meeting of Protestants in St. George's Fields, who marched to the House of Commons and burst into the lobby. For five days (June 2–7), owing to the want of energy shown by the authorities, London was at the mercy of the mob, who burned down not fewer than 72 private houses, with four or five strong gaols. The Lord Mayor was tried and convicted of criminal negligence. Gordon was tried on a charge of high treason and acquitted in 1781.

The Gordon Riots.

In 1789 the first French Revolution commenced with the meeting of the National Assembly on June 17 and the storming of the Bastille on July 14. In

French Revolution.

1790 a new Constitution was forced upon the King, who in 1791 attempted to escape from France, but was stopped at Varennes and brought back to Paris. In 1792 the ill success of the French arms against the Continental powers caused a fresh outburst of revolutionary excitement at Paris, and on August 10 the Tuilleries was stormed by the mob, an event which was followed by a terrible massacre, lasting five days (Sept. 2–7), of imprisoned royalists. On September 21 France was declared a Republic, and in January, 1793, Louis XVI. was executed. The Reign of Terror followed in the same year, and the execution of the Queen. In 1795 the Government of the Directory was established, accompanied by the rise to power of Napoleon I

England in Cowper's youth.

Of the social and political life of England in Cowper's day—or rather that of which he had experience as a young man—a modern writer has given a gloomy picture. It was a world from which the spirit of poetry seemed to have fled. Spiritual religion was almost extinct. The Church was little better than a political force. The clergy were idle and neglectful of their duties, often sordid and corrupt, fanatics in their Toryism, and cold, rationalistic, and almost heathen in their preachings. The society of the day was one of hard and heartless polish and fashionable immorality, devoted to a giddy round of theatre-going, card-parties, and balls. Among the common people religion was almost extinct. Ignorance and brutality reigned in the cottage. Drunkenness and profanity[1] reigned in palace and cottage alike. Thus on page 68 Cowper writes:

[1] Cf. note to p. 101, l. 15.

"Heathenish parents can only bring up heathenish children; an assertion nowhere oftener or more clearly illustrated than at Olney, where children, seven years of age, infest the streets every evening with curses and with songs to which it would be unseemly to give their proper epithet."[1] Gambling, cock-fighting, and bull-baiting were the amusements of the people. Political life was corrupt from the top of the scale to the bottom. Society was intensely aristocratic; no duties towards the lower classes were acknowledged; and each rank was divided from that below it by a sharp line, which precluded brotherhood or sympathy. Of humanity there was as little as there was of religion. It was the age of the criminal law which hanged men for petty thefts, of lifelong imprisonment for debt, of the unreformed prison system, and of the press-gang. That the slave-trade was iniquitous hardly any one suspected.[2]

Revival of Poetry.

But a change was at hand, and two revivals—one literary, and the other, religious—were in progress, in both of which Cowper took no inconsiderable part. It is to him chiefly, along with Thomson, Gray, and Crabbe, that we owe that great revolution in popular taste and sentiment which substituted the "romantic" for the "classical" type in poetic literature—a revolution which was ushered in by the publication in 1765 of Bishop Percy's *Reliques of Ancient English Poetry*. In Cowper's verse a simple and natural, almost colloquial, style takes the place of that pompous and artificial

---

[1] Cf. also p. 37, ll. 4-10.

[2] See *Cowper*, "English Men of Letters" Series; and compare Cowper's own sketch in *Tirocinium*, 813-858.

style which Pope had brought into favour; and he is one of the leaders in the reaction—"a morning star which heralded another sunrise"[1]—from the hard conventionalism and cold, unreal sentiment of the Queen Anne school of poetry, to the picturesque freshness and genuine human feeling which was to attain a yet nobler development in the hands of a Scott, a Shelley, and a Wordsworth.

Revival of Religion.

With the religious revival of 1738, of which Whitfield and Wesley were the leaders, Cowper was even more in sympathy. It expressed a revolt from the religious deadness of the time, and its aim was to carry religion and morality to the masses of the population. But it did more than this; its action upon the Church broke the lethargy of the clergy, till the fox-hunting parson and the absentee rector became at last impossible. A fresh moral enthusiasm arose in the nation at large, the profligacy of the upper classes gradually disappeared, and a new philanthropic impulse established Sunday schools, raised hospitals, sent John Howard on his visits to the prisons of England and Europe, supported Burke in his plea for the Hindoo, and Clarkson and Wilberforce in their crusade against the iniquity of the slave trade.[2] Of this moral and religious movement Cowper was the poetical exponent; and his indignant denunciations of national offences against piety and morality, with the intense religious feeling that animates his writings, mark him out from among the poets of his day, and indeed from among all other English poets.

---

[1] *Quarterly Review*, 1849.

[2] See Green's *History of the English People*, vol. iv., pp. 273-4.

Cowper's CHARACTER: (a) His natural cheerfulness.

Cowper was of an amiable and cheerful disposition, and his natural gaiety of temperament often shows itself in his poetry, and especially in his letters. This geniality of disposition is shown by the impersonality of his satire, and often leads him to pardon in the individual what he condemns in the abstract. Thus, though strongly objecting to tobacco-smoking, he is indulgent to the practice in the case of his friends Newton and Bull. The pessimism with which he has been charged, seems to have been the outcome, partly of the hypochondria from which he constantly suffered,[1] and partly of his theology, which inculcated and emphasized the irretrievable corruption of human nature, ever pursued by the vengeance of an angry God.

(b) His refinement of taste.

At the same time, Cowper is never unctuous, and though he sometimes indulges in a censorious tone of thought and expression, no trace of religious cant is to be found in his writings; the refined and delicate taste that is one of his most striking characteristics, governs, with hardly an exception, his frequent references to spiritual matters. Here and there, it is true, he betrays a fanatical antipathy to natural science,[2] and his religious asceticism leads him sometimes to denounce amusements which we now justly deem innocent. But

---

[1] Cf. *To Lady Hesketh*, Nov. 23, 1785: "I have, indeed, a most troublesome stomach, and which does not improve as I grow older"; and *To Newton*, Dec. 3, 1785: "Having been for some years troubled with an inconvenient stomach; and, lately, with a stomach that will digest nothing without help." "He had dreadful stomach complaints," writes Dr. Currie to W. Roscoe, "and drank immense quantities of tea."

[2] As in *Task*, iii. 150-190.

it is seldom that his strictures are marked by a spirit of religious intolerance.[1] Thus, writing to his friend Hurdis on the practice of dancing, he says; "I will not tease you with graver arguments on the subject, especially as I have a hope that years, and the study of the Scripture, and His Spirit whose word it is, will in due time bring you to my way of thinking. I am not one of those sages who require that young men should be as old as themselves before they have had time to be so."[2]

(c) His shyness.

Another characteristic of Cowper was his excessive shyness, which has been already illustrated by his morbid shrinking from the Parliamentary clerkship, and which led to a passionate love of retirement and seclusion. He calls himself "naturally the shyest of mankind," and describes how at Olney he "lived the life of a solitary," unvisited by a single neighbour.[3] "I was never fond of company," he tells Newton, "and especially disliked it in the country";[4] and on page 89 he speaks of his "fear of strangers." A new visitor generally disconcerted him, and when he is told that a "lady of quality" awaits him in the parlour, "he feels his spirits sink ten degrees." And he concludes his account of the occurrence with "I am a shy animal, and want much kindness to make me easy. Such I shall be to my dying day."[5]

(d) His tenderness of disposition.

A natural concomitant of this shyness was a sympathetic tenderness of disposition, which was a per-

---

[1] As somewhat in the case of the Misagathus episode, *Task*, vi. 483-559.

[2] P. 121, ll. 27-32. [3] *To Hurdis*, Aug. 9, 1791.

[4] P. 67, ll. 6, 7. [5] P. 124, ll. 17-25.

petual protest against the hardness of the world around him, and which showed itself in his love for animals. Besides his hares, his spaniel, his goldfinches, and his cat, all of which his poetry has enshrined, at one time we find "eight pair of tame pigeons" waiting for their breakfast every morning from his hand;[1] and, at another, a pet linnet is let out of its cage, "to whisk about the room a little" and then be shut up again.[2] He kept, too, a tame mouse while he was a schoolboy at Westminster.[3] Very characteristic is a passage in one of his letters where, referring to his attachment to animals he says: "All the notice that we lords of creation vouchsafe to bestow on the creatures, is generally to abuse them; it is well therefore that here and there a man should be found a little womanish, or perhaps a little childish in this matter, who will make amends by kissing, by coaxing, and laying them in one's bosom."[4] At the time of his second derangement, he seems to have been perfectly indifferent to what happened to his belongings with one characteristic exception, his cat, which was consigned to the care of Hill; and again, thirty-two years later, when he is sinking into the depths of hypochondria, he cannot close the touching letter to Buchanan without an inquiry after his "poor birds."[5]

(1) Towards animals.

Some of his most exquisite verses are those in which he describes the innocent happiness of beast or bird that people his sylvan haunts,[6] and the passage in which he inculcates kindness to animals has become classical

[1] *To Unwin*, Sept. 21, 1799

[2] P. 6, ll. 34-36.

[3] P. 83, l. 29 *et seq.*

[4] P. 121, ll. 2-8.

[5] P. 139, ll. 20-23.

[6] *Task*, vi. 305 *et seq.*

on that theme.[1] He cannot dismiss the subject of the waggoner plodding beside his load in winter, without a plea for the "poor beasts" that drag it—"Ah, treat them kindly!"[2]

(2) Towards the poor.

This gentle sensibility showed itself too in his friendly attitude towards the poor and his sympathetic descriptions of their hardships and sorrows. "All his tenderest, deepest, holiest, sympathies were theirs."[3] His letters contain not a few compassionate references to the sufferings of the poverty-stricken lace-makers of Olney,[4] and what a realistic and touching picture has he drawn in the *Task*[5] of the poor cottager's winter evening—each sad detail accurately worked in with unadorned directness. There is a world of simple pathos in the single line I have italicized—

> "The taper soon extinguished, which I saw
> *Dangled along at the cold finger's end*
> Just when the day declined."

(*e*) His love of Nature.

Lastly, Cowper was pre-eminently a lover of Nature. Slighted as it was in his day, "the country," he writes, "wins me still";[6] and the only poets that could please him in his youth were those

> "whose lyre was tuned
> To Nature's praises."[7]

"O! I could spend," he writes,[8] "whole days and moonlight nights in feeding upon a lovely prospect! My eyes drink the rivers as they flow." And in a letter from his greenhouse to Unwin, he declares that

---

[1] *Task*, vi. 560 *et seq.* [2] *Ib.*, iv. 370 *et seq.*; see also ll. 147, 148.
[3] *Blackwood's Magazine*, 1834. [4] Cf. pp. 25, 29.
[5] iv. 374-398. [6] *Task*, iv. 694; see note to my edition.
[7] *Ib.*, 704, 705. [8] P. 8, ll. 10-12.

"the beauties of the spot are themselves an interruption; my attention is called upon by those very myrtles, by a double row of grass pinks just beginning to blossom, and by a bed of beans already in bloom."[1] And again: "Everything I see in the fields is to me an object, and I can look at the same rivulet, or at a handsome tree, every day of my life with new pleasure. This indeed is partly the effect of a natural taste for rural beauty, and partly the effect of habit; for I never in all my life have let slip the opportunity of breathing fresh air, and of conversing with nature, when I could fairly catch it."[2] The tender care with which he has studied her varied effects is sufficient proof of the love he felt for her, illustrated as it is so frequently and exquisitely in his verse. Take for instance his description of the play of light and shade under the "graceful arch" of an avenue of trees:

> "Beneath
> The chequered earth seems restless as a flood
> Brushed by the wind. So sportive is the light
> Shot through the boughs, it dances as they dance,
> Shadow and sunshine intermingling quick,
> And darkening and enlightening, as the leaves
> Play wanton, every moment, every spot."[3]

Or, if we pass to his enumeration of the plants in a greenhouse, how picturesquely accurate are the epithets he employs, and with what loving delight does he linger over the picture:

> "The spiry myrtle with unwithering leaf
> Shines there, and flourishes. The golden boast
> Of Portugal and Western India there,
> The ruddier orange and the paler lime,

[1] P. 33, ll. 4-8. [2] *To Unwin*, Nov. 10, 1788. [3] *Task*, i. 343-349.

Peep through their polished foliage at the storm,
And seem to smile at what they need not fear.
The amomum there with intermingling flowers
And cherries hangs her twigs. Geranium boasts
Her crimson honours; and the spangled beau,
Ficoides, glitters bright the winter long."[1]

(1) He prefers well-ordered Nature.

As has been said of Tennyson, so it is true of Cowper, that the Nature he loved was of the well-ordered and well-regulated kind, rather than the Nature of mountains and rocks and shaggy forests. He delights in the trim avenue, the carefully-tended garden, the sheltered walk, the Wilderness with its "well-rolled" paths. Writing of his visit to Hayley at Eartham, he says: "The cultivated appearance of Weston suits my frame of mind far better than wild hills that aspire to be mountains, covered with vast unfrequented woods, and here and there affording a peep between their summits at the distant ocean. Within doors all was hospitality and kindness, but the scenery *would* have its effect; and though delightful in the extreme to those who had spirits to bear it, was too gloomy for me."[2]

(2) His view of Nature differs from Words-worth's

Though Cowper, like Wordsworth, was a reverent student of Nature's lore, he never thought, like him, of idealizing her as a power that may enable us to "see into the life of things," and of listening for her hidden voices. He depicts her outward features with loving fidelity, but sees no soul behind them. The only spiritual significance Nature has for him is that she affords a proof of the wisdom and goodness of the

---

[1] *Task*, iii. 570-579.

[2] P. 132, ll. 22-29. See also *To Lady Hesketh*, Sept. 9, 1792.

Creator. At the same time he approaches nearer to Wordsworth's idealism than such a writer as Thomson did, who merely reproduces her picturesque effects. He can contemplate her as a whole, and in one passage at least in his poetry we find a flash of still profounder imaginative insight. For the solitary man, he tells us, not only animals but shrubs and trees have speech easy to be understood, and then follows this couplet:

> "After long drought, when rains abundant fall,
> *He hears the herbs and flowers rejoicing all*,"[1]

the latter line of which almost startingly reminds us of the great poet of Nature.

Cowper's Letters: (a) Their excellence.

Cowper has received from Southey the high praise of being "the best of English letter-writers"—an opinion with which most true critics will agree. Walpole's and Gray's and, above all, Charles Lamb's letters are inimitable of their kind, but Cowper's combine so many of the qualities that go to produce excellence in letter-writing, that they remain, if not unequalled, at least unsurpassed in English literature.

(b) Not written for publication.

Unlike Pope, Cowper did not write his letters with a view to their publication. So far from that, he never had the faintest idea that such a fate might be in store for them, and is inclined himself to set little value upon them. "As you are pleased," he tells Unwin, "to desire my letters, I am the more pleased with writing them, though, at the same time, I must needs testify my surprise that you should think them worth receiving, as

[1] *The Needless Alarm*, 59, 60.

I seldom send one that I think favourably of myself."[1] And referring to "a very clever letter" that he had received from Henry Cowper, he says that he "answered it as well as he could, but not in kind. I seem to myself immoderately stupid on epistolary occasions, and especially when I wish to shine."[2] He frequently complains of the dearth of subjects for his letters, and tells us how he "often finds himself reduced to the necessity, the disagreeable necessity, of writing about himself."[3]

(c) Their subjectivity.

And this brings us to a special point of interest in his letters, viz., their subjectivity. They are full of the writer himself, his doings and experiences, and the personal touches with which they abound are introduced without the slightest tinge of self-consciousness—which is the first quality of good letter-writing. He is in the fullest sympathy with his correspondents, and opens his heart to them freely and unreservedly; and hence the interest and value that attach to his letters as materials of the best kind for his biography.

(d) Their naturalness.

Another excellence in the letters is their perfect naturalness and sincerity. There is no *pose*, no pretentiousness, about them. As Robert Hall remarks, "To an air of inimitable ease and carelessness they unite a high degree of correctness, such as would result only from the clearest intellect, combined with the most finished taste." Careless they may be, but they are never slovenly; and the pure, idiomatic English in which they are expressed makes them admirable as a school-book. For Cowper has an abhorrence of

---

[1] P. 5, l. 30 *et seq.* [2] P. 96, ll. 25-28.

[3] P. 9, ll. 17-21; and cf. p. 22, ll. 20-24; p. 34, ll. 19-22.

affectation of any kind, and his language and his thoughts are both so clear and simple that we are never at a loss for his meaning; and it is this genuineness of the man that invests his letters with moral dignity as well as with literary excellence.

(e) No premeditation.

Cowper has told us something of his method, or rather absence of method, of writing—which was to "scribble away, and write his uppermost thoughts, and those only."[1] In the same letter he deprecates the praise that had been given to his letters as tending to spoil him quite as a letter-writer. "For," he writes, "I found this consequence attending or likely to attend the eulogium you bestowed—if my friend thought me witty before, he shall think me ten times more witty hereafter—where I joked once, I will joke five times, and, for one sensible remark, I will send him a dozen." Here we see the secret of Cowper's charm: he "scribbles away," there is little or no premeditation, he puts down whatever he has in his mind at the time. Thus in another letter he writes: "I have often found . . . when a great penury of matter has seemed to threaten me with an utter impossibility of hatching a letter, that nothing is necessary but to put pen to paper, and go on, in order to conquer all difficulties."[2] And again: "I had need take care, when I begin a letter, that the subject with which I set off be of some importance; for before I can exhaust it, be it what it may, I have generally filled my paper."[3] And, once more, he tells Lady Hesketh, "As to method, you know as well

---

[1] *To Unwin*, June 8, 1780. [2] P. 22, ll. 21-25.
[3] P. 111, ll. 8-11.

as I, that it is never more out of its place than in a letter."[1]

(*f*) Their humour and fancy.

While full of sympathetic affection for his correspondents, Cowper's letters are remarkable for their delicate humour and light-hearted play of fancy. This is seen more especially in his letters to Lady Hesketh, to whom he writes in a spirit of graceful *abandon* that is very charming. But even in his more sober compositions, such as those addressed to Newton, his "whisking wit" breaks out ever and anon; and it is to him that he sends the rhyming letter on page 19, which is to "keep him still, though against his will, dancing away, alert and gay." Cowper is rather fond of these jingles. "Here sit *I*," he writes to Bagot, "calling myself *shy*, yet have published by the *by*, two great volumes of poe*try*."[2] And on page 22 he winds up a letter to Newton with

"I nothing add but this—that *still I am*
Your most affectionate and humble
WILLIAM."

Another letter[3] ends with

"We send you a cheese,
In hopes it will please:
If so, your mother
Will send you another."

What a delightfully humorous description he gives us on page 27 of the waiter at the coffee-house, who "raises the teapot to the ceiling with his right hand, while in his left the teacup descending almost to the floor, receives a limpid stream!" And how frequently do we

---

[1] P. 86, l. 31 *et seq.*
[2] P. 124, ll. 26, 27.
[3] To *Unwin*, June 12, 1782.

come across such inimitable touches as the following: "I thank you for the snip of cloth, commonly called a pattern. At present I have two coats, and but one back. If at any time hereafter I should find myself possessed of fewer coats, or more backs, it will be of use to me."[1] Again, "First came the barber; who, after having embellished the outside of my head, has left the inside just as unfurnished as he found it";[2] with which we may compare a passage on page 9: "The effects of time seem to have taken place rather on the outside of my head than within it. What was brown is become gray, but what was foolish remains foolish still." He closes a letter to Lady Hesketh on page 124 with "Our affectionate hearts all lay themselves at your pettitoes," and writing to the same lady of the walks round Weston, some of them "unapproachable by you either on foot or in your carriage," he says: "Had you twenty toes (whereas I suppose you have but ten) you could not reach them; and coach wheels have never been seen there since the flood."[3] The last paragraph of the letter to Rose on page 112 is another instance of this light humour, a vein of which runs through the letter to Mrs. Throckmorton on page 116; and his defence of Milton against Dr. Johnson's strictures (p. 5) concludes with a very happy stroke of satire: "Oh! I could thrash his old jacket till I made his pension jingle in his pockets." Of Cowper's play of fancy, mentioned above, we have charming specimens, full of quiet fun and gentle satire, in his imagined sketch of life in antediluvian times,[4] and in his delicious picture[5] of the flying philosopher,

---

[1] P. 100, ll. 10-13. [2] *To Unwin*, July 27, 1780.
[3] P. 98, ll. 21-23. [4] P. 43. [5] P. 40, l. 31 *et seq.*

"ascending by his own comparative levity," and "steering himself by the help of a pasteboard rudder attached to his posteriors."

(g) Their images

Cowper, again, appeals to his readers in the aptness and point of his images. Excellent is his comparison of Johnson, his publisher, to some vicious horses that he has known: "They would not budge till they were spurred, and when they were spurred, they would kick. So did he; his temper was somewhat disconcerted: but his pace was quickened, and I was contented."[1] Describing to Unwin his discovery of a bird's nest with two eggs in it, which "by and by will be fledged, and tailed, and get wing-feathers, and fly," he continues: "My case is somewhat similar to that of the parent bird. My nest is in a little nook. Here I brood and hatch, and in due time my progeny takes wing and whistles."[2] How strikingly appropriate, again, is the following simile: "As when the sea is uncommonly agitated, the water finds its way into creeks and holes of rocks, which in its calmer state it never reaches, in like manner the effect of these turbulent times is felt even at Orchard Side, where in general we live as undisturbed by the political elements," etc.[3] Admirable, too, is the image with which he illustrates his contention that a poem may have lines that cannot be made smoother without being the worse for it: "There is a roughness on a plum which nobody that understands fruit would rub off, though the plum would be much more polished without it."[4] And when he declines Lady Hesketh's services for the Poet-Laureate-

[1] P. 65, ll. 10-13. [2] P. 66, ll. 20-24.
[3] P. 47, ll. 7-14. [4] P. 119, ll. 21-24.

ship, his ready wit at once provides him with an expressive metaphor: "It would be (he tells her) a leaden extinguisher clapped on all the fire of my genius."[1]

(h) Their incidents.

It has been frequently remarked in how interesting and delightful a manner Cowper could describe the most trivial occurrences, and this is one of the great charms of his correspondence. Like Swift, he could write well upon a broomstick. His letters are full of these little incidents and pictures which are unsurpassed for their shrewdness, their sly humour or their delicate sentiment, their descriptive fidelity, and the excellence of their literary execution. As examples we may take his account of the escape of one of his hares in the letter to Newton on page 10; the story of his goldfinches with which the letter to Unwin on page 36 closes; the highly amusing description of the visit of that "most loving, kissing, kind-hearted gentleman," the Parliamentary candidate, on pages 47 and 48, together with the Homeric encounter that grew out of the Elections, which is delineated in the succeeding letter; the manner of his deliverance from a decayed tooth on page 102; how he was "in at the death" of a fox, narrated on pages 104 and 105; and his admirable representation on page 135 of his meeting with the Milton of his dream. How perfect in its Addisonian humour is the picture that he draws on page 30 of the "conference" of Olney townsmen on the new treaty of peace in the blacksmith's shed: "Some held their hands behind them, some had them folded across

[1] P. 117, ll. 18-20.

their bosom, and others had thrust them into their breeches pockets. Every man's posture bespoke a pacific turn of mind," etc. The account too of his interview with the Northampton clerk on page 99, and of his engaging to supply him with mortuary verses, is excellent; ending, as it does, with the triumphant remark, "A fig for poets who write epitaphs upon individuals! I have written *one*, that serves *two hundred* persons."

(*i*) Their happy phrases. As might be expected with Cowper's ready wit, his keen sense of the proportion of things, and his gift of insight into the motives and feelings of others, we find scattered up and down his letters a good many shrewd, pithy comments and happy phrases and remarks. A few examples may be quoted:

"The happiness we cannot call our own, we yet seem to possess, while we sympathise with our friends who can" (p. 28, ll. 5-7).

"The earth is a grain of sand, but the spiritual interests of man are commensurate with the heavens" (p. 31, ll. 30, 31).

"I have just time to observe that time is short, and by the time I have made the observation, time is gone" (p. 42, l. 30 *et seq.*).

"Critics did not originally beget authors; but authors made critics" (p. 50, ll. 33, 34).

"Those events that prove the prelude to our greatest success, are often apparently trivial in themselves, and such as seemed to promise nothing" (p. 64, ll. 28-30).

"Fame begets favour; and one talent, if it be rubbed a little bright by use and practice, will procure a man more friends than a thousand virtues" (p. 66, ll. 5-8).

"I would that every fastidious judge of authors were himself obliged to write; there goes more to the composition of a volume than many critics imagine" (p. 111, ll. 24-26).

"I could never find that I had learned half so much of a

woman's real character by dancing with her, as by conversing with her at home, where I could observe her behaviour at the table, at the fireside, and in all the trying circumstances of domestic life. We are all good when we are pleased; but she is the good woman, who wants not a fiddle to sweeten her" (p. 121, ll. 19-25).

(*k*) Their literary criticisms: (1) Of others.

Cowper's good sense and intellectual penetration are also illustrated by his literary criticisms, which are often excellent. It is true that he had not wholly emancipated himself from the conventional taste and sentiment that marked the Artificial School of poetry, and we find instances of this in the high praise he gives to Prior's *Henry and Emma*,[1] that frigid modernized version of a spirited old ballad, and in his passing expression of approval of Blackmore's *Creation*. He is, however, juster than Dr. Johnson in his estimate of the latter author, whom he rightly designates as having "written more absurdities in verse than any writer of our country."[2] On the other hand, the eulogium he pronounces upon Prior's ballad is the more remarkable in view of the very sensible observations upon ballads and ballad-writing that he makes in a subsequent letter.[3] But with his almost passionate defence of his favourite Milton against the attack of Dr. Johnson we can feel altogether in sympathy, and acknowledge the admirable truth of his criticism when he writes: "I am convinced . . . that he (Johnson) has no ear for poetical numbers, or that it was stopped by prejudice against the harmony of Milton's. Was there ever anything so delightful as the music of the *Paradise Lost*? It is like that of a fine organ; has the fullest

[1] P. 24, ll. 10-21. [2] P. 21, ll. 26-28. [3] Pp. 37, 38.

and the deepest tones of majesty, with all the softness and elegance of the Dorian flute: variety without end, and never equalled, unless perhaps by Virgil."[1] Cowper's fondness for "Vinny" Bourne, his old usher at Westminster, makes him a partial judge of that writer's Latin poems, placing them, as he does, above those of Tibullus and Propertius, and on a level with Ovid's.[2] But his estimate of Watts, a genuine poet (as Mr. Palgrave[3] has pointed out), displays no little critical discernment. "A man," he calls him, "of true poetical ability; careless, indeed, for the most part, and inattentive too often to those niceties which constitute elegance of expression, but frequently sublime in his conceptions, and masterly in his execution."[4] Cowper's criticism of Pope, too, shows admirable point and insight: "He was certainly a mechanical maker of verses," but, "with the unwearied application of a plodding Flemish painter, who draws a shrimp with the most minute exactness, he had all the genius of one of the first masters. Never, I believe, were such talents and such drudgery united." And then how well he goes on to contrast Dryden's method: "But I admire Dryden most, who has succeeded by mere dint of genius, and in spite of a laziness and carelessness almost peculiar to himself. His faults are numberless, and so are his beauties. His faults are those of a great man, and his beauties are such (at least sometimes) as Pope, with all his touching and retouching, could never equal."[5] Cowper's strictures upon the styles of Robertson and Gibbon[6] are, perhaps, too strongly expressed, in his desire to give

[1] P. 5, ll. 12-19. [2] P. 15, ll. 18-20. [3] *Treasury of Sacred Song*, p. 349.
[4] P. 21, ll. 8-11. [5] P. 23, ll. 6-22. [6] P. 36, ll. 10-23.

point to an antithesis; and his critical observations, however excellent, upon such writers as Beattie and Blair[1] have little attraction for the modern reader.

(2) Of himself.

Perhaps, however, the most interesting remarks of this nature that are found in Cowper's letters, are those that relate to his own compositions. We can trace the history of their production to a large extent in his correspondence; for there he often tells us how the subjects of his poems came to be suggested to his mind, explains his aims and methods in writing them, or defends himself against adverse criticism. This is especially so in the case of his Second Volume, which included the *Task*, and the letters on pages 52–66 form a body of information and comment of peculiar interest to students of that delightful poem. Passages too, there are, dealing with this topic, of a more general character, which well repay attentive perusal. The following, for instance, is a truth that is often apt to be forgotten: "Inequalities there must be always and in every work of length. There are level parts of every subject, parts which we cannot with propriety attempt to elevate. They are by nature humble, and can only be made to assume an awkward and uncouth appearance by being mounted."[2] The whole of page 88 is an admirable piece of literary criticism, which is well supplemented by the remarks contained in the subsequent letter of remonstrance to his publisher; and we can feel the revulsion from the so-called "correctness" of Pope and his compeers that was taking place, as we read: "Give me a manly rough line, with a deal of

---

[1] P. 50, ll. 8-23. [2] P. 78, ll. 17-21.

meaning in it, rather than a whole poem of musical periods, that have nothing but their oily smoothness to recommend them!"[1]

(*l*) Their praise of retirement.

As in the *Task*, so in his letters, there is one topic to which Cowper continually recurs—the praise of retirement and country life. Both his prose and his poetry are redolent of home and the domestic hearth. He is supremely contented "in the low vale of life," delighting in the thought that he is at a safe distance from the "great Babel" of the outer world. "I am," he writes to Thomas Park,[2] "as you say, a hermit, and probably an irreclaimable one, having a horror of London that I cannot express, nor indeed very easily account for." Hence the heartfelt enjoyment with which he paints the pleasures of the country as opposed to those of the town, of "fireside enjoyments, homeborn happiness," as opposed to the theatre, the rout, and the card-party. Little home scenes and touches are frequently to be met with in his letters, such as this: "Here are two rustics, and your humble servant in company. One of the ladies has been playing at battledore and shuttlecock. A little dog in the meantime, howling under the chair of the former, performed in the vocal way, to admiration."[3] Or this: "We were sitting yesterday after dinner, the two ladies and myself, very composedly, and without the least apprehension of any such intrusion in our snug parlour, one lady knitting, the other netting, and the gentleman winding worsted, when," etc.[4] "I see the winter approaching," he tells Hill, "without much concern . . .

[1] P. 119, ll. 10-13.
[2] May 17, 1793.
[3] P. 27, ll. 25-30.
[4] P. 47, ll. 14-18.

the long evenings have their comforts too, and there is hardly to be found upon the earth, I suppose, so snug a creature as an Englishman by his fireside in the winter. I mean, however, an Englishman that lives in the country, for in London it is not very easy to avoid intrusion. I have two ladies to read to, sometimes more, but never less."[1] To Newton he writes: "My passion for retirement is not at all abated, after so many years spent in the most sequestered state, but rather increased";[2] and mentioning to Lady Hesketh the departure of Lady Austen, he tells her that now "we have seldom any company at all."[3] The general impression made upon our minds by his letters recalls the picture he gives us in the *Task*—the "intimate delights" of the winter evening, the snug parlour, the close-drawn curtains shutting out the "freezing blast," the bubbling and hissing tea-urn, the happy group round the fire, the needle "plying its busy task" to the accompaniment of the book read aloud or the song sung to the guitar, the modest supper, and the social converse with which the evening ends.[4]

The Post: (a) Letters.

The Postal arrangements of Cowper's day may, to a large extent, be gathered from his letters. The postage rate was high, varying according to distance, and was paid by the recipient[5] not by the sender of the letter, postage stamps not being yet introduced. Thus the postage of a letter of Cowper's to Lady Hesketh (of which I possess a facsimile), dated June 1, 1798, con-

[1] P. 42, ll. 4-12. [2] P. 35, ll. 2-4. [3] P. 82, ll. 19, 20.
[4] Bk. iv., ll. 35 *et seq.*, 158 *et seq.*
[5] Cf. p. 7, l. 18; p. 126, ll. 11-14.

sisting of a single sheet, and sent from East Dereham to Bath, was eightpence. This letter was re-directed by the Bath postmaster and sent on to Clifton, near Bristol, where Lady Hesketh was then staying, and a total charge of elevenpence was made for it. One sheet only was allowed for single postage, so that we often find Cowper telling his correspondents that he has no room for writing more.[1] Two or three sheets involved double or treble postage.[2] No envelopes were used, the sheet, which was of quarto size, being merely folded and sealed. The back of the sheet was consequently left blank for the address, except that, under stress of matter, the writer could utilize the sides of the page that were folded underneath the two ends. This practice appears to explain Cowper's expression when he speaks of filling *four* sides of a sheet.[3] He mentions, in one place, his intention of using a second sheet as a "case" for the first, by leaving a space blank for the address on the outside of it.[4]

(*b*) Franks. The postage of a letter being so expensive, Cowper as far as possible employed "franks," *i.e.* sheets signed on the back by a member of either House of Parliament. During a Dissolution, therefore, no franks were available,[5] but otherwise they were so common that Cowper often uses the word "frank" as synonymous with "letter."[6] Letters thus franked went free up to the year 1764, but after that date, to avoid abuses of the privilege, the whole of the address, with the date on which the letter was despatched,[7] as well as the

[1] P. 5, l. 26. [2] P. 14, l. 21; p. 81, ll. 12, 13.
[3] P. 44, l. 2. [4] P. 84, ll. 13-15.
[5] P. 47, ll. 1-4. [6] P. 13, l. 14. [7] P. 58, ll. 28-32.

signature, had to be in the Member's own hand-writing. Owing to his aristocratic connexions and his friendship with Mr. Robert Smith and others, Cowper was generally able to obtain as many franks as he required. Thus he would sometimes receive from Unwin a large quantity at a time on which to write his poems, so as to send them to his printer free of charge.[1]

(c) Mail coaches.

From the year 1784 letters were carried by mail-coaches, heavier articles being conveyed by waggon,[2] though, for speedier transit, parcels could, at greater cost, be sent by coach.[3] Newport Pagnell was Cowper's nearest post-town, and the mail-coach deposited the Olney letter-bag at the *Swan* inn[4] of that town, whence it was sent on to Olney. Cowper sometimes complains of the negligence of the hostess of the *Swan* in the late delivery of letters.[5] The post arrived at Olney three times a week till the end of 1787, when a daily post was introduced.[6]

Cowper's Correspondents:

It remains to append short notices of those to whom the letters contained in this volume are addressed.

Mrs. Cowper.

Frances Maria Cowper was the wife of General Cowper, her first cousin, and both were first cousins to the poet. She was the daughter of Dr. John Cowper's sister, and sister to the Rev. Martin Madan, the author of *Thelypthora*. The correspondence between her and Cowper originated in her sending him a copy of Pearsall's *Meditations*, and is almost entirely of a religious character.

---

[1] P. 16, ll. 17, 18; p. 58, ll. 29-32. [2] P. 44, l. 29; p. 75, l. 21. [3] P. 138, l. 5. [4] P. 86, l. 3. [5] P. 93, ll. 14-21. [6] P. 103, ll. 22-28.

Hill. *Joseph Hill* was Cowper's schoolfellow at Westminster and one of the seven members of the Nonsense Club. He was a lawyer and a man of good business habits, and, greatly to the benefit of the poet, took charge of his finances.

Unwin. *William Cawthorne Unwin* was the son of the Rev. Morley and Mary Unwin, and first became intimate with Cowper at Huntingdon. He was educated at Christ's College, Cambridge, and, like his father, belonged to the Evangelical party in the Church of England. In July, 1769, he became Rector of Stock, near Ramsden, in Essex. He died of typhus fever at Winchester on November 29, 1786, at the age of forty-one, leaving a widow and three young children.

Newton. *Rev. John Newton* (born 1726, died 1807) was one of the leading spirits of the Evangelical movement. After a wild youth spent at sea, he became religious, entered the Church, and in 1764 became curate of Olney. In January, 1780, he removed to the living of St. Mary Woolnoth, in London, when Cowper's correspondence with him begins. In 1750 he married Mrs. Newton. Miss Mary Catlett, the *Mrs. Newton* to whom several of Cowper's letters are addressed.

Bull. *Rev. William Bull* was an Independent minister of Newport Pagnell, five miles from Olney. To him Newton, on his departure, introduced Cowper, and they became so intimate that it became the custom for him to dine with the poet regularly once a fortnight.

Lady Hesketh. *Harriet, Lady Hesketh*, was the eldest daughter of Ashley Cowper, the poet's uncle, and the sister of Theodora. She married Sir Thomas Hesketh, who died in 1778. Cowper wrote several letters to her from Huntingdon, but their religious tone found no sympathy with her. After twenty years, however, the publication of the *Task* caused a renewal of their correspondence to Cowper's great delight.

Rose.

Samuel Rose was the son of Dr. William Rose, a schoolmaster at Chiswick. On his way to London from Glasgow University he paid a visit to the poet at Olney, January 18, 1787. Rose gave him a copy of the newly published poems of Burns, and they became great friends. His house in London was one of the places where Cowper rested during the return journey from Eartham to Weston. He died in 1804 in his 38th year.

Mrs. King.

Mrs. King was the wife of the Rev. John King, Rector of Pertenhall, in Bedfordshire. She had been a friend of Cowper's brother John, and having read the *Task*, wrote in February, 1788, a friendly letter to the poet, and subsequently sent him some unpublished poems of his brother's. In September, 1790, she and Mr. King visited Cowper at Weston. She died February 6, 1793.

Mrs. Bodham.

Ann Bodham was one of the daughters of the Rev. Roger Donne, Cowper's uncle, Rector of Catfield, in Norfolk, and wife of the Rev. Thomas Bodham, Rector of Mattishall, in the same county. She was Cowper's playfellow in childhood, and renewed her intercourse with him by sending him, in 1790, his mother's picture.

John Johnson.

John Johnson was nephew to the preceding, being the son of her sister Catherine, who married Mr. John Johnson, of Ludham. In January, 1790, being at that time a young man of twenty and a student of Caius College, Cambridge, he sought out the poet at Weston. He became a clergyman, and died in 1833.

Mrs. Throckmorton.

Maria Throckmorton was the wife of Mr. (afterwards Sir) John Courtenay Throckmorton, the son of Sir Robert Throckmorton. They resided at Weston Hall, in Weston Underwood, a mile from Olney. They were Roman Catholics, but Cowper became very intimate with them, and Weston Lodge, the house to which he removed from Orchard Side, Olney, belonged to them. Upon the death of Sir Robert in 1791, the Throckmortons left Weston, and went to live at the family seat of Bucklands, in Berkshire.

Joseph Johnson.

Joseph Johnson was Cowper's publisher, and his place of business was No. 72, St. Paul's Churchyard, London. He was introduced to the poet by Newton.

Buchanan.

Rev. John Buchanan was curate of Ravenstone and Weston Underwood, and lived only a few doors from Weston Lodge.

Hurdis.

Rev. James Hurdis was Rector of Bishopstone, in Sussex, and author of a once popular poem entitled *The Village Curate.* In 1793 he was appointed Professor of Poetry at Oxford.

Bagot.

Rev. Walter Bagot was Rector of Blithfield, Staffordshire, and was, with his four brothers, a schoolfellow of the poet at Westminster. In 1782, having read and liked Cowper's first volume, he renewed his acquaintance with him, and visited him several times at Olney, subscribing twenty pounds towards his translation of Homer. One of his brothers, Charles (who took the name of Chester), resided at Chicheley, five miles from Olney. Another brother was Lewis (complimented in *Tirocinium*), who became successively Bishop of Bristol, Norwich, and St. Asaph.

Clotworthy Rowley, of Tendring Hall, near Stoke-by-Nayland, was a fellow-Templar of Cowper, with whom he had corresponded in his early days. The correspondence was renewed in December, 1787, when Rowley, who was then living at Dublin, returned some books which Cowper had lent him twenty-five years previously. **Rowley.**

Rev. W. Greatheed was a Nonconformist minister residing at Newport Pagnell. **Greatheed.**

Catherine Courtenay was the wife of Mr. George Courtenay, to whom she (then Miss Stapleton) was married in June, 1792. He was the younger brother of John Throckmorton; but, upon John's succeeding to the title in 1791, took the name of Courtenay and came to reside at Weston Hall. She was most helpful to Cowper in making a fair copy of his Homer. **Mrs. Courtenay.**

William Hayley (born 1745, died 1820) was educated at Trinity Hall, Cambridge, and was the author of several epistles in verse and of a poem, formerly famous, entitled *The Triumphs of Temper*. In 1774 he removed to Eartham, and gave himself up to the pleasures of building, gardening, and literature. He had been engaged by the publishers Boydell and Nicholl to write a life of Milton, and it had been represented that he and Cowper were rivals. He accordingly, in February, 1792, wrote a friendly letter to Cowper, enclosing a graceful sonnet addressed to the poet, assuring him that he had been unaware of Cowper's Milton scheme, and expressing his belief that their **Hayley.**

respective labours would not clash. In May, 1792, Hayley visited Cowper at Weston, a visit which the poet returned in August of the same year. In November, 1793, Hayley paid him a second visit, and a third in April, 1794.

Park *Thomas Park* was the author of *Sonnets and Miscellaneous Poems* and the editor of Walpole's *Royal and Noble Authors.* In February, 1792, he sent Cowper a parcel containing "Cursory Remarks," a copy of Fletcher's *Faithful Shepherdess*, and a friendly letter, which formed the commencement of a correspondence between them. In May, 1793, he presented the poet with a copy of Chapman's translation of *Homer.*

Mrs. Smith. *Charlotte Smith*, novelist and poet, was introduced to Cowper at Eartham. She sent him a copy of her novel, *The Old Manor House*, published in 1793, and dedicated her poem of *The Emigrants* to him. She died in 1806.

SELECTIONS FROM

COWPER'S LETTERS.

COWPER'S LETTERS.

TO MRS. COWPER.

Huntingdon, October 20, 1766.

MY DEAR COUSIN—I am very sorry for poor Charles's illness, and hope you will soon have cause to thank God for his complete recovery. We have an epidemical fever in this country likewise, which leaves behind it a continual sighing, almost to suffocation; not that I have seen any instance of it, for, blessed be God! our family have hitherto escaped it; but such was the account I heard of it this morning.

I am obliged to you for the interest you take in my welfare, and for your inquiring so particularly after the manner in which my time passes here. As to amusements—I mean what the world calls such—we have none; the place, indeed, swarms with them, and cards and dancing are the professed business of almost all the *gentle* inhabitants of Huntingdon. We refuse to take part in them, or to be accessories to this way of murdering our time, and by so doing have acquired the name of Methodists. Having told you how we *do not* spend our time, I will next say how we do. We breakfast commonly between eight and nine; till eleven we read either the Scripture, or the sermons of some faithful preacher of those holy mysteries; at eleven we attend divine service, which is performed here twice every day; and from twelve to three we separate, and amuse ourselves as we please. During that interval I either read in my own apartment, or walk, or ride, or work in the garden. We seldom sit an hour after dinner; but, if the weather permits, adjourn to the garden, where, with Mrs. Unwin and her son, I have generally the pleasure of religious conversation till tea-time. If it rains, or is too windy for walking, we either converse within doors, or sing some hymns of Martin's collection; and by the help of Mrs. Unwin's harpsichord, make up a tolerable concert, in which our hearts, I hope, are the best and most musical performers. After tea we sally forth to walk in good earnest. Mrs. Unwin is a good walker, and we have generally travelled about four miles before we see home again. When the days are short, we make this excursion in the former part of the day, between church-time and dinner. At night we read and converse, as before, till supper, and commonly finish the evening either with hymns or a sermon, and last of all the family are called to prayers. I need not tell *you* that such a life as this is consistent with the utmost cheerfulness; accordingly we are all happy, and dwell together in unity as brethren. Mrs. Unwin has almost a maternal affection for me, and I have something very like a filial one for her; and her son and I are brothers. Blessed be the God of our salvation for such companions, and for such a life; above all, for a heart to like it!

I have had many anxious thoughts about taking orders, and I believe every new convert is apt to think himself called upon for that purpose; but it has pleased God, by means which there is no need to particularise, to give me full satisfaction as to the propriety of declining it; indeed they who have the least idea of what I have suffered from the dread of public exhibitions, will readily excuse my never attempting them hereafter. In the meantime, if it please the Almighty, I may be an instrument of turning many to the truth in a private way, and I hope that my endeavours in this way have not been entirely unsuccessful. Had I the zeal of Moses, I should want an Aaron to be my spokesman.—Yours ever, my dear cousin,

W. C.

TO JOSEPH HILL, ESQ.

July 13, 1777.

My dear Friend—You need not give yourself any further trouble to procure me the South Sea Voyages. Lord Dartmouth, who was here about a month since, and was so kind as to pay me two visits, has furnished me with both Cook's and Forster's. 'Tis well for the poor natives of those distant countries that our national expenses cannot be supplied by cargoes of yams and bananas. Curiosity, therefore, being once satisfied, they may possibly be permitted for the future to enjoy their riches of that kind in peace.

If, when you are most at leisure, you can find out Baker upon the Microscope, or Vincent Bourne's Latin Poems, the last edition, and send them, I shall be obliged to you. Either, or both, if they can be easily found.—I am yours affectionately,

Wm. Cowper.

TO JOSEPH HILL, ESQ.

Oct. 2, 1779.

My dear Friend—You begin to count the remaining days of the vacation, not with impatience, but through unwillingness to see the end of it. For the mind of man, at least of most men, is equally busy in anticipating the evil and the good. That word *anticipation* puts me in remembrance of the pamphlet of that name, which, if you purchased, I should be glad to borrow. I have seen only an extract from it in the Review, which made me laugh heartily, and wish to peruse the whole.

The newspaper informs me of the arrival of the Jamaica fleet. I hope it imports some pine-apple plants for me. I have a good frame and a good bed prepared to receive them. I send you annexed a fable, in which the pine-apple makes a figure, and shall be glad if you like the taste of it. Two pair of soles, with shrimps, which arrived last night, demand my acknowledgements. You have heard that when Arion performed upon the harp, the fish followed him. I really have no design to fiddle you out of more fish, but if you should esteem my verses worthy of such a price, though I shall never be so renowned as he was, I shall think myself equally indebted to the muse that helps me.

My affectionate respects attend Mrs. Hill. She has put Mr. Wright to the expense of building a new hot-house: the plants produced by the seeds she gave me, having grown so large as to require an apartment by themselves.—Yours,

Wm. Cowper.

TO THE REV. WILLIAM UNWIN.

October 31, 1779.

My dear Friend—I wrote my last letter merely to inform you that I had nothing to say, in answer to which you have said nothing. I admire the propriety of your conduct, though I am a loser by it. I will endeavour to say something now, and shall hope for something in return.

I have been well entertained with Johnson's biography, for which I thank you: with one exception, and that a swinging one, I think he has acquitted himself with his usual good sense and sufficiency. His treatment of Milton is unmerciful to the last degree. A pensioner is not likely to spare a republican, and the Doctor, in order, I suppose, to convince his royal patron of the sincerity of his monarchical principles, has belaboured that great poet's character with the most industrious cruelty. As a man, he has hardly left him the shadow of one good quality. Churlishness in his private life, and a rancorous hatred of everything royal in his public, are the two colours with which he has smeared all the canvas. If he had any virtues, they are not to be found in the Doctor's picture of him, and it is well for Milton that some sourness in his temper is the only vice with which his memory has been charged; it is evident enough that if his biographer could have discovered more, he would not have spared him. As a poet, he has treated him with severity enough, and has plucked one or two of the most beautiful feathers out of his Muse's wing, and trampled them under his great foot. He has passed sentence of condemnation upon Lycidas, and has taken occasion, from that charming poem, to expose to ridicule (what is indeed ridiculous enough) the childish prattlement of pastoral compositions, as if Lycidas was the prototype and pattern of them all. The liveliness of the description, the sweetness of the numbers, the classical spirit of antiquity that prevails in it, go for nothing. I am convinced, by the way, that he has no ear for poetical numbers, or that it was stopped by prejudice against the harmony of Milton's. Was there ever any thing so delightful as the music of the *Paradise Lost?* It is like that of a fine organ; has the fullest and the deepest tones of majesty, with all the softness and elegance of the Dorian flute: variety without end, and never equalled, unless perhaps by Virgil. Yet the Doctor has little or nothing to say upon this copious theme, but talks something about the unfitness of the English language for blank verse, and how apt it is, in the mouth of some readers, to degenerate into declamation. Oh! I could thrash his old jacket till I made his pension jingle in his pockets.

I could talk a good while longer, but I have no room. Our love attends yourself, Mrs. Unwin, and Miss Shuttleworth, not forgetting the two miniature pictures at your elbow.—Yours affectionately, W. C.

TO THE REV. WILLIAM UNWIN.

February 27, 1780.

My dear Friend—As you are pleased to desire my letters, I am the more pleased with writing them, though, at the same time, I must needs testify my surprise that you should think them worth receiving, as I seldom send one that I think favourably of myself. This is not to be understood as an imputation upon your taste or judgement, but as an encomium upon my own modesty and humility, which I desire you to remark well. It is a just observation of Sir Joshua Reynolds, that though men of ordinary talents may be highly satisfied with their own productions, men of true genius never are. Whatever be their subject, they always seem to themselves to fall short of it, even when they seem to others most to excel. And for this reason,—because they have a certain sublime sense of perfection, which other men are strangers to, and which they themselves in their performances are not able to exemplify. Your servant, Sir Joshua! I little thought of seeing you when I began, but as you have popped in, you are welcome.

When I wrote last, I was a little inclined to send you a copy of verses entitled the Modern Patriot, but was not quite pleased with a line or two which I found it difficult to mend, therefore did not. At night I read Mr. Burke's speech in the newspaper, and was so well pleased with his proposals for a reformation, and with the temper in which he made them, that I began to think better of his cause, and burnt my verses. Such is the lot of the man who writes upon the subject of the day; the aspect of affairs changes in an hour or two, and his opinion with it; what was just and well-deserved satire in the morning, in the evening becomes a libel; the author commences his own judge, and while he condemns with unrelenting severity what he so lately approved, is sorry to find that he has laid his leaf-gold upon touchwood, which crumbled away under his fingers. Alas! what can I do with my wit? I have not enough to do great things with, and these little things are so fugitive, that while a man catches at the subject, he is only filling his hand with smoke. I must do with it as I do with my linnet: I keep him for the most part in a cage, but now and then set open the door that he may whisk about the room a little, and then shut him up again. My whisking wit has produced the following, the subject of which is more important than the manner in which I have treated it seems to imply, but a fable may speak truth, and all truth is sterling; I only premise, that in the philosophical tract in the Register, I found it asserted that the glow-worm is the nightingale's proper food.

The officer of a regiment, part of which is quartered here, gave one of the soldiers leave to be drunk six weeks, in hopes of curing him by satiety. He *was* drunk six weeks, and is so still, as often as he can find an opportunity. One vice may swallow up another, but no coroner in the state of ethics ever brought in his verdict, when a vice died, that it was—*felo de se.*

Thanks for all you have done, and all you intend; the biography will be particularly welcome. My truly affectionate respects attend you all.—Yours, WM. COWPER.

When you feel postage a burden, send me some franks.

TO THE REV. JOHN NEWTON.

May 3, 1780.

DEAR SIR—You indulge me in such a variety of subjects, and allow me such a latitude of excursion in this scribbling employment, that I have no excuse for silence. I am much obliged to you for swallowing such boluses as I send you, for the sake of my gilding, and verily believe that I am the only man alive, from whom they would be welcome to a palate like yours. I wish I could make them more splendid than they are, more alluring to the eye, at least, if not more pleasing to the taste; but my leaf gold is tarnished, and has received such a tinge from the vapours that are ever brooding over my mind, that I think it no small proof of your partiality to me, that you will read my letters. I am not fond of longwinded metaphors; I have always observed, that they halt at the latter end of their progress, and so do mine. I deal much in ink indeed, but not such ink as is employed by poets, and writers of essays. Mine is a harmless fluid, and guilty of no deceptions but such as may prevail without the least injury to the person imposed on. I draw mountains, valleys, woods, and streams, and ducks, and dab-chicks. I admire them myself, and Mrs. Unwin admires them ; and her praise, and my praise put together, are fame enough for me. O ! I could spend whole days and moonlight nights in feeding upon a lovely prospect ! My eyes drink the rivers as they flow. If every human being upon earth could think for one quarter of an hour as I have done for many years, there might perhaps be many miserable men among them, but not an unawakened one could be found from the arctic to the antarctic circle. At present, the difference between them and me is greatly to their advantage. I delight in baubles, and know them to be so ; for rested in, and viewed without a reference to their Author, what is the earth,—what are the planets,—what is the sun itself but a bauble? Better for a man never to have seen them, or to see them with the eyes of a brute, stupid and unconscious of what he beholds, than not to be able to say, "The Maker of all these wonders is my friend !" Their eyes have never been opened, to see that they are trifles ; mine have been, and will be till they are closed for ever. They think a fine estate, a large conservatory, a hothouse rich as a West Indian garden, things of consequence ; visit them with pleasure, and muse upon them with ten times more. I am pleased with a frame of four lights, doubtful whether the few pines it contains will ever be worth a farthing ; amuse myself with a greenhouse which Lord Bute's gardener could take upon his back, and walk away with ; and when I have paid it the accustomed visit, and watered it, and given it air, I say to myself—"This is not mine, it is a plaything lent me for the present ; I must leave it soon."

W. C.

TO MRS. COWPER, PARK STREET, GROSVENOR SQUARE.

July 20, 1780.

My dear Cousin—Mr. Newton having desired me to be of the party, I am come to meet him. You see me sixteen years older, at the least, than when I saw you last; but the effects of time seem to have taken place rather on the outside of my head than within it. What was brown is become gray, but what was foolish remains foolish still. Green fruit must rot before it ripens, if the season is such as to afford it nothing but cold winds and dark clouds, that interrupt every ray of sunshine. My days steal away silently, and march on (as poor mad King Lear would have made his soldiers march) as if they were shod with felt; not so silently but that I hear them; yet were it not that I am always listening to their flight, having no infirmity that I had not when I was much younger, I should deceive myself with an imagination that I am still young.

I am fond of writing as an amusement, but do not always find it one. Being rather scantily furnished with subjects that are good for any thing, and corresponding only with those who have no relish for such as are good for nothing, I often find myself reduced to the necessity, the disagreeable necessity, of writing about myself. This does not mend the matter much; for though in a description of my own condition, I discover abundant materials to employ my pen upon, yet as the task is not very agreeable to *me*, so I am sufficiently aware that it is likely to prove irksome to others. A painter who should confine himself in the exercise of his art to the drawing of his own picture, must be a wonderful coxcomb, if he did not soon grow sick of his occupation; and be peculiarly fortunate, if he did not make others as sick as himself.

Remote as your dwelling is from the late scene of riot and confusion, I hope that though you could not but hear the report, you heard no more, and that the roarings of the mad multitude did not reach you. That was a day of terror to the innocent, and the present is a day of still greater terror to the guilty. The law was for a few moments like an arrow in the quiver, seemed to be of no use, and did no execution; now it is an arrow upon the string, and many, who despised it lately, are trembling as they stand before the point of it.

I have talked more already than I have formerly done in three visits:—you remember my taciturnity, never to be forgotten by those who knew me. Not to depart entirely from what might be, for aught I know, the most shining part of my character, I here shut my mouth, make my bow, and return to Olney. W. C.

TO THE REV. JOHN NEWTON.

August 21, 1780.

THE following occurrence ought not to be passed over in silence, in a place where so few notable ones are to be met with. Last Wednesday night, while we were at supper, between the hours of eight and nine, I heard an unusual noise in the back parlour, as if one of the hares was entangled, and endeavouring to disengage herself. I was just going to rise from table, when it ceased. In about five minutes, a voice on the outside of the parlour door inquired if one of my hares had got away. I immediately rushed into the next room, and found that my poor favourite Puss had made her escape. She had gnawed in sunder the strings of a lattice-work, with which I thought I had sufficiently secured the window, and which I preferred to any other sort of blind, because it admitted plenty of air. From thence I hastened to the kitchen, where I saw the redoubtable Thomas Freeman, who told me, that having seen her, just after she had dropped into the street, he attempted to cover her with his hat, but she screamed out, and leaped directly over his head. I then desired him to pursue as fast as possible, and added Richard Coleman to the chase, as being nimbler, and carrying less weight than Thomas; not expecting to see her again, but desirous to learn, if possible, what became of her. In something less than an hour, Richard returned, almost breathless, with the following account. That soon after he began to run, he left Tom behind him, and came in sight of a most numerous hunt of men, women, children, and dogs; that he did his best to keep back the dogs, and presently outstripped the crowd, so that the race was at last disputed between himself and Puss;—she ran right through the town, and down the lane that leads to Dropshort; a little before she came to the house, he got the start and turned her; she pushed for the town again, and soon after she entered it, sought shelter in Mr. Wagstaff's tanyard, adjoining to old Mr. Drake's. Sturge's harvest men were at supper, and saw her from the opposite side of the way. There she encountered the tanpits full of water; and while she was struggling out of one pit, and plunging into another, and almost drowned, one of the men drew her out by the ears, and secured her. She was then well washed in a bucket, to get the lime out of her coat, and brought home in a sack at ten o'clock.

This frolic cost us four shillings, but you may believe we did not grudge a farthing of it. The poor creature received only a little hurt in one of her claws, and in one of her ears, and is now almost as well as ever.

I do not call this an answer to your letter, but such as it is I send it, presuming upon that interest which I know you take in my minutest concerns, which I cannot express better than in the words of Terence a little varied—*Nihil mei a te alienum putas.*—Yours, my dear friend, W. C.

TO THE REV. WILLIAM UNWIN.

May 1, 1781.

Your mother says I *must* write, and *must* admits of no apology; I might otherwise plead, that I have nothing to say, that I am weary, that I am dull, that it would be more convenient therefore for you, as well as for myself, that I should let it alone; but all these pleas, and whatever pleas besides either disinclination, indolence, or necessity might suggest, are overruled, as they ought to be, the moment a lady adduces her irrefragable argument, *you must.* You have still however one comfort left, that what I must write, you may, or may not read, just as it shall please you; unless Lady Anne at your elbow should say, you *must* read it, and then like a true knight you will obey without looking out for a remedy.

I do not love to harp upon strings that, to say the least, are not so musical as one would wish. But you I know have many a time sacrificed your own feelings to those of others, and where an act of charity leads you, are not easily put out of your way. This consideration encourages me just to insinuate that your silence on the subject of a certain nomination is distressful to more than you would wish, in particular to the little boy whose clothes are outgrown and worn out; and to his mother, who is unwilling to furnish him with a new suit, having reason to suppose that the long blue petticoat would soon supersede it, if she should.

In the press, and speedily will be published, in one volume octavo, price three shillings, Poems, by William Cowper, of the Inner Temple, Esq. You may suppose, by the size of the publication, that the greatest part of them have been long kept secret, because you yourself have never seen them: but the truth is, that they are most of them, except what you have in your possession, the produce of the last winter. Two-thirds of the compilation will be occupied by four pieces, the first of which sprung up in the month of December, and the last of them in the month of March. They contain, I suppose, in all, about two thousand and five hundred lines; are known, or to be known in due time, by the names of *Table Talk—The Progress of Error—Truth—Expostulation.* Mr. Newton writes a Preface, and Johnson is the publisher. The principal, I may say the only reason why I never mentioned to you, till now, an affair which I am just going to make known to all the world, (if *that* Mr. All-the-world should think it worth his knowing,) has been this; that till within these few days, I had not the honour to know it myself. This may seem strange, but it is true; for not knowing where to find underwriters who would choose to insure them; and not finding it convenient to a purse like mine, to run any hazard, even upon the credit of my own ingenuity, I was very much in doubt for some weeks, whether any bookseller would be willing to subject himself to an ambiguity, that might prove very expensive in case of a bad market. But Johnson has heroically set all peradventures at defiance, and takes the whole charge upon himself. So out I come. I shall be glad of my Translations from Vincent Bourne, in your next frank. My Muse will lay herself at your feet immediately on her first public appearance.—Yours, my dear friend, W. C.

TO THE REV. WILLIAM UNWIN.

May 23, 1781.

My dear Friend—If a writer's friends have need of patience, how much more the writer! Your desire to see my muse in public, and mine to gratify you, must both suffer the mortification of delay. I expected that my trumpeter would have informed the world by this time of all that is needful for them to know upon such an occasion; and that an advertising blast, blown through every newspaper, would have said—"The poet is coming!"—But man, especially man that writes verse, is born to disappointments, as surely as printers and booksellers are born to be the most dilatory and tedious of all creatures. The plain English of this magnificent preamble is, that the season of publication is just elapsed, that the town is going into the country every day, and that my book cannot appear till they return, that is to say, not till next winter.

This misfortune however comes not without its attendant advantage; I shall now have, what I should not otherwise have had, an opportunity to correct the press myself; no small advantage upon any occasion, but especially important, where poetry is concerned! A single erratum may knock out the brains of a whole passage, and that perhaps, which of all others the unfortunate poet is the most proud of. Add to this, that now and then there is to be found in a printing-house a presumptuous intermeddler, who will fancy himself a poet too, and what is still worse, a better than he that employs him. The consequence is, that with cobbling, and tinkering, and patching on here and there a shred of his own, he makes such a difference between the original and the copy, that an author cannot know his own work again. Now as I choose to be responsible for nobody's dulness but my own, I am a little comforted, when I reflect that it will be in my power to prevent all such impertinence; and yet not without your assistance. It will be quite necessary, that the correspondence between me and Johnson should be carried on without the expense of postage, because proof sheets would make double or treble letters, which expense, as in every instance it must occur twice, first when the packet is sent, and again when it is returned, would be rather inconvenient to me, who, as you perceive, am forced to live by my wits, and to him, who hopes to get a little matter no doubt by the same means. Half a dozen franks therefore to me, and *totidem* to him, will be singularly acceptable, if you can, without feeling it in any respect a trouble, procure them for me.

My neckcloths being all worn out, I intend to wear stocks, but not unless they are more fashionable than the former. In that case, I shall be obliged to you if you will buy me a handsome stock-buckle, for a very little money; for twenty or twenty-five shillings perhaps a second-hand affair may be purchased that will make a figure at Olney.

I am much obliged to you for your offer to support me in

a translation of Bourne. It is but seldom, however, and never except for my amusement, that I translate, because I find it disagreeable to work by another man's pattern ; I should at least be sure to find it so in a business of any length. Again, *that* is epigrammatic and witty in Latin, which would be perfectly insipid in English ; and a translator of Bourne would frequently find himself obliged to supply what is called the turn, which is in fact the most difficult, and the most expensive part of the whole composition, and could not perhaps, in many instances, be done with any tolerable success. If a Latin poem is neat, elegant, and musical, it is enough ; but English readers are not so easily satisfied. To quote myself, you will find, in comparing the Jackdaw with the original, that I was obliged to sharpen a point which, though smart enough in the Latin, would, in English, have appeared as plain, and as blunt, as the tag of a lace. I love the memory of Vinny Bourne. I think him a better Latin poet than Tibullus, Propertius, Ausonius, or any of the writers in *his* way, except Ovid, and not at all inferior to *him*. I love him too with a love of partiality, because he was usher of the fifth form at Westminster, when I passed through it. He was so good-natured, and so indolent, that I lost more than I got by him ; for he made me as idle as himself. He was such a sloven, as if he had trusted to his genius as a cloak for every thing that could disgust you in his person ; and indeed in his writings he has almost made amends for all. His humour is entirely original ; he can speak of a magpie or a cat in terms so exquisitely appropriated to the character he draws, that one would suppose him animated by the spirit of the creature he describes. And with all this drollery there is a mixture of rational, and even religious reflection at times : and always an air of pleasantry, good-nature, and humanity, that makes him, in my mind, one of the most amiable writers in the world. It is not common to meet with an author who can make you smile, and yet at nobody's expense ; who is always entertaining, and yet always harmless; and who, though always elegant, and classical to a degree not always found even in the classics themselves, charms more by the simplicity and playfulness of his ideas, than by the neatness and purity of his verse; yet such was poor Vinny. I remember seeing the Duke of Richmond set fire to his greasy locks, and box his ears to put it out again.

Since I began to write long poems, I seem to turn up my nose at the idea of a short one. I have lately entered upon one, which, if ever finished, cannot easily be comprised in much less than a thousand lines! But this must make part of a second publication, and be accompanied, in due time, by others not yet thought of; for it seems (which I did not know till the bookseller had occasion to tell me so) that single pieces stand no chance, and that nothing less than a volume will go down. You yourself afford me a proof of the certainty of this intelligence, by sending me franks which nothing less than a volume can fill. I have accordingly sent you one, but am obliged to add, that had the wind been in any other point of the compass, or, blowing as it does from the east, had it been less boisterous, you must have been contented with a much shorter letter, but the abridgement of every other occupation is very favourable to that of writing.

I am glad I did not expect to hear from you by this post, for the boy has lost the bag in which your letter must have been enclosed;—another reason for my prolixity!—Yours affectionately, W. C.

TO THE REV. JOHN NEWTON.

July 7, 1781.

My dear Friend—Mr. Old brought us the acceptable news of your safe arrival. My sensations at your departure were far from pleasant, and Mrs. Unwin suffered more upon the occasion than when you first took leave of Olney. When we shall meet again, and in what circumstances, or whether we shall meet or not, is an article to be found no where but in that volume of Providence which belongs to the current year, and will not be understood till it is accomplished. This I know, that your visit was most agreeable here. It was so even to me, who, though I live in the midst of many agreeables, am but little sensible of their charms. But when you came, I determined, as much as possible, to be deaf to the suggestions of despair; that if I could contribute but little to the pleasure of the opportunity, I might not dash it with unseasonable melancholy, and, like an instrument with a broken string, interrupt the harmony of the concert.

Lady Austen, waving all forms, has paid us the first visit; and not content with showing us that proof of her respect, made handsome apologies for her intrusion. We returned the visit yesterday. She is a lively, agreeable woman; has seen much of the world, and accounts it a great simpleton, as it is. She laughs and makes laugh, and keeps up a conversation without seeming to labour at it.

I had rather submit to chastisement now, than be obliged to undergo it hereafter. If Johnson, therefore, will mark with a marginal Q, those lines that he or his object to as not sufficiently finished, I will willingly retouch them, or give a reason for my refusal. I shall moreover think myself obliged by any hints of that sort, as I do already to somebody, who, by running here and there two or three paragraphs into one, has very much improved the arrangement of my matter. I am apt, I know, to fritter it into too many pieces, and, by doing so, to disturb that order to which all writings must owe their perspicuity, at least in a considerable measure. With all that carefulness of revisal I have exercised upon the sheets as they have been transmitted to me, I have been guilty of an oversight, and have suffered a great fault to escape me, which I shall be glad to correct if not too late.

In the *Progress of Error*, a part of the Young Squire's

apparatus, before he yet enters upon his travels, is said to be

> —— Memorandum-book to minute down
> The several posts, and where the chaise broke down.

Here, the reviewers would say, is not only "down," but "down derry down" into the bargain, the word being made to rhyme to itself. This never occurred to me till last night, just as I was stepping into bed. I should be glad, however, to alter it thus—

> With memorandum-book for every town,
> And every inn, and where the chaise broke down.

I have advanced so far in *Charity*, that I have ventured to give Johnson notice of it, and his option whether he will print it now or hereafter. I rather wish he may choose the present time, because it will be a proper sequel to *Hope*, and because I am willing to think it will embellish the collection. Mrs. Unwin purposes to send a couple of ducks by next Friday's diligence, when I imagine this last production will have a place in the basket.

Whoever means to take my phiz will find himself sorely perplexed in seeking for a fit occasion. That I shall not give him one is certain; and if he steals one, he must be as cunning and quick-sighted a thief as Autolycus himself. His best course will be to draw a face, and call it mine, at a venture. They who have not seen me these twenty years will say, It may possibly be a striking likeness now, though it bears no resemblance to what he was: time makes great alterations. They who know me better will say perhaps, Though it is not perfectly the thing, yet there is somewhat of the cast of his countenance. If the nose was a little longer, and the chin a little shorter, the eyes a little smaller, and the forehead a little more protuberant, it would be just the man. And thus, without seeing me at all, the artist may represent me to the public eye, with as much exactness as yours has bestowed upon you, though, I suppose, the original was full in his view when he made the attempt.

We are both as well as when you left us. Our hearty affections wait upon yourself and Mrs. Newton, not forgetting Euphrosyne, the laughing lady.—Yours, my dear Sir,

Wm. Cowper.

TO THE REV. JOHN NEWTON.

July 12, 1781.

My very dear Friend—I am going to send, what when you have read, you may scratch your head, and say, I suppose, there's nobody knows, whether what I have got, be verse or not: by the tune and the time, it ought to be rhyme; but if it be, did you ever see, of late or of yore, such a ditty before? The thought did occur, to me and to her, as Madam and I, did walk and not fly, over hills and dales, with spreading sails, before it was dark, to Weston Park.

I have writ Charity, not for popularity, but as well as I could, in hopes to do good; and if the Reviewer should say "to be sure, the gentleman's Muse, wears Methodist shoes; you may know by her pace, and talk about grace, that she and her bard have little regard, for the taste and fashions, and ruling passions, and hoidening play, of the modern day; and though she assume a borrowed plume, and now and then wear a tittering air, 'tis only her plan, to catch if she can, the giddy and gay, as they go that way, by a production, on a new construction. She has baited her trap in hopes to snap all that may come, with a sugar-plum."——His opinion in this, will not be amiss; 'tis what I intend, my principal end; and if I succeed, and folks should read, till a few are brought to a serious thought, I shall think I am paid, for all I have said, and all I have done, though I have run, many a time, after a rhyme, as far as from hence, to the end of my sense, and by hook or crook, write another book, if I live and am here, another year.

I have heard before, of a room with a floor, laid upon springs, and such like things, with so much art, in every part, that when you went in, you was forced to begin a minuet pace, with an air and a grace, swimming about, now in and now out, with a deal of state, in a figure of eight, without pipe or string, or any such thing ; and now I have writ, in a rhyming fit, what will make you dance, and as you advance, will keep you still, though against your will, dancing away, alert and gay, till you come to an end of what I have penn'd ; which that you may do, ere Madam and you are quite worn out with jigging about, I take my leave, and here you receive a bow profound, down to the ground, from your humble me— W. C.

P.S.—When I concluded, doubtless you did think me right, as well you might, in saying what I said of Scott ; and then it was true, but now it is due to him to note, that since I wrote, himself and he has visited we.

TO THE REV. JOHN NEWTON.

The Greenhouse, Sept. 18, 1781.

My dear Friend—I return your preface, with many thanks for so affectionate an introduction to the public. I have observed nothing that in my judgement required alteration, except a single sentence in the first paragraph, which I have not obliterated, that you may restore it if you please, by obliterating my interlineation. My reason for proposing an amendment of it was, that your meaning did not strike me, which therefore I have endeavoured to make more obvious. The rest is what I would wish it to be. You say, indeed, more in my commendation than I can modestly say of myself : but something will be allowed to the partiality of friendship, on so interesting an occasion.

I have no objection in the world to your conveying a copy

to Dr. Johnson ; though I well know that one of his pointed sarcasms, if he should happen to be displeased, would soon find its way into all companies, and spoil the sale. He writes, indeed, like a man that thinks a great deal, and that sometimes thinks religiously : but report informs me that he has been severe enough in his animadversions upon Dr. Watts, who was nevertheless, if I am in any degree a judge of verse, a man of true poetical ability ; careless, indeed, for the most part, and inattentive too often to those niceties which constitute elegance of expression, but frequently sublime in his conceptions, and masterly in his execution. Pope, I have heard, had placed him once in the Dunciad ; but on being advised to read before he judged him, was convinced that he deserved other treatment, and thrust somebody's blockhead into the gap, whose name, consisting of a monosyllable, happened to fit it. Whatever faults, however, I may be chargeable with as a poet, I cannot accuse myself of negligence. I never suffer a line to pass till I have made it as good as I can ; and though my doctrines may offend this king of critics, he will not, I flatter myself, be disgusted by slovenly inaccuracy, either in the numbers, rhymes, or language. Let the rest take its chance. It is possible he may be pleased ; and if he should, I shall have engaged on my side one of the best trumpeters in the kingdom. Let him only speak as favourably of me as he has spoken of Sir Richard Blackmore (who, though he shines in his poem called Creation, has written more absurdities in verse than any writer of our country), and my success will be secured.

I have often promised myself a laugh with you about your pipe, but have always forgotten it when I have been writing, and at present I am not much in a laughing humour. You will observe, however, for your comfort and the honour of that same pipe, that it hardly falls within the line of my censure. You never fumigate the ladies, or force them out of company ; nor do you use it as an incentive to hard drinking. Your friends, indeed, have reason to complain that it frequently deprives them of the pleasure of your own conversation while it leads you either into your study or your garden ; but in all other respects it is as innocent a pipe as can be. Smoke away, therefore ; and remember that if one poet has condemned the practice, a better than he (the witty and elegant Hawkins Browne,) has been warm in the praise of it.

Retirement grows, but more slowly than any of its predecessors. Time was when I could with ease produce fifty, sixty, or seventy lines in a morning : now, I generally fall short of thirty, and am sometimes forced to be content with a dozen. It consists at present, I suppose, of between six and seven hundred ; so that there are hopes of an end, and I dare say Johnson will give me time enough to finish it.

I nothing add but this—that *still I am*
Your most affectionate and humble

WILLIAM.

TO THE REV. WILLIAM UNWIN.

Jan. 5, 1782.

MY DEAR FRIEND—Did I allow myself to plead the common excuse of idle correspondents, and esteem it a sufficient reason for not writing, that I have nothing to write about, I certainly should not write now. But I have so often found, on similar occasions, when a great penury of matter has seemed to threaten me with an utter impossibility of hatching a letter, that nothing is necessary but to put pen to paper, and go on, in order to conquer all difficulties,—that, availing myself of past experience, I now begin with a most assured persuasion, that sooner or later, one idea naturally suggesting another, I shall come to a most prosperous conclusion.

In the last Review, I mean in the last but one, I saw

Johnson's critique upon Prior and Pope. I am bound to acquiesce in his opinion of the latter, because it has always been my own. I could never agree with those who preferred him to Dryden ; nor with others, (I have known such, and persons of taste and discernment too,) who could not allow him to be a poet at all. He was certainly a mechanical maker of verses, and in every line he ever wrote, we see indubitable marks of the most indefatigable industry and labour. Writers who find it necessary to make such strenuous and painful exertions, are generally as phlegmatic as they are correct ; but Pope was, in this respect, exempted from the common lot of authors of that class. With the unwearied application of a plodding Flemish painter, who draws a shrimp with the most minute exactness, he had all the genius of one of the first masters. Never, I believe, were such talents and such drudgery united. But I admire Dryden most, who has succeeded by mere dint of genius, and in spite of a laziness and carelessness almost peculiar to himself. His faults are numberless, but so are his beauties. His faults are those of a great man, and his beauties are such, (at least sometimes,) as Pope, with all his touching and retouching, could never equal. So far, therefore, I have no quarrel with Johnson. But I cannot subscribe to what he says of Prior. In the first place, though my memory may fail me, I do not recollect that he takes any notice of his Solomon ; in my mind the best poem, whether we consider the subject of it, or the execution, that he ever wrote. In the next place, he condemns him for introducing Venus and Cupid into his love-verses, and concludes it impossible his passion could be sincere, because when he would express it he has recourse to fables. But when Prior wrote, those deities were not so obsolete as now. His contemporary writers, and some that succeeded him, did not think them beneath their notice. Tibullus, in reality, disbelieved their existence as much as we do ; yet Tibullus is allowed to be the prince of all poetical inamoratos, though he mentions them in almost every page. There is a fashion in these things, which the Doctor seems to have forgotten. But what shall we say of his old fusty-rusty remarks upon Henry and Emma? I agree with him, that morally considered both the knight and his lady are bad characters, and that each exhibits an example which ought not to be followed. The man dissembles in a way that would have justified the woman had she renounced him; and the woman resolves to follow him at the expense of delicacy, propriety, and even modesty itself. But when the critic calls it a dull dialogue, who but a critic will believe him? There are few readers of poetry of either sex, in this country, who cannot remember how that enchanting piece has bewitched them, who do not know, that instead of finding it tedious, they have been so delighted with the romantic turn of it, as to have overlooked all its defects, and to have given it a consecrated place in their memories, without ever feeling it a burthen. I wonder almost, that, as the Bacchanals served Orpheus, the boys and girls do not tear this husky, dry commentator limb from limb, in resentment of such an injury done to their darling poet. I admire Johnson as a man of great erudition and sense; but when he sets himself up for a judge of writers upon the subject of love, a passion which I suppose he never felt in his life, he might as well think himself qualified to pronounce upon a treatise on horsemanship, or the art of fortification.

The next packet I receive will bring me, I imagine, the last proof sheet of my volume, which will consist of about three hundred and fifty pages honestly printed. My public *entrée* therefore is not far distant.

Had we known that the last cheeses were naught, we would not have sent you these. Your mother has however enquired for and found a better dairy, which she means shall furnish you with cheese another year.—Yours, W. C.

TO MRS. NEWTON.

Nov. 23, 1782.

My dear Madam—The soles with which you favoured us were remarkably fine. Accept our thanks for them; thanks likewise for the trouble you take in vending my poems, and still more for the interest you take in their success. My authorship is undoubtedly pleased when I hear that they are approved either by the great or the small; but to be approved by the great, as Horace observed many years ago, is fame indeed. Having met with encouragement, I consequently wish to write again; but wishes are a very small part of the qualifications necessary for such a purpose. Many a man who has succeeded tolerably well in his first attempt, has spoiled all by the second. But it just occurs to me that I told you so once before, and if my memory had served me with the intelligence a minute sooner, I would not have repeated the observation now.

The winter sets in with great severity. The rigour of the season, and the advanced price of grain, are very threatening to the poor. It is well with those that can feed upon a promise, and wrap themselves up warm in the robe of salvation. A good fire-side and a well-spread table are but very indifferent substitutes for these better accommodations; so very indifferent, that I would gladly exchange them both, for the rags and the unsatisfied hunger of the poorest creature that looks forward with hope to a better world, and weeps tears of joy in the midst of penury and distress. What a world is this! How mysteriously governed, and, in appearance left to itself. One man, having squandered thousands at a gaming-table, finds it convenient to travel; gives his estate to somebody to manage for him; amuses himself a few years in France and Italy; returns, perhaps, wiser than he went, having acquired knowledge which, but for his follies, he would never have acquired; again makes a splendid figure at home, shines in the senate, governs his country as its minister, is admired for his abilities, and, if successful, adored, at least by a party. When he dies he is praised as a demi-god, and his monument records every thing but his vices. The exact contrast of such a picture is to be found in many cottages at Olney. I have no need to describe them ; you know the characters I mean. They love God, they trust him, they pray to him in secret, and though he means to reward them openly, the day of recompense is delayed. In the mean time they suffer every thing that infirmity and poverty can inflict upon them. Who would suspect, that has not a spiritual eye to discern it, that the fine gentleman was one whom his Maker had in abhorrence, and the wretch last-mentioned, dear to him as the apple of his eye? It is no wonder that the world, who are not in the secret, find themselves obliged, some of them, to doubt a Providence, and others, absolutely to deny it, when almost all the real virtue there is in it, is to be found living and dying in a state of neglected obscurity, and all the vices of others cannot exclude them from the privilege of worship and honour! But behind the curtain the matter is explained ; very little, however, to the satisfaction of the great.

If you ask me why I have written thus, and to you especially, to whom there was no need to write thus, I can only reply, that having a letter to write, and no news to communicate, I picked up the first subject I found, and pursued it as far as was convenient for my purpose.

Mr. Newton and I are of one mind on the subject of patriotism. Our dispute was no sooner begun than it ended. It would be well, perhaps, if, when two disputants begin to engage, their friends would hurry each into a separate chaise, and order them to opposite points of the compass. Let one travel twenty miles east ; the other as many west ; then let them write their opinions by the post. Much altercation and chafing of the spirit would be prevented ; they would sooner come to a right understanding, and running away from each other, would carry on the combat more judiciously, in exact proportion to the distance.

My love to that gentleman, if you please; and tell him, that, like him, though I love my country, I hate its follies and its sins, and had rather see it scourged in mercy, than judicially hardened by prosperity.

Mrs. Unwin is not very well, but better than she has been. She adds her love to both.—Yours, my dear Madam, as ever,

WM. COWPER.

TO JOSEPH HILL, ESQ.

Dec. 7, 1782.

MY DEAR FRIEND—At seven o'clock this evening, being the seventh of December, I imagine I see you in your box at the coffee-house. No doubt the waiter, as ingenious and adroit as his predecessors were before him, raises the teapot to the ceiling with his right hand, while in his left the teacup descending almost to the floor, receives a limpid stream; limpid in its descent, but no sooner has it reached its destination, than frothing and foaming to the view, it becomes a roaring syllabub. This is the nineteenth winter since I saw you in this situation; and if nineteen more pass over me before I die, I shall still remember a circumstance we have often laughed at.

How different is the complexion of your evenings and mine!—yours, spent amid the ceaseless hum that proceeds from the inside of fifty noisy and busy periwigs; mine, by a domestic fireside, in a retreat as silent as retirement can make it; where no noise is made but what we make for our own amusement. For instance, here are two rustics, and your humble servant in company. One of the ladies has been playing on the harpsichord, while I, with the other, have been playing at battledore and shuttlecock. A little dog, in the mean time, howling under the chair of the former, performed, in the vocal way, to admiration. This entertainment over, I began my letter, and having nothing more important to communicate, have given you an account of it. I know you love dearly to be idle, when you can find an opportunity to be so; but as such opportunities are rare with you, I thought it possible that a short description of the idleness I enjoy might give you pleasure. The happiness we cannot call our own, we yet seem to possess, while we sympathise with our friends who can.

The papers tell me that peace is at hand, and that it is at a great distance; that the siege of Gibraltar is abandoned, and that it is to be still continued. It is happy for me, that though I love my country, I have but little curiosity. There was a time when these contradictions would have distressed me, but I have learnt by experience that it is best for little people like myself to be patient, and to wait till time affords the intelligence which no speculations of theirs can ever furnish.

I thank you for a fine cod with oysters, and hope that ere long, I shall have to thank you for procuring me Elliott's medicines. Every time I feel the least uneasiness in either eye, I tremble lest, my Æsculapius being departed, my infallible remedy should be lost for ever. Adieu. My respects to Mrs. Hill.—Yours, faithfully, WM. COWPER.

TO THE REV. WILLIAM UNWIN.

Jan. 19, 1783.

MY DEAR WILLIAM—Not to retaliate, but for want of opportunity, I have delayed writing. From a scene of the most uninterrupted retirement, we have passed at once into a state of constant engagement; not that our society is much multiplied,—the addition of an individual has made all this difference. Lady Austen and we pass our days alternately at each other's *chateau*. In the morning I walk with one or other of the ladies, and in the afternoon wind thread. Thus did Hercules, and thus probably did Samson, and thus do I;

and were both those heroes living, I should not fear to challenge them to a trial of skill in that business, or doubt to beat them both. As to killing lions, and other amusements of that kind, with which they were so delighted, I should be their humble servant, and beg to be excused.

Having no frank, I cannot send you Mr. Smith's two letters as I intended. We corresponded as long as the occasion required, and then ceased. Charmed with his good sense, politeness, and liberality to the poor, I was indeed ambitious of continuing a correspondence with him, and told him so. Perhaps I had done more prudently had I never proposed it. But warm hearts are not famous for wisdom, and mine was too warm to be very considerate on such an occasion. I have not heard from him since, and have long given up all expectation of it. I know he is too busy a man to have leisure for me, and ought to have recollected it sooner. He found time to do much good, and to employ us as his agents in doing it, and that might have satisfied me. Though laid under the strictest injunctions of secrecy, both by him, and by you on his behalf, I consider myself as under no obligation to conceal from you the remittances he made. Only, in my turn, I beg leave to request secrecy on your part, because, intimate as you are with him, and highly as he values you, I cannot yet be sure that the communication would please him, his delicacies on this subject being as singular as his benevolence. He sent forty pounds, twenty at a time. Olney has not had such a friend this many a day; nor has there been an instance at any time of a few poor families so effectually relieved, or so completely encouraged to the pursuit of that honest industry by which, their debts being paid, and the parents and children comfortably clothed, they are now enabled to maintain themselves. Their labour was almost in vain before; but now it answers; it earns them bread, and all their other wants are plentifully supplied. —Yours, my dear friend, W. C.

TO THE REV. JOHN NEWTON.

Jan. 26, 1783.

My dear Friend—It is reported among persons of the best intelligence at Olney—the barber, the schoolmaster, and the drummer of a corps quartered at this place, that the belligerent powers are at last reconciled, the articles of the treaty adjusted, and that peace is at the door. I saw this morning, at nine o'clock, a group of about twelve figures very closely engaged in a conference, as I suppose, upon the same subject. The scene of consultation was a blacksmith's shed, very comfortably screened from the wind, and directly opposed to the morning sun. Some held their hands behind them, some had them folded across their bosom, and others had thrust them into their breeches pockets. Every man's posture bespoke a pacific turn of mind; but the distance being too great for their words to reach me, nothing transpired. I am willing, however, to hope that the secret will not be a secret long, and that you and I, equally interested in the event, though not, perhaps, equally well-informed, shall soon have an opportunity to rejoice in the completion of it. The powers of Europe have clashed with each other to a fine purpose; that the Americans, at length declared independent, may keep themselves so, if they can; and that what the parties, who have thought proper to dispute upon that point, have wrested from each other in the course of the conflict, may be, in the issue of it, restored to the proper owner. Nations may be guilty of a conduct that would render an individual infamous for ever; and yet carry their heads high, talk of their glory, and despise their neighbours. Your opinions and mine, I mean our political ones, are not exactly of a piece, yet I cannot think otherwise upon this subject than I have always done. England, more, perhaps, through the fault of her generals, than her councils, has in some instances acted with a spirit of cruel animosity she was never chargeable with till now. But this is the worst that can be said. On the other hand, the Americans, who, if they had contented themselves with a struggle for lawful liberty, would have deserved applause, seem to me to have incurred the guilt of parricide, by renouncing their parent, by making her ruin their favourite object, and by associating themselves with her worst enemy, for the accomplishment of their purpose. France, and of course Spain, have acted a treacherous, a thievish part. They have stolen America from England, and whether they are able to possess themselves of that jewel or not hereafter, it was doubtless what they intended. Holland appears to me in a meaner light than any of them. They quarrelled with a friend for an enemy's sake. The French led them by the nose, and the English have thrashed them for suffering it. My views of the contest being, and having been always such, I have consequently brighter hopes for England than her situation some time since seemed to justify. She is the only injured party. America may, perhaps, call her the aggressor ; but if she were so, America has not only repelled the injury, but done a greater. As to the rest, if perfidy, treachery, avarice, and ambition, can prove their cause to have been a rotten one, those proofs are found upon them. I think, therefore, that whatever scourge may be prepared for England, on some future day, her ruin is not yet to be expected.

Acknowledge, now, that I am worthy of a place under the shed I described, and that I should make no small figure among the *quidnuncs* of Olney.

I wish the society you have formed may prosper. Your subjects will be of greater importance, and discussed with more sufficiency. The earth is a grain of sand, but the spiritual interests of man are commensurate with the heavens.

Pray remind Mr. Bull, who has too much genius to have a good memory, that he has an account to settle for Mrs. Unwin with her grocer, and give our love to him. Accept for yourself and Mrs. Newton your just share of the same commodity, with our united thanks for a very fine barrel of oysters. This, indeed, is rather commending the barrel than its contents. I should say, therefore, for a barrel of very fine oysters.—Yours, my dear friend, as ever, W. C.

TO THE REV. WILLIAM BULL.

June 3, 1783.

My dear Friend—My greenhouse, fronted with myrtles, and where I hear nothing but the pattering of a fine shower and the sound of distant thunder, wants only the fumes of your pipe to make it perfectly delightful. Tobacco was not known in the golden age. So much the worse for the golden age. This age of iron, or lead, would be insupportable without it; and therefore we may reasonably suppose that the happiness of those better days would have been much improved by the use of it. We hope that you and your son are perfectly recovered. The season has been most unfavourable to animal life; and I, who am merely animal, have suffered much by it.

Though I should be glad to write, I write little or nothing. The time for such fruit is not yet come; but I expect it, and I wish for it. I want amusement; and, deprived of that, have none to supply the place of it. I send you, however, according to my promise to send you every thing, two stanzas composed at the request of Lady Austen. She wanted words to a tune she much admired, and I gave her these on Peace. —Yours, W. C.

TO THE REV. WILLIAM UNWIN.

June 8, 1783.

My dear William—Our severest winter, commonly called the spring, is now over, and I find myself seated in my favourite recess, the greenhouse. In such a situation, so silent, so shady, where no human foot is heard, and where only my myrtles presume to peep in at the window, you may suppose I have no interruption to complain of, and that my thoughts are perfectly at my command. But the beauties of the spot are themselves an interruption ; my attention is called upon by those very myrtles, by a double row of grass pinks just beginning to blossom, and by a bed of beans already in bloom ; and you are to consider it, if you please, as no small proof of my regard, that though you have so many powerful rivals, I disengage myself from them all, and devote this hour entirely to you.

You are not acquainted with the Rev. Mr. Bull, of Newport ; perhaps it is as well for you that you are not. You would regret still more than you do, that there are so many miles interposed between us. He spends part of the day with us to-morrow. A dissenter, but a liberal one ; a man of letters and of genius ; master of a fine imagination, or rather not master of it,—an imagination which, when he finds himself in the company he loves, and can confide in, runs away with him into such fields of speculation, as amuse and enliven every other imagination that has the happiness to be of the party. At other times he has a tender and delicate sort of melancholy in his disposition, not less agreeable in its way. No men are better qualified for companions in such a world as this, than men of such a temperament. Every scene of life has two sides, a dark and a bright one, and the mind that has an equal mixture of melancholy and vivacity is best of all qualified for the contemplation of either ; it can be lively without levity, and pensive without dejection. Such a man is Mr. Bull. But—he smokes tobacco. Nothing is perfect,—

Nihil est ab omni
Parte beatum.

I find that your friend Mr. Fytche has lost his cause ; and more mortifying still, has lost it by a single voice. Had I been a peer, he should have been secure of mine ; for I am persuaded that if conditional presentations were in fashion, and if every minister held his benefice, as the judges their office, upon the terms of *quamdiu bene se gesserit,* it would be better for the cause of religion, and more for the honour of the Establishment. There ought to be discipline somewhere; and if the Bishops will not exercise it, I do not see why lay patrons should have their hands tied. If I remember your state of the case, (and I never heard it stated but by you,) my reflections upon it are pertinent. It is however long since we talked about it, and I may possibly misconceive it at present: if so, they go for nothing. I understand that he presented upon condition, that if the parson proved immoral or negligent, he should have liberty to call upon him either for his resignation or the penalty. If I am wrong, correct me.

On the other side I send you a something, a song if you please, composed last Thursday—the incident happened the day before.—Yours, W. C.

TO THE REV. JOHN NEWTON.

July 27, 1783.

My dear Friend—You cannot have more pleasure in receiving a letter from me, than I should find in writing it, were it not almost impossible in such a place to find a subject.

I live in a world abounding with incidents, upon which many grave, and perhaps some profitable observations might be made; but those incidents never reaching my unfortunate ears, both the entertaining narrative and the reflection it might suggest are to me annihilated and lost. I look back to the past week, and say, what did it produce? I ask the same question of the week preceding, and duly receive the same answer from both,—nothing!—A situation like this, in which I am as unknown to the world, as I am ignorant of all that passes in it; in which I have nothing to do but to think, would exactly suit me, were my subjects of meditation as agreeable as my leisure is uninterrupted. My passion for retirement is not at all abated, after so many years spent in the most sequestered state, but rather increased ;—a circumstance I should esteem wonderful to a degree not to be accounted for, considering the condition of my mind, did I not know, that we think as we are made to think, and of course approve and prefer, as Providence, who appoints the bounds of our habitation, chooses for us. Thus am I both free and a prisoner at the same time. The world is before me; I am not shut up in the Bastille ; there are no moats about my castle, no locks upon my gates, of which I have not the key ;—but an invisible, uncontrollable agency, a local attachment, an inclination more forcible than I ever felt, even to the place of my birth, serves me for prison-walls, and for bounds which I cannot pass. In former years I have known sorrow, and before I had ever tasted of spiritual trouble. The effect was an abhorrence of the scene in which I had suffered so much, and a weariness of those objects which I had so long looked at with an eye of despondency and dejection. But it is otherwise with me now. The same cause subsisting, and in a much more powerful degree, fails to produce its natural effect. The very stones in the garden-walls are my intimate acquaintance. I should miss almost the minutest object, and be disagreeably affected by its removal, and am persuaded that were it possible I could leave this incommodious nook for a twelvemonth, I should return to it again with rapture, and be transported with the sight of objects which to all the world beside would be at least indifferent; some of them perhaps, such as the ragged thatch and the tottering walls of the neighbouring cottages, disgusting. But so it is, and it is so, because here is to be my abode, and because such is the appointment of *Him* that placed me in it.—

Iste terrarum mihi prœter omnes
Angulus ridet.

It is the place of all the world I love the most, not for any happiness it affords me, but because here I can be miserable with most convenience to myself and with the least disturbance to others.

You wonder, and (I dare say) unfeignedly, because you do not think yourself entitled to such praise, that I prefer your style, as an historian, to that of the two most renowned writers of history the present day has seen. That you may not suspect me of having said more than my real opinion will warrant, I will tell you why. In your style I see no affectation. In every line of theirs I see nothing else. They disgust me always, Robertson with his pomp and his strut, and Gibbon with his finical and French manners. You are as correct as they. You express yourself with as much precision. Your words are ranged with as much propriety, but you do not set your periods to a tune. They discover a perpetual desire to exhibit themselves to advantage, whereas your subject engrosses you. They sing, and you say; which, as history is a thing to be said, and not sung, is, in my judgement, very much to your advantage. A writer that despises their tricks, and is yet neither inelegant nor inharmonious, proves himself, by that single circumstance, a man of superior judgement and ability to them both. You have my reasons. I honour a manly character, in which good sense, and a desire of doing good, are the predominant features;—but affectation is an emetic. W. C.

TO THE REV. WILLIAM UNWIN.

August 4, 1783.

My dear William—I feel myself sensibly obliged by the interest you take in the success of my productions. Your feelings upon the subject are such as I should have myself, had I an opportunity of calling Johnson aside to make the enquiry you purpose. But I am pretty well prepared for the worst, and so long as I have the opinion of a few capable judges in my favour, and am thereby convinced that I have neither disgraced myself nor my subject, shall not feel myself disposed to any extreme anxiety about the sale. To aim with success at the spiritual good of mankind, and to become popular by writing on scriptural subjects, were an unreasonable ambition, even for a poet to entertain, in days like these. Verse may have many charms, but has none powerful enough to conquer the aversion of a dissipated age to such instruction. Ask the question therefore boldly, and be not mortified even though he should shake his head, and drop his chin; for it is no more than we have reason to expect. We will lay the fault upon the vice of the times, and we will acquit the poet.

I am glad you were pleased with my Latin ode, and indeed with my English dirge, as much as I was myself. The tune laid me under a disadvantage, obliging me to write in Alexandrines; which I suppose would suit no ear but a French one; neither did I intend any thing more than that the subject and the words should be sufficiently accommodated to the music. The ballad is a species of poetry, I believe, peculiar to this country, equally adapted to the drollest and the most tragical subjects. Simplicity and ease are its proper characteristics. Our forefathers excelled in it; but we moderns have lost the art. It is observed, that we have few good English odes. But to make amends, we have many excellent ballads, not inferior perhaps in true poetical merit to some of the very best odes that the Greek or Latin languages have to boast of. It is a sort of composition I was ever fond of, and if graver matters had not called me another way, should have addicted myself to it more than to any other. I inherited a taste for it from my father, who succeeded well in it himself, and who lived at a time when the best pieces in that way were produced. What can be prettier than Gay's ballad, or rather Swift's, Arbuthnot's, Pope's, and Gay's, in the What do ye call it—" 'Twas when the seas were roaring?" I have been well informed that they all contributed, and that the most celebrated association of clever fellows this country ever saw did not think it beneath them to unite their strength and abilities in the composition of a song. The success however answered to their wishes, and our puny days will never produce such another. The ballads that Bourne has translated, beautiful in themselves, are still more beautiful in his version of them, infinitely surpassing, in my judgement, all that Ovid or Tibullus have left behind them. They are quite as elegant, and far more touching and pathetic than the tenderest strokes of either.

So much for ballads, and ballad writers. "A worthy subject," you will say, "for a man whose head might be filled with better things;"—and *it is* filled with better things, but to so ill a purpose, that I thrust into it all manner of topics that may prove more amusing; as for instance, I have two goldfinches, which in the summer occupy the greenhouse. A few days since, being employed in cleaning out their cages, I placed that which I had in hand upon the table, while the other hung against the wall: the windows and the doors stood wide open. I went to fill the fountain at the pump, and on my return was not a little surprised to find a goldfinch sitting on the top of the cage I had been cleaning, and singing to and kissing the goldfinch within. I approached him, and he discovered no fear; still nearer, and he discovered none. I advanced my hand towards him, and he took no notice of it. I seized him, and supposed I had caught a new bird, but casting my eye upon the other cage perceived my mistake. Its inhabitant, during my absence, had contrived to find an opening, where the wire had been a little bent, and made no other use of the escape it afforded him, than to salute his friend, and to converse with him more intimately than he had done before. I returned him to his proper mansion, but in vain. In less than a minute he had thrust his little person through the aperture again, and again perched upon his neighbour's cage, kissing him, as at the first, and singing, as if transported with the fortunate adventure. I could not but respect such friendship, as for the sake of its gratification had twice declined an opportunity to be free, and, consenting to their union, resolved that for the future one cage should hold them both. I am glad of such incidents; for at a pinch, and when I need entertainment, the versification of them serves to divert me.—Yours ever,

W. C.

TO THE REV. WILLIAM UNWIN.

Sept. 29, 1783.

My dear William—We are sorry that you and your household partake so largely of the ill effects of this unhealthy season. You are happy however in having hitherto escaped the epidemic fever, which has prevailed much in this part of the kingdom, and carried many off. Your mother and I are well. After more than a fortnight's indisposition, which slight appellation is quite adequate to the description of all I suffered, I am at length restored by a grain or two of emetic tartar. It is a tax I generally pay in autumn. By this time, I hope, a purer ether than we have seen for months, and these brighter suns than the summer had to boast, have cheered your spirits, and made your existence more comfortable. We are rational; but we are animal too, and therefore subject to the influences of the weather. The cattle in the fields show evident symptoms of lassitude and disgust in an unpleasant season; and we, their lords and masters, are constrained to sympathize with them: the only difference between us is, that they know not the cause of their dejection, and we do,—but, for our humiliation, are equally at a loss to cure it. Upon this account I have sometimes wished myself a philosopher. How happy, in comparison with myself, does the sagacious investigator of nature seem, whose fancy is ever employed in the invention of *hypotheses*, and his reason in the support of them! While he is accounting for the origin of the winds, he has no leisure to attend to their influence upon himself; and while he considers what the sun is made of, forgets that he has not shone for a month. One project indeed supplants another. The *vortices* of Descartes gave way to the gravitation of Newton, and this again is threatened by the electrical fluid of a modern. One generation blows bubbles, and the next breaks them. But in the mean time your philosopher is a happy man. He escapes a thousand inquietudes to which the indolent are subject, and finds his occupation, whether it be the pursuit of a butterfly, or a demonstration, the wholesomest exercise in the world. As he proceeds, he applauds himself. His discoveries, though eventually perhaps they prove but dreams, are to him realities. The world gaze at him, as he does at new phenomena in the heavens, and perhaps understand him as little. But this does not prevent their praises, nor at all disturb him in the enjoyment of that self-complacence, to which his imaginary success entitles him. He wears his honours while he lives, and if another strips them off when he has been dead a century, it is no great matter; he can then make shift without them.

I have said a great deal upon this subject, and know not what it all amounts to. I did not intend a syllable of it when I began. But *currente calamo*, I stumbled upon it. My end is to amuse myself and you. The former of these two points is secured. I shall be happy if I do not miss the latter.

By the way, what is your opinion of these air-balloons? I am quite charmed with the discovery. Is it not possible (do you suppose) to convey such a quantity of inflammable air into the stomach and abdomen, that the philosopher, no longer gravitating to a centre, shall ascend by his own comparative levity, and never stop till he has reached the medium exactly *in equilibrio* with himself? May he not by the help of a pasteboard rudder, attached to his posteriors, steer himself in that purer element with ease; and again by a slow and gradual discharge of his aerial contents, recover his former tendency to the earth, and descend without the smallest danger or inconvenience? These things are worth inquiry; and (I dare say) they will be inquired after as they deserve. The *pennæ non homini datæ* are likely to be less regretted than they were; and perhaps a flight of academicians and a covey of fine ladies may be no uncommon spectacle in the next generation. A letter which appeared in the public prints last week convinces me, that the learned are not without hopes of some such improvement upon this discovery. The author is a sensible and ingenious man, and under a reasonable apprehension that the ignorant may feel themselves inclined to laugh upon a subject that affects himself with the utmost seriousness, with much good manners and management bespeaks their patience, suggesting many good consequences that may result from a course of experiments upon this machine, and amongst others, that it may be of use in ascertaining the shape of continents and islands, and the face of wide-extended and far distant countries; an end not to be hoped for, unless by these means of extraordinary elevation the human prospect may be immensely enlarged, and the philosopher, exalted to the skies, attain a view of the whole hemisphere at once. But whether he is to ascend by the mere inflation of his person, as hinted above, or whether in a sort of bandbox, supported upon balloons, is not yet apparent, nor (I suppose) even in his own idea perfectly decided.—Yours, my dear William, W. C.

TO JOSEPH HILL, ESQ.

Oct. 20, 1783.

I SHOULD not have been thus long silent, had I known with certainty where a letter of mine might find you. Your summer excursions however are now at an end, and addressing a line to you in the centre of the busy scene in which you spend your winter, I am pretty sure of my mark.

I see the winter approaching without much concern, though a passionate lover of fine weather and the pleasant scenes of summer; but the long evenings have their comforts too, and there is hardly to be found upon the earth, I suppose, so snug a creature as an Englishman by his fireside in the winter. I mean however an Englishman that lives in the country, for in London it is not very easy to avoid intrusion. I have two ladies to read to, sometimes more, but never less. At present we are circumnavigating the globe, and I find the old story with which I amused myself some years since, through the great felicity of a memory not very retentive, almost new. I am however sadly at a loss for Cook's voyage, can you send it? I shall be glad of Foster's too. These together will make the winter pass merrily, and you will much oblige me. W. C.

TO THE REV. JOHN NEWTON.

Nov. 30, 1783.

My dear Friend—I have neither long visits to pay nor to receive, nor ladies to spend hours in telling me that which might be told in five minutes, yet often find myself obliged to be an economist of time, and to make the most of a short opportunity. Let our station be as retired as it may, there is no want of playthings and avocations, nor much need to seek them, in this world of ours. Business, or what presents itself to us, under that imposing character, will find us out, even in the stillest retreat, and plead its importance, however trivial in reality, as a just demand upon our attention. It is wonderful how by means of such real or seeming necessities, my time is stolen away. I have just time to observe that time is short, and by the time I have made the observation, time is gone. I have wondered in former days at the patience of the Antediluvian world; that they could endure a life almost millenary, with so little variety as seems to have fallen to their share. It is probable that they had much fewer employments than we. Their affairs lay in a narrower compass; their libraries were indifferently furnished; philosophical researches were carried on with much less industry and acuteness of penetration, and fiddles, perhaps, were not even invented. How then could seven or eight hundred years of life be supportable? I have asked this question formerly, and been at a loss to resolve it; but I think I can answer it now. I will suppose myself born a thousand years before Noah was born or thought of. I rise with the sun; I worship; I prepare my breakfast; I swallow a bucket of goat's milk, and a dozen good sizeable cakes. I fasten a new string to my bow, and my youngest boy, a lad of about thirty years of age, having played with my arrows till he has stript off all the feathers, I find myself obliged to repair them. The morning is thus spent in preparing for the chase, and it is become necessary that I should dine. I dig up my roots; I wash them; I boil them; I find them not done enough, I boil them again; my wife is angry; we dispute; we settle the point; but in the mean time the fire goes out, and must be kindled again. All this is very amusing. I hunt; I bring home the prey; with the skin of it I mend an old coat, or I make a new one. By this time the day is far spent; I feel myself fatigued, and retire to rest. Thus what with tilling the ground and eating the fruit of it, hunting and walking, and running, and mending old clothes, and sleeping and rising again, I can suppose an inhabitant of the primæval world so much occupied, as to sigh over the shortness of life, and to find at the end of many centuries, that they had all slipt through his fingers, and were passed away like a shadow. What wonder then that I, who live in a day of so much greater refinement, when there is so much more to be wanted, and wished, and to be enjoyed, should feel myself now and then pinched in point of opportunity, and at some loss for leisure to fill four sides of a sheet like this? Thus, however, it is, and if the ancient gentlemen to whom I have referred, and their complaints of the disproportion of time to the occasions they had for it, will not serve me as an excuse, I must even plead guilty, and confess that I am often in haste, when I have no good reason for being so.

This by way of introduction; now for my letter. Mr. Scott is desired by Mr. De Coetlegon to contribute to the Theological Review, of which, I suppose, that gentleman is a manager. He says he has insured your assistance, and at the same time desires mine, either in prose or verse. He did well to apply to you, because you can afford him substantial help; but as for me, had he known me better, he would never have suspected me for a theologian, either in rhyme or otherwise.

Lord Dartmouth's Mr. Wright spent near two hours with me this morning; a respectable old man, whom I always see with pleasure, both for his master's sake and for his own. I was glad to learn from him that his lordship has better health than he has enjoyed for some years.—Believe me, my dear friend, your affectionate Wm. Cowper.

TO THE REV. WILLIAM UNWIN.

March 21, 1784.

My dear William—I thank you for the entertainment you have afforded me. I often wish for a library, often regret my folly in selling a good collection; but I have one in Essex. It is rather remote, indeed, too distant for occasional reference; but it serves the purpose of amusement, and a waggon being a very suitable vehicle for an author, I find myself commodiously supplied. Last night I made an end of reading Johnson's Prefaces; but the number of poets whom he has vouchsafed to chronicle being fifty-six, there must be many with whose history I am not yet acquainted. These, or some of these, if it suits you to give them a part of your chaise, when you come, will be heartily welcome. I am very much the biographer's humble admirer. His uncommon share of good sense, and his forcible expression, secure to him that tribute from all his readers. He has a penetrating insight into character, and a happy talent of correcting the popular opinion, upon all occasions where it is erroneous; and this he does with the boldness of a man who will think for himself, but, at the same time, with a justness of sentiment that convinces us he does not differ from others through affectation, but because he has a sounder judgement. This remark, however, has his narrative for its object, rather than his critical performance. In the latter, I do not think him always just, when he departs from the general opinion. He finds no beauties in Milton's Lycidas. He pours contempt upon Prior, to such a degree, that were he really as undeserving of notice as he represents him, he ought no longer to be numbered among the poets. These, indeed, are the two capital instances in which he has offended me. There are others less important, which I have not room to enumerate, and in which I am less confident that he is wrong. What suggested to him the thought that the Alma was written in imitation of Hudibras, I cannot conceive. In former years, they were both favourites of mine, and I often read them; but never saw in them the least resemblance to each other; nor do I now, except that they are composed in verse of the same measure. After all, it is a melancholy observation, which it is impossible not to make, after having run through this series of poetical lives, that where there were such shining talents, there should be so little virtue. These luminaries of our country seem to have been kindled into a brighter blaze than others, only that their spots might be more noticed! So much can nature do for our intellectual part, and so little for our moral. What vanity, what petulance in Pope! How painfully sensible of censure, and yet how restless in provocation! To what mean artifices could Addison stoop, in hopes of injuring the reputation of his friend! Savage, how sordidly vicious, and the more condemned for the pains that are taken to palliate his vices. Offensive as they appear through a veil, how would they disgust without one. What a sycophant to the public taste was Dryden; sinning against his feelings, lewd in his writings, though chaste in his conversation. I know not but one might search these eight volumes with a candle, as the prophet says, to find a man, and not find one, unless, perhaps, Arbuthnot were he.

I shall begin Beattie this evening, and propose to myself much satisfaction in reading him. In him, at least, I shall find a man whose faculties have now and then a glimpse from Heaven upon them;—a man, not indeed in possession of much evangelical light, but faithful to what he has, and never neglecting an opportunity to use it. How much more respectable such a character, than that of thousands who would call him blind, and yet have not the grace to practise half his virtues! He, too, is a poet, and wrote the Minstrel. The specimens which I have seen of it pleased me much. If you have the whole, I should be glad to read it. I may, perhaps, since you allow me the liberty, indulge myself here and there with a marginal annotation, but shall not use that allowance wantonly, so as to deface the volumes.

Your mother wishes you to buy for her ten yards and a half of yard-wide Irish, from two shillings to two shillings and sixpence per yard; and my head will be equally obliged to you for a hat, of which I enclose a string that gives you the circumference. The depth of the crown must be four inches and one-eighth. Let it not be a round slouch, which I abhor, but a smart well-cocked fashionable affair. A fashionable hat likewise for your mother; a black one if they are worn, otherwise chip.—Yours, my dear William,

W. C.

TO THE REV. JOHN NEWTON.

March 29, 1784.

My dear Friend—It being his majesty's pleasure that I should yet have another opportunity to write before he dissolves the parliament, I avail myself of it with all possible alacrity. I thank you for your last, which was not the less welcome for coming, like an extraordinary gazette, at a time when it was not expected.

As when the sea is uncommonly agitated, the water finds its way into creeks and holes of rocks, which in its calmer state it never reaches, in like manner the effect of these turbulent times is felt even at Orchard side, where in general we live as undisturbed by the political element, as shrimps or cockles that have been accidentally deposited in some hollow beyond the water mark, by the usual dashing of the waves. We were sitting yesterday after dinner, the two ladies and myself, very composedly, and without the least apprehension of any such intrusion in our snug parlour, one lady knitting, the other netting, and the gentleman winding worsted, when to our unspeakable surprise a mob appeared before the window; a smart rap was heard at the door, the boys halloo'd, and the maid announced Mr. Grenville. Puss was unfortunately let out of her box, so that the candidate, with all his good friends at his heels, was refused admittance at the grand entry, and referred to the back door, as the only possible way of approach.

Candidates are creatures not very susceptible of affronts, and would rather, I suppose, climb in at a window, than be absolutely excluded. In a minute, the yard, the kitchen, and the parlour, were filled. Mr. Grenville advancing toward me shook me by the hand with a degree of cordiality that was extremely seducing. As soon as he and as many more as could find chairs were seated, he began to open the intent of his visit. I told him I had no vote, for which he readily gave me credit. I assured him I had no influence, which he was not equally inclined to believe, and the less, no doubt, because Mr. Ashburner, the drapier, addressing himself to me at this moment, informed me that I had a great deal. Supposing that I could not be possessed of such a treasure without knowing it, I ventured to confirm my first assertion, by saying, that if I had any I was utterly at a loss to imagine where it could be, or wherein it consisted. Thus ended the conference. Mr. Grenville squeezed me by the hand again, kissed the ladies, and withdrew. He kissed likewise the maid in the kitchen, and seemed upon the whole a most loving, kissing, kind-hearted gentleman. He is very young, genteel, and handsome. He has a pair of very good eyes in his head, which not being sufficient as it should seem for the many nice and difficult purposes of a senator, he has a third also, which he wore suspended by a ribband from his buttonhole. The boys halloo'd, the dogs barked, Puss scampered, the hero, with his long train of obsequious followers, withdrew. We made ourselves very merry with the adventure, and in a short time settled into our former tranquillity, never probably to be thus interrupted more. I thought myself, however, happy in being able to affirm truly that I had not that influence for which he sued; and which, had I been possessed of it, with my present views of the dispute between the Crown and the Commons, I must have refused him, for he is on the side of the former. It is comfortable to be of no consequence in a world where one cannot exercise any without disobliging somebody. The town however seems to be much at his service, and if he be equally successful throughout the county, he will undoubtedly gain his election. Mr. Ashburner perhaps was a little mortified, because it was evident that I owed the honour of this visit to his misrepresentation of my importance. But had he thought proper to assure Mr. Grenville that I had three heads, I should not I suppose have been bound to produce them.

Mr. Scott, who you say was so much admired in your pulpit, would be equally admired in his own, at least by all capable judges, were he not so apt to be angry with his congregation. This hurts him, and had he the understanding and eloquence of Paul himself, would still hurt him. He seldom, hardly ever indeed, preaches a gentle, well-tempered sermon, but I hear it highly commended : but warmth of temper, indulged to a degree that may be called scolding, defeats the end of preaching. It is a misapplication of his powers, which it also cripples, and teases away his hearers. But he is a good man, and may perhaps outgrow it.

Many thanks for the worsted, which is excellent. We are as well as a spring hardly less severe than the severest winter will give us leave to be. With our united love, we conclude ourselves yours and Mrs. Newton's affectionate and faithful

W. C.
M. U.

TO THE REV. JOHN NEWTON.

April 26, 1784.

My dear Friend—We are truly sorry that you have been indisposed. It is well however to have passed through such a season and to have fared no worse. A cold and a sore-throat are troublesome things, but in general an ague is more troublesome ; and in this part of the world few have escaped one. I have lately been an invalid myself, and have just recovered from a rheumatic pain in my back, the most excruciating of the sort I ever felt. There was talk of bleeding and blistering, but I escaped with only an embrocation and a box of pills. Mr. Grindon attended me, who though he fidgets about the world as usual, is, I think, a dying man, having had some time since a stroke of apoplexy, and lately a paralytic one. His loss will be felt in this country. Though I do not think him absolutely an Æsculapius, I believe him to be as skilful as most of his fraternity in the neighbourhood, besides which, he has the merit of being extremely cautious, a very necessary quality in a practitioner upon the constitutions of others.

We are glad that your book runs. It will not indeed satisfy those whom nothing could satisfy but your accession to their party ; but the liberal will say you do well, and it is in the opinion of such men only that you can feel yourself interested.

I have lately been employed in reading Beattie and Blair's Lectures. The latter I have not yet finished, I find the former the most agreeable of the two, indeed the most entertaining writer upon dry subjects that I ever met with. His imagination is highly poetical, his language easy and elegant, and his manner so familiar that we seem to be conversing with an old friend, upon terms of the most sociable intercourse, while we read him. Blair is on the contrary rather stiff, not that his style is pedantic, but his air is formal. He is a sensible man, and understands his subjects, but too conscious that he is addressing the public, and too solicitous about his success, to indulge himself for a moment in that play of fancy which makes the other so agreeable. In Blair we find a scholar, in Beattie both a scholar and an amiable man ; indeed so amiable, that I have wished for his acquaintance ever since I read his book. Having never in my life perused a page of Aristotle, I am glad to have had an opportunity of learning more than (I suppose) he would have taught me, from the writings of two modern critics. I felt myself too a little disposed to compliment my own acumen upon the occasion. For though the art of writing and composing was never much my study, I did not find that they had any great news to tell me. They have assisted me in putting my own observations into some method, but have not suggested many, of which I was not by some means or other previously apprized. In fact, critics did not originally beget authors ; but authors made critics. Common sense dictated to writers the necessity of method, connexion, and thoughts congruous to the nature of their subject ;

genius prompted them with embellishments, and then came the critics. Observing the good effects of an attention to these items, they enacted laws for the observance of them in time to come, and having drawn their rules for good writing from what was actually well written, boasted themselves the inventors of an art which yet the authors of the day had already exemplified. They are however useful in their way, giving us at one view a map of the boundaries which propriety sets to fancy; and serving as judges, to whom the public may at once appeal, when pestered with the vagaries of those who have had the hardiness to transgress them.

The candidates for this county have set an example of economy, which other candidates would do well to follow, having come to an agreement on both sides to defray the expenses of their voters, but to open no houses for the entertainment of the rabble; a reform however which the rabble did not at all approve of, and testified their dislike of it by a riot. A stage was built, from which the orators had designed to harangue the electors. This became the first victim of their fury. Having very little curiosity to hear what gentlemen could say who would give them nothing better than words, they broke it in pieces, and threw the fragments upon the hustings. The sheriff, the members, the lawyers, the voters, where instantly put to flight. They rallied, but were again routed by a second assault, like the former. They then proceeded to break the windows of the inn to which they had fled; and a fear prevailing that at night they would fire the town, a proposal was made by the freeholders to face about and endeavour to secure them. At that instant a rioter, dressed in a merry andrew's jacket, stepped forward, and challenged the best man among them. Olney sent the hero to the field, who made him repent of his presumption. Mr. Ashburner was he. Seizing him by the throat, he shook him,—he threw him to the earth, he made the hollowness of his skull resound by the application of his fists, and dragged him into custody without the least damage to his person. Animated by this example, the other freeholders followed it: and in five minutes twenty-eight out of thirty ragamuffins were safely lodged in gaol.

Adieu, my dear friend; writing makes my back ache, and my paper is full.—We love you, and are yours,

W. AND M.

TO THE REV. WILLIAM UNWIN.

Oct. 10, 1784.

MY DEAR WILLIAM—I send you four quires of verse, which having sent, I shall dismiss from my thoughts, and think no more of, till I see them in print. I have not after all found time or industry enough to give the last hand to the points. I believe, however, they are not very erroneous, though in so long a work, and in a work that requires nicety in this particular, some inaccuracies will escape. Where you find any, you will oblige me by correcting them.

In some passages, especially in the second book, you will observe me very satirical. Writing on such subjects I could not be otherwise. I can write nothing without aiming at least at usefulness: it were beneath my years to do it, and still more dishonourable to my religion. I know that a reformation of such abuses as I have censured is not to be expected from the efforts of a poet; but to contemplate the world, its follies, its vices, its indifference to duty, and its strenuous attachment to what is evil, and not to reprehend, were to approve it. From this charge at least I shall be clear, for I have neither tacitly nor expressly flattered either its characters or its customs. I have paid one, and only one compliment, which was so justly due, that I did not know how to withhold it, especially having so fair an occasion;—I forget myself, there is another in the first book to Mr. Throckmorton,—but the compliment I mean is to Mr. Smith. It is however so managed, that nobody but himself can make the application, and you, to whom I disclose the secret; a delicacy on my part, which so much delicacy on his obliged me to the observance of.

What there is of a religious cast in the volume I have thrown towards the end of it, for two reasons; first, that I might not revolt the reader at his entrance,—and secondly, that my best impressions might be made last. Were I to write as many volumes as Lope de Vega, or Voltaire, not one of them would be without this tincture. If the world like it not, so much the worse for them. I make all the concessions I can, that I may please them, but I will not please them at the expense of conscience.

My descriptions are all from nature: not one of them second-handed. My delineations of the heart are from my own experience: not one of them borrowed from books, or in the least degree conjectural. In my numbers, which I have varied as much as I could, (for blank verse without variety of numbers is no better than bladder and string,) I have imitated nobody, though sometimes perhaps there may be an apparent resemblance; because at the same time that I would not imitate, I have not affectedly differed.

If the work cannot boast a regular plan, (in which respect however I do not think it altogether indefensible,) it may yet boast, that the reflections are naturally suggested always by the preceding passage, and that except the fifth book, which is rather of a political aspect, the whole has one tendency; to discountenance the modern enthusiasm after a London life, and to recommend rural ease and leisure, as friendly to the cause of piety and virtue.

If it pleases you I shall be happy, and collect from your pleasure in it an omen of its general acceptance.—Yours, my dear friend, W. C.

TO THE REV. WILLIAM UNWIN.

Oct. 20, 1784.

My dear William—Your letter has relieved me from some anxiety, and given me a good deal of positive pleasure. I have faith in your judgement, and an implicit confidence in the sincerity of your approbation. The writing of so long a poem is a serious business ; and the author must know little of his own heart, who does not in some degree suspect himself of partiality to his own production ; and who is he that would not be mortified by the discovery, that he had written five thousand lines in vain ? The poem however which you have in hand will not of itself make a volume so large as the last, or as a bookseller would wish. I say this, because when I had sent Johnson five thousand verses, he applied for a thousand more. Two years since, I began a piece which grew to the length of two hundred, and there stopped. I have lately resumed it, and (I believe) shall finish it. But the subject is fruitful, and will not be comprised in a smaller compass than seven or eight hundred verses. It turns on the question, whether an education at school or at home be preferable, and I shall give the preference to the latter. I mean that it shall pursue the track of the former,—that is to say, that it shall visit Stock in its way to publication. My design also is to inscribe it to you. But you must see it first; and if, after having seen it, you should have any objection, though it should be no bigger than the tittle of an *i*, I will deny myself that pleasure, and find no fault with your refusal. I have not been without thoughts of adding John Gilpin at the tail of all. He has made a good deal of noise in the world, and perhaps it may not be amiss to show, that though I write generally with a serious intention, I know how to be occasionally merry. The Critical Reviewers charged me with an attempt at humour. John having been more celebrated upon the score of humour than most pieces that have appeared in modern days, may serve to exonerate me from the imputation: but in this article I am entirely under your judgement, and mean to be set down by it. All these together will make an octavo like the last. I should have told you, that the piece which now employs me, is in rhyme. I do not intend to write any more blank. It is more difficult than rhyme, and not so amusing in the composition. If, when you make the offer of my book to Johnson, he should stroke his chin, and look up to the ceiling and cry—"Humph!"—anticipate him (I beseech you) at once, by saying—"that you know I should be sorry that he should undertake for me to his own disadvantage, or that my volume should be in any degree pressed upon him. I make him the offer merely because I think he would have reason to complain of me, if I did not."—But that punctilio once satisfied, it is a matter of indifference to me what publisher sends me forth. If Longman should have difficulties, which is the more probable, as I understand from you that he does not in these cases see with his own eyes, but will consult a brother poet, take no pains to conquer them. The idea of being hawked about, and especially of your being the hawker, is insupportable. Nichols (I have heard) is the most learned printer of the present day. He may be a man of taste as well as of learning; and I suppose that you would not want a gentleman usher to introduce you. He prints the Gentleman's Magazine, and may serve us, if the others should decline; if not, give yourself no farther trouble about the matter. I may possibly envy authors, who can afford to publish at their own expense, and in that case should write no more. But the mortification would not break my heart.

I can easily see that you may have very reasonable objections to my dedicatory proposal. You are a clergyman, and I have banged your order. You are a child of *Alma Mater*, and I have banged her too. Lay yourself therefore under no constraints that I do not lay you under, but consider yourself as perfectly free.

With our best love to you all, I bid you heartily farewell. I am tired of this endless scribblement. Adieu !—Yours,

W. C.

TO THE REV. JOHN NEWTON.

Oct. 30, 1784.

My dear Friend—I am now reading a book which you have never read, and will probably never read—Knox's Essays. Perhaps I should premise, that I am driven to such reading by the want of books that would please me better, neither having any, nor the means of procuring any. I am not sorry, however, that I have met with him; though when I have allowed him the praise of being a sensible man, and in *his* way a good one, I have allowed him all that I can afford. Neither his style pleases me, which is sometimes insufferably dry and hard, and sometimes ornamented even to an Harveian tawdriness; nor his manner, which is never lively without being the worse for it: so unhappy is he in his attempts at character and narration. But writing chiefly on the manners, vices, and follies of the modern day, to me he is at least so far useful, as that he gives me information upon points concerning which I neither *can* nor *would* be informed except by hearsay. Of such information, however, I have need, being a writer upon those subjects myself, and a satirical writer too. It is fit, therefore, in order that I may find fault in the right place, that I should know where fault may properly be found.

I am again at Johnson's in the shape of a poem in blank verse, consisting of six books, and called The Task. I began it about this time twelvemonth, and writing sometimes an hour in a day, sometimes half a one, and sometimes two hours, have lately finished it. I mentioned it not sooner, because almost to the last I was doubtful whether I should ever bring it to a conclusion, working often in such distress of mind, as, while it spurred me to the work, at the same time threatened to disqualify me for it. My bookseller I suppose will be as tardy as before. I do not expect to be born into the world till the month of March, when I and the crocuses shall peep together. You may assure yourself that I shall take my first opportunity to wait on you. I mean likewise to gratify myself by obtruding my Muse upon Mr. Bacon.

Adieu, my dear friend! we are well and love you.—Yours, and Mrs. Newton's,

W. C.

TO THE REV. WILLIAM UNWIN.

Nov. 1, 1784.

My dear Friend—Were I to delay my answer, I must yet write without a frank at last, and may as well therefore write without one now, especially feeling, as I do, a desire to thank you for your friendly offices so well performed. I am glad for your sake, as well as for my own, that you succeeded in the first instance, and that the first trouble proved the last. I am willing too to consider Johnson's readiness to accept a second volume of mine, as an argument that at least he was no loser by the former; I collect from it some reasonable hope that the volume in question may not wrong him neither. My imagination tells me, (for I know you interest yourself in the success of my productions,) that your heart fluttered when you approached his door, and that it felt itself discharged of a burthen when you came out again. You did well to mention it at the Thorntons; they will now know that you do not pretend to a share in my confidence, whatever be the value of it, greater than you actually possess. I wrote to Mr. Newton by the last post, to inform him that I was gone to the press again. He will be surprised, and perhaps not pleased: but I think he cannot complain, for he keeps his own authorly secrets without participating them with me. I do not think myself in the least degree injured by his reserve; neither should I, were he to publish a whole library without favouring me with any previous notice of his intentions. In these cases it is no violation of the laws of friendship not to communicate, though there must be a friendship where the communication is made. But many reasons may concur in disposing a writer to keep his work a secret, and none of them injurious to his friends. The influence of one I have felt myself, for which none of them would blame me,—I mean the desire of surprising agreeably. And if I have denied myself this pleasure in your instance, it was only to give myself a greater, by eradicating from your mind any little weeds of suspicion, that might still remain in it, that any man living is nearer to me than yourself. Had not this consideration forced up the lid of my strong box like a lever, it would have kept its contents with an inviolable closeness to the last; and the first news that either you or any of my friends would have had of the Task, they would have received from the public papers. But you know now, that neither as poet, nor as man, do I give to any man a precedence in my estimation at your expense.

I am proceeding with my new work (which at present I feel myself much inclined to call by the name of Tirocinium) as fast as the Muse permits. It has reached the length of seven hundred lines, and will probably receive an addition of two or three hundred more. When you see Mr. Smith, perhaps you will not find it difficult to procure from him half a dozen franks, addressed to yourself, and dated the fifteenth of December, in which case, they will all go to the post filled with my lucubrations, on the evening of that day. I do not name an earlier, because I hate to be hurried; and Johnson cannot want it sooner than, thus managed, it will reach him.

I am not sorry that John Gilpin, though hitherto he has

been nobody's child, is likely to be owned at last. Here and there I can give him a touch that I think will mend him, the language in some places not being quite so quaint and old-fashioned as it should be ; and in one of the stanzas there is a false rhyme. When I have thus given the finishing stroke to his figure, I mean to grace him with two mottoes, a Greek and a Latin one, which, when the world shall see that I have only a little one of three words to the volume itself, and none to the books of which it consists, they will perhaps understand as a stricture upon that pompous display of literature, with which some authors take occasion to crowd their titles. Knox, in particular, who is a sensible man too, has not, I think, fewer than half a dozen to his Essays.—Adieu, W. C.

TO THE REV. JOHN NEWTON.

Nov. 27, 1784.

My dear Friend—All the interest that you take in my new publication, and all the pleas that you urge in behalf of your right to my confidence, the moment I had read your letter, struck me as so many proofs of your regard ; of a friendship, in which distance and time make no abatement. But it is difficult to adjust opposite claims to the satisfaction of all parties. I have done my best, and must leave it to your candour to put a just interpretation upon all that has passed, and to give me credit for it, as a certain truth, that whatever seeming defects, in point of attention and attachment to you, my conduct on this occasion may have appeared to have been chargeable with, I am in reality as clear of all real ones as you would wish to find me.

I send you enclosed, in the first place, a copy of the advertisement to the reader, which accounts for my title, not otherwise easily accounted for ;—secondly, what is called an argument, or a summary of the contents of each book, more circumstantial and diffuse by far than that which I have sent to the press. It will give you a pretty accurate acquaintance with my matter, though the tenons and mortises, by which the several passages are connected, and let into each other, cannot be explained in a syllabus ;—and lastly, an extract, as you desired. The subject of it I am sure will please you ; and as I have admitted into my description no images but what are scriptural, and have aimed as exactly as I could at the plain and simple sublimity of the scripture language, I have hopes the manner of it may please you too. As far as the numbers and diction are concerned, it may serve pretty well for a sample of the whole. But the subjects being so various, no single passage can in all respects be a specimen of the book at large.

My principal purpose is to allure the reader, by character, by scenery, by imagery, and such poetical embellishments, to the reading of what may profit him. Subordinately to this, to combat that predilection in favour of a metropolis, that beggars and exhausts the country, by evacuating it of all its principal inhabitants : and collaterally, and as far as is consistent with this double intention, to have a stroke at vice, vanity, and folly, wherever I find them. I have not spared the Universities. A letter which appeared in the General Evening Post of Saturday, said to have been received by a general officer, and by him sent to the press, as worthy of public notice, and which has all the appearance of authenticity, would alone justify the severest censure of those bodies, if any such justification were wanted. By way of supplement to what I have written on this subject, I have added a poem, called Tirocinium, which is in rhyme. It treats of the scandalous relaxation of discipline, that obtains in almost all schools universally, but especially in the largest, which are so negligent in the article of morals, that boys are debauched in general the moment they are capable of being so. It recommends the office of tutor to the father, where there is no real impediment ; the expedient of a domestic tutor, where there is; and the disposal of boys into the hands of a respectable country clergyman, who limits his attention to two, in all cases where they cannot be conveniently educated at home. Mr. Unwin happily affording me an instance in point, the poem is inscribed to him. You will now I hope command your hunger to be patient, and be satisfied with the luncheon that I send, till dinner comes. That piecemeal perusal of the work, sheet by sheet, would be so disadvantageous to the work itself, and therefore so uncomfortable to me, that, I dare say, you will waive your desire of it. A poem, thus disjointed, cannot possibly be fit for any body's inspection but the author's.

Tully's rule—"*Nulla dies sine lineâ*"—will make a volume in less time than one would suppose. I adhered to it so rigidly, that though more than once I found three lines as many as I had time to compass, still I wrote; and finding occasionally, and as it might happen, a more fluent vein, the abundance of one day made me amends for the barrenness of another. But I do not mean to write blank verse again. Not having the music of rhymes, it requires so close an attention to the pause and the cadence, and such a peculiar mode of expression, as render it, to me at least, the most difficult species of poetry that I have ever meddled with.

I am obliged to you, and to Mr. Bacon, for your kind remembrance of me when you meet. No artist can excel as he does, without the finest feelings; and every man that has the finest feelings is, and must be, amiable.—Adieu, my dear friend! Affectionately yours, W. C.

TO THE REV. JOHN NEWTON.

Dec. 11, 1784.

My dear Friend—Having imitated no man, I may reasonably hope that I shall not incur the disadvantage of a comparison with my betters. Milton's manner was peculiar.

So is Thomson's. He that should write like either of them, would, in my judgement, deserve the name of a copyist, but not of a poet. A judicious and sensible reader therefore, like yourself, will not say that my manner is not good, because it does not resemble theirs, but will rather consider what it is in itself. Blank verse is susceptible of a much greater diversification of manner, than verse in rhyme : and why the modern writers of it have all thought proper to cast their numbers alike, I know not. Certainly it was not necessity that compelled them to it. I flatter myself however that I have avoided that sameness with others, which would entitle me to nothing but a share in one common oblivion with them all. It is possible that, as the reviewer of my former volume found cause to say that he knew not to what class of writers to refer me, the reviewer of this, whosoever he shall be, may see occasion to remark the same singularity. At any rate, though as little apt to be sanguine as most men, and more prone to fear and despond, than to overrate my own productions, I am persuaded that I shall not forfeit any thing by this volume that I gained by the last.

As to the title, I take it to be the best that is to be had. It is not possible that a book, including such a variety of subjects, and in which no particular one is predominant, should find a title adapted to them all. In such a case, it seemed almost necessary to accommodate the name to the incident that gave birth to the poem ; nor does it appear to me, that because I performed more than my task, therefore the Task is not a suitable title. A house would still be a house, though the builder of it should make it ten times as big as he at first intended. I might indeed, following the example of the Sunday newsmonger, call it the Olio. But I should do myself wrong ; for though it have much variety, it has, I trust, no confusion.

For the same reason none of the interior titles apply themselves to the contents at large of that book to which they belong. They are, every one of them, taken either from the leading, (I should say the introductory,) passage of that particular book, or from that which makes the most conspicuous figure in it. Had I set off with a design to write upon a gridiron, and had I actually written near two hundred lines upon that utensil, as I have upon the Sofa, the Gridiron should have been my title. But the Sofa being, as I may say, the starting-post from which I addressed myself to the long race that I soon conceived a design to run, it acquired a just pre-eminence in my account, and was very worthily advanced to the titular honour it enjoys, its right being at least so far a good one, that no word in the language could pretend a better.

The Time-piece appears to me, (though by some accident the import of that title has escaped you,) to have a degree of propriety beyond the most of them. The book to which it belongs is intended to strike the hour that gives notice of approaching judgement, and dealing pretty largely in the *signs* of the *times*, seems to be denominated, as it is, with a sufficient degree of accommodation to the subject.

As to the word *worm*, it is the very appellation which Milton himself, in a certain passage of the Paradise Lost, gives to the serpent. Not having the book at hand, I cannot now refer to it; but I am sure of the fact. I am mistaken, too, if Shakspeare's Cleopatra do not call the asp, by which she thought fit to destroy herself, by the same name. But not having read the play these five-and-twenty years, I will not affirm it. They are, however, without all doubt, convertible terms. A worm is a small serpent, and a serpent is a large worm. And when an epithet significant of the most terrible species of those creatures is adjoined, the idea is surely sufficiently ascertained. No animal of the vermicular or serpentine kind is crested, but the most formidable of all.

We do not often see, or rather feel, so severe a frost before Christmas. Unexpected, at least by me, it had like to have been too much for my greenhouse, my myrtles having found themselves yesterday morning in an atmosphere so cold that the mercury was fallen eight degrees below the freezing point.

We are truly sorry for Mrs. Newton's indisposition, and shall be glad to hear of her recovery. We are most liable to colds at this season, and at this season a cold is most difficult of cure.

Be pleased to remember us to the young ladies, and to all under your roof and elsewhere, who are mindful of us.—And believe me, your affectionate, WM. COWPER.

TO THE REV. WILLIAM UNWIN.

April 30, 1785.

MY DEAR FRIEND—I return you thanks for a letter so warm with the intelligence of the celebrity of John Gilpin. I little thought, when I mounted him upon my Pegasus, that he would become so famous. I have learned also, from Mr. Newton, that he is equally renowned in Scotland, and that a lady there had undertaken to write a second part, on the subject of Mrs. Gilpin's return to London, but not succeeding in it as she wished, she dropped it. He tells me likewise, that the head master of St. Paul's school, (who he is I know not,) has conceived, in consequence of the entertainment that John has afforded him, a vehement desire to write to me. Let us hope he will alter his mind; for should we even exchange civilities upon the occasion, Tirocinium will spoil all. The great estimation however in which this knight of the stone-bottles is held, may turn out a circumstance propitious to the volume of which his history will make a part. Those events that prove the prelude to our greatest success, are often apparently trivial in themselves, and such as seemed to promise nothing. The disappointment that Horace mentions is reversed—We design a mug, and it proves a hogshead.

It is a little hard, that I alone should be unfurnished with a printed copy of this facetious story. When you visit London next, you must buy the most elegant impression of it, and bring it with you. I thank you also for writing to Johnson. I likewise wrote to him myself. Your letter and mine together have operated to admiration. There needs nothing more but that the effect be lasting, and the whole will soon be printed. We now draw towards the middle of the fifth book of the Task. The man, Johnson, is like unto some vicious horses, that I have known. They would not budge till they were spurred, and when they were spurred, they would kick.—So did he ; his temper was somewhat disconcerted : but his pace was quickened, and I was contented.

I was very much pleased with the following sentence in Mr. Newton's last ;—"I am perfectly satisfied with the propriety of your proceeding as to the publication."—Now therefore we are friends again. Now he once more enquires after the work, which, till he had disburthened himself of this acknowledgement, neither he nor I, in any of our letters to each other, ever mentioned. Some side-wind has wafted to him a report of those reasons by which I justified my conduct. I never made a secret of them, but both your mother and I have studiously deposited them with those who we thought were most likely to transmit them to him. They wanted only a hearing, which once obtained, their solidity and cogency were such that they were sure to prevail.

You mention Bensley. I formerly knew the man you mention, but his elder brother much better. We were schoolfellows, and he was one of a club of seven Westminster men, to which I belonged, who dined together every Thursday. Should it please God to give me ability to perform the poet's part to some purpose, many whom I once called friends, but who have since treated me with a most magnificent indifference, will be ready to take me by the hand again, and some, whom I never held in that estimation, will, like Bensley, (who was but a boy when I left London,) boast of a connexion with me which they never had. Had I the virtues, and graces, and accomplishments of St. Paul himself, I might have them at Olney, and nobody would care a button about me, yourself and one or two more excepted. Fame begets favour; and one talent, if it be rubbed a little bright by use and practice, will procure a man more friends than a thousand virtues. Dr. Johnson, I remember, in the life of one of our poets, (I believe of Savage,) says, that he retired from the world, flattering himself that he should be regretted. But the world never missed him. I think his observation upon it is, that the vacancy made by the retreat of any individual is soon filled up; that a man may always be obscure, if he chooses to be so; and that he, who neglects the world, will be by the world neglected.

Your mother and I walked yesterday in the Wilderness. As we entered the gate, a glimpse of something white, contained in a little hole in the gate-post, caught my eye. I looked again, and discovered a bird's nest, with two tiny eggs in it. By and by they will be fledged, and tailed, and get wing-feathers, and fly. My case is somewhat similar to that of the parent bird. My nest is in a little nook. Here I brood and hatch, and in due time my progeny takes wing and whistles.

We wait for the time of your coming with pleasant expectation.—Yours truly, W. C.

TO THE REV. JOHN NEWTON.

Sept. 24, 1785.

My dear Friend—I am sorry that an excursion, which you would otherwise have found so agreeable, was attended with so great a drawback upon its pleasures as Miss Cunningham's illness must needs have been. Had she been able to bathe in the sea, it might have been of service to her; but

I knew her weakness and delicacy of habit to be such as did not encourage any very sanguine hopes that the regimen would suit her. I remember Southampton well, having spent much time there; but though I was young, and had no objections on the score of conscience either to dancing or cards, I never was in the assembly-room in my life. I never was fond of company, and especially disliked it in the country. A walk to Netley Abbey, or to Freemantle, or to Redbridge, or a book by the fire-side, had always more charms for me than any other amusement that the place afforded. I was also a sailor, and being of Sir Thomas Hesketh's party, who was himself born one, was often pressed into the service. But though I gave myself an air, and wore trowsers, I had no genuine right to that honour, disliking much to be occupied in great waters, unless in the finest weather. How they contrive to elude the wearisomeness that attends a sea life, who take long voyages, you know better than I; but for my own part, I seldom have sailed so far as from Hampton river to Portsmouth, without feeling the confinement irksome, and sometimes to a degree that was almost insupportable. There is a certain perverseness, of which I believe all men have a share, but of which no man has a larger share than I;—I mean that temper, or humour, or whatever it is to be called, that indisposes us to a situation, though not unpleasant in itself, merely because we cannot get out of it. I could not endure the room in which I now write, were I conscious that the door were locked. In less than five minutes I should feel myself a prisoner, though I can spend hours in it, under an assurance that I may leave it when I please, without experiencing any tedium at all. It was for this reason, I suppose, that the yacht was always disagreeable to me. Could I have stepped out of it into a corn-field or a garden, I should have liked it well enough; but being surrounded with water, I was as much confined in it as if I had been surrounded by fire, and did not find that it made me any adequate compensation for such an abridgement of my liberty.

I make little doubt but Noah was glad when he was enlarged from the ark; and we are sure that Jonah was, when he came out of the fish; and so was I to escape from the good sloop the Harriet.

In my last, I wrote you word that Mr. Perry was given over by his friends, and pronounced a dead man by his physician. Just when I had reached the end of the foregoing paragraph, he came in. His errand hither was to bring two letters, which I enclose; one is to yourself, in which he will give you, I doubt not, such an account both of his body and mind, as will make all that I might say upon those subjects superfluous. The only consequences of his illness seem to be, that he looks a little pale, and that though always a most excellent man, he is still more angelic than he was. Illness sanctified is better than health. But I know a man who has been a sufferer by a worse illness than his, almost these fourteen years, and who at present is only the worse for it.

Mr. Scott called upon us yesterday: he is much inclined to set up a Sunday school, if he can raise a fund for the purpose. Mr. Jones has had one some time at Clifton; and Mr. Unwin writes me word that he has been thinking of nothing else day and night, for a fortnight. It is a wholesome measure, that seems to bid fair to be pretty generally adopted, and for the good effects that it promises, deserves well to be so. I know not, indeed, while the spread of the gospel continues so limited as it is, how a reformation of manners, in the lower class of mankind, can be brought to pass; or by what other means the utter abolition of all principle among them, moral as well as religious, can possibly be prevented. Heathenish parents can only bring up heathenish children; an assertion no where oftener or more clearly illustrated than at Olney; where children, seven years of age, infest the streets every evening with curses and with songs, to which it would be unseemly to give their proper epithet. Such urchins as these could not be so diabolically accomplished, unless by the connivance of their parents. It is well, indeed, if in some instances their parents be not themselves their instructors. Judging by their proficiency, one can hardly suppose any other. It is, therefore, doubtless an act of the greatest charity to snatch them out of such hands, before the inveteracy of the evil shall have made it desperate. Mr. Teedon, I should imagine, will be employed as a teacher, should this expedient be carried into effect. I know not, at least, that we have any other person among us so well qualified for the service. He is indisputably a Christian man, and miserably poor, whose revenues need improvement, as much as any children in the world can possibly need instruction.

Mrs. Unwin hopes that a hare, which she sent before Mrs. Newton went her journey, arrived safe. By this week's coach she also sent three fowls and a ham, with cabbages, of whose safe arrival she will likewise be glad to hear. She has long been troubled with a pain in her side, which we take to be of the spasmodic kind, but is otherwise well. She joins with me in love to yourself and Mrs. Newton, and to the young ladies; neither do we forget Sally Johnson.—Believe me, my dear friend, with true affection, yours, W. C.

TO LADY HESKETH.

October 12, 1785.

My dear Cousin—It is no new thing with you to give pleasure. But I will venture to say that you do not often give more than you gave me this morning. When I came down to breakfast, and found upon the table a letter franked by my uncle, and when opening that frank I found that it contained a letter from you, I said within myself—"This is just as it should be. We are all grown young again, and the days that I thought I should see no more are actually returned." You perceive, therefore, that you judged well when you conjectured that a line from you would not be disagreeable to me. It could not be otherwise than, as in fact it proved, a most agreeable surprise, for I can truly boast of an affection for you that neither years nor interrupted intercourse have at all abated. I need only recollect how much I valued you once, and with how much cause, immediately to feel a revival of the same value; if that can be said to revive which at the most has only been dormant for want of employment. But I slander it when I say that it has slept. A thousand times have I recollected a thousand scenes, in which our two selves have formed the whole of the drama, with the greatest pleasure; at times, too, when I had no reason to suppose that I should ever hear from you again. I have laughed with you at the Arabian Nights' Entertainment, which afforded us, as you well know, a fund of merriment that deserves never to be forgot. I have walked with you to Netley Abbey, and have scrambled with you over hedges in every direction; and many other feats we have performed together upon the field of my remembrance, and all within these few years. Should I say within this twelvemonth I should not transgress the truth. The hours that I have spent with you were among the pleasantest of my former days, and are therefore chronicled in my mind so deeply as to fear no erasure. Neither do I forget my poor friend Sir Thomas. I should remember him indeed, at any rate, on account of his personal kindness to myself; but the last testimony that he gave of his regard for you endears him to me still more. With his uncommon understanding (for with many peculiarities he had more sense than any of his acquaintance), and with his generous sensibilities, it was hardly possible that he should not distinguish you as he has done. As it was the last, so it was the best proof that he could give of a judgment that never deceived him when he would allow himself leisure to consult it.

You say that you have often heard of me; that puzzles

me. I cannot imagine from what quarter; but it is no matter. I must tell you, however, my cousin, that your information has been a little defective. That I am happy in my situation is true; I live, and have lived these twenty years, with Mrs. Unwin, to whose affectionate care of me during the far greater part of that time it is, under Providence, owing that I live at all. But I do not account myself happy in having been for thirteen of those years in a state of mind that has made all that care and attention necessary; an attention and a care that have injured her health, and which, had she not been uncommonly supported, must have brought her to the grave. But I will pass to another subject; it would be cruel to particularise only to give pain, neither would I by any means give a sable hue to the first letter of a correspondence so unexpectedly renewed.

I am delighted with what you tell me of my uncle's good health. To enjoy any measure of cheerfulness at so late a day is much. But to have that late day enlivened with the vivacity of youth is much more, and in these post-diluvian times a rarity indeed. Happy for the most part are parents who have daughters. Daughters are not apt to outlive their natural affections, which a son has generally survived even before his boyish years are expired. I rejoice particularly in my uncle's felicity, who has three female descendants from his little person, who leave him nothing to wish for upon that head.

My dear cousin, dejection of spirits, which I suppose may have prevented many a man from becoming an author, made me one. I find constant employment necessary, and therefore take care to be constantly employed. Manual occupations do not engage the mind sufficiently, as I know by experience, having tried many. But composition, especially of verse, absorbs it wholly. I write, therefore, generally three hours in a morning, and in an evening I transcribe. I read also, but less than I write, for I must have bodily exercise, and therefore never pass a day without it.

You ask me where I have been this summer. I answer, at Olney. Should you ask me where I spent the last seventeen summers, I should still answer at Olney. Ay, and the winters also; I have seldom left it, and except when I attended my brother in his last illness, never, I believe, a fortnight together.

Adieu, my beloved cousin, I shall not always be thus nimble in reply, but shall always have great pleasure in answering you when I can.—Yours, my dear friend and cousin,

W. C.

TO LADY HESKETH.

Olney, November 9, 1785.

My dearest Cousin, whose last most affectionate letter has run in my head ever since I received it, and which I now sit down to answer two days sooner than the post will serve me—I thank you for it, and with a warmth for which I am sure you will give me credit, though I do not spend many words in describing it. I do not seek *new* friends, not being altogether sure that I should find them, but have unspeakable pleasure in being still beloved by an old one. I hope that now our correspondence has suffered its last interruption, and that we shall go down together to the grave, chatting and chirping as merrily as such a scene of things as this will permit.

I am happy that my poems have pleased you. My volume has afforded me no such pleasure at any time, either while I was writing it or since its publication, as I have derived from yours and my uncle's opinion of it. I make certain allowances for partiality, and for that peculiar quickness of taste with which you both relish what you like, and, after all drawbacks upon those accounts duly made, find myself rich in the measure of your approbation that still remains. But, above all, I honour "John Gilpin," since it was he who first encouraged you to write. I made him on purpose to laugh at, and he served his purpose well; but I am now in debt to him for a more valuable acquisition than all the laughter in the world amounts to, the recovery of my intercourse with you, which is to me inestimable.

My benevolent and generous cousin, when I was once asked if I wanted anything, and given delicately to understand that the inquirer was ready to supply all my occasions, I thankfully and civilly, but positively declined the favour. I neither suffer, nor have suffered any such inconveniences as I had not much rather endure than come under obligations of that sort to a person comparatively with yourself a stranger to me. But to you I answer otherwise. I know you thoroughly, and the liberality of your disposition; and have that consummate confidence in the sincerity of your wish to serve me that delivers me from all awkward constraint, and from all fear of trespassing by acceptance. To you therefore I reply, yes. Whensoever, and whatsoever, and in what manner soever you please; and add, moreover, that my affection for the giver is such as will increase to me tenfold the satisfaction that I shall have in receiving. It is necessary, however, that I should let you a little into the state of my finances, that you may not suppose them more narrowly circumscribed than they are. Since Mrs. Unwin and I have lived at Olney we have had but one purse, although during the whole of that time, till lately, her income was nearly double mine. Her revenues indeed are now in some measure reduced, and do not much exceed my own; the worst consequence of this is that we are forced to deny ourselves some things which hitherto we have been better able to afford, but they are such things as neither life, nor the well-being of life, depend upon. My own income has been better than it is, but when it was best it would not have enabled me to live as my connexions demanded that I should, had it not been combined with a better than itself, at least at this end of the kingdom. Of this I had full proof during three months that I spent in lodgings at Huntingdon, in which time, by the help of good management, and a clear notion of economical matters, I contrived to spend the income of a twelvemonth. Now, my beloved cousin, you are in possession of the whole case as it stands. Strain no points to your own inconvenience or hurt, for there is no need of it, but indulge yourself in communicating (no matter what) that you can spare without missing it, since by so doing you will be sure to add to the comforts of my life one of the sweetest that I can enjoy,—a token and proof of your affection.

In the affair of my next publication, toward which you also offer me so kindly your assistance, there will be no need that you should help me in the manner that you propose. It will be a large work, consisting, I should imagine, of six volumes at least. The twelfth of this month I shall have spent a year upon it, and it will cost me more than another. I do not love the booksellers well enough to make them a present of such a labour, but intend to publish by subscription. Your vote and interest, my dear cousin, upon the occasion, if you please, but nothing more. I will trouble you with some papers of proposals when the time shall come, and am sure that you will circulate as many for me as you can. Now, my dear, I am going to tell you a secret. It is a great secret, that you must not whisper even to your cat. No creature is at this moment apprised of it but Mrs. Unwin and her son. I am making a new translation of Homer, and am on the point of finishing the twenty-first book of the *Iliad.* The reasons upon which I undertake this Herculean labour, and by which I justify an enterprise in which I seem so effectually anticipated by Pope, although in fact he has not anticipated me at all, I may possibly give you, if you wish for them, when I can find nothing more interesting to say, a period which I do not conceive to be very near! I have not answered many things in your letter, nor can do it at present for want of room. I cannot believe but that I should know you, nothwithstanding all that time may have done.

There is not a feature of your face, could I meet it upon the road by itself, that I should not instantly recollect. I should say, that is my cousin's nose, or those are her lips and her chin, and no woman upon earth can claim them but herself. As for me, I am a very smart youth of my years. I am not indeed grown gray so much as I am grown bald. No matter. There was more hair in the world than ever had the honour to belong to me. Accordingly, having found just enough to curl a little at my ears, and to intermix with a little of my own that still hangs behind, I appear, if you see me in an afternoon, to have a very decent head-dress, not easily distinguished from my natural growth; which being worn with a small bag, and a black ribbon about my neck, continues to me the charms of my youth, even on the verge of age. Away with the fear of writing too often.—Yours, my dearest cousin, W. C.

P.S.—That the view I give you of myself may be complete, I add the two following items,—that I am in debt to nobody, and that I grow fat.

TO LADY HESKETH.

Olney, Dec. 6, 1785.

My dearest Cousin—I write not *upon* my desk, but *about* it. Having in vain expected it by the waggon that followed your letter, I again expected it by the next; and thinking it likely that it might arrive last night at Sherrington, I sent a man over thither this morning, hoping to see him return with it; but again I am disappointed. I have felt an impatience to receive it that you yourself have taught me, and now think it necessary to let you know that it is not come, lest it should perhaps be detained in London, by the negligence of somebody to whom you might entrust the packing of it, or its carriage to the inn.

I shall be obliged to be more concise than I choose to be

when I write to you, for want of time to indulge myself in writing more. How, will you say, can a man want time, who lives in the country, without business, and without neighbours, who visits nobody, and who is visited himself so seldom? My dear, I have been at the races this morning, and have another letter to write this evening; the post sets out at seven, and it is now drawing near to six. A fine day, you will say, for the races, and the better, no doubt, because it has rained continually ever since the morning. At what races do you suppose that I have been? I might leave you to guess, but loving you too well to leave you under the burthen of an employment that must prove for ever vain, I will even tell you, and keep you no longer in suspense. I have been at Troy, where the principal heroes of the Iliad have been running for such a prize as our jockeys would disdain to saddle a horse for; and yet I assure you they acquitted themselves most nobly, though a kettle and a frying-pan were to reward their labours.

I never answered your question concerning my strong partiality to a common. I well remember making the speech of which you remind me, and the very place where I made it was upon a common, in the neighbourhood of Southampton, the name of which, however, I have forgot. But I perfectly recollect that I boasted of the sagacity that you mention just after having carried you over a dirty part of the road that led to it. My nostrils have hardly been regaled with those wild odours from that day to the present. We have no such here. If there ever were any such in this country, the enclosures have long since destroyed them; but we have a scent in the fields about Olney, that to me is equally agreeable, and which, even after attentive examination, I have never been able to account for. It proceeds, so far as I can find, neither from herb, nor tree, nor shrub: I should suppose therefore that it is in the soil. It is exactly the scent of amber when it has been rubbed hard, only more potent. I have never observed it except in hot weather, or in places where the sun shines powerfully, and from which the air is excluded. I had a strong poetical desire to describe it when I was writing the Common-scene in the Task, but feared lest the unfrequency of such a singular property in the earth, should have tempted the reader to ascribe it to a fanciful nose, at least to have suspected it for a deliberate fiction.

I have been as good as my word, and have sent for the doctor; but having left him the whole week to choose out of, am uncertain on what day I shall fall under his consideration. I have been in his company. He is quite a gentleman, and a very sensible one; and as to skill in his profession, I suppose that he has few superiors.

Mrs. Unwin, (who begs to be mentioned to you with affectionate respect,) sits knitting my stockings at my elbow, with a degree of industry worthy of Penelope herself. You will not think this an exaggeration when I tell you that I have not bought a pair these twenty years, either of thread, silk, or worsted.

Adieu, my most beloved cousin; if you get this before I have an answer to my last, let me soon have an answer to them both.—Truly yours, WM. COWPER.

TO LADY HESKETH.

Jan. 10, 1786.

IT gave me great pleasure that you found my friend Unwin, what I was sure you would find him, a most agreeable man. I did not usher him in with the marrow-bones and cleavers of high-sounding panegyric, both because I was certain that whatsoever merit he had, your discernment would mark it, and because it is possible to do a man material injury by making his praise his harbinger. It is easy to raise expectation to such a pitch, that the reality, be it ever so excellent, must necessarily fall below it.

I hold myself much indebted to Mr. ———, of whom I have the first information from yourself, both for his friendly disposition towards me, and for the manner in which he marks the defects in my volume. An author must be tender indeed to wince on being touched so gently. It is undoubtedly as he says, and as you and my uncle say. You cannot be all mistaken, neither is it at all probable that any of you should be so. I take it for granted therefore that there are inequalities in the composition, and I do assure you, my dear, most faithfully, that if it should reach a second edition, I will spare no pains to improve it. It may serve me for an agreeable amusement perhaps when Homer shall be gone and done with. The first edition of poems has generally been susceptible of improvement. Pope, I believe, never published one in his life that did not undergo variations; and his longest pieces, many. I will only observe, that inequalities there must be always, and in every work of length. There are level parts of every subject, parts which we cannot with propriety attempt to elevate. They are by nature humble, and can only be made to assume an awkward and uncouth appearance by being mounted. But, again, I take it for granted that this remark does not apply to the matter of your objection. You were sufficiently aware of it before, and have no need that I should suggest it as an apology, could it have served that office, but would have made it for me yourself. In truth, my dear, had you known in what anguish of mind I wrote the whole of that poem, and under what perpetual interruptions from a cause that has since been removed, so that sometimes I had not an opportunity of writing more than three lines at a sitting, you would long since have wondered as much as I do myself, that it turned out any thing better than Grub Street.

My cousin, give yourself no trouble to find out any of the Magi to scrutinize my Homer. I can do without them; and if I were not conscious that I have no need of their help, I would be the first to call for it. Assure yourself that I intend to be careful to the utmost line of all possible caution, both with respect to language and versification. I will not send a verse to the press, that shall not have undergone the strictest examination.

A subscription is surely on every account the most eligible mode of publication. When I shall have emptied the purses of my friends, and of their friends, into my own, I am still free to levy contributions upon the world at large, and I shall then have a fund to defray the expenses of a new edition. I have ordered Johnson to print the proposals immediately, and hope that they will kiss your hands before the week is expired.

I have had the kindest letter from Josephus that I ever had. He mentioned my purpose to one of the masters of Eton, who replied, that "such a work is much wanted."—Affectionately yours, W. C.

TO LADY HESKETH.

Jan. 16, 1786.

MY DEAREST COUSIN—You do not ask me, my dear, for an explanation of what I could mean by *anguish of mind*, and by *the perpetual interruptions* that I mentioned. Because you *do not* ask, and because your reason for not asking consists of a delicacy and tenderness peculiar to yourself, for that very cause I will tell you. A wish so suppressed is more irresistible than many wishes plainly uttered. Know then that in the year 73 the same scene that was acted at St. Alban's, opened upon me again at Olney, only covered with a still deeper shade of melancholy, and ordained to be of much longer duration. I was suddenly reduced from my wonted rate of understanding to an almost childish imbecility. I did not indeed lose my senses, but I lost the power to exercise them. I could return a rational answer even to a difficult question, but a question was necessary, or I never spoke at all. This state of mind was accompanied, as I suppose it to be in most instances of the kind, with misapprehension of things and persons that made me a very untractable patient. I believed that every body hated me, and that Mrs. Unwin hated me most of all; was convinced that all my food was poisoned, together with ten thousand megrims of the same stamp. I would not be more circumstantial than is necessary. Dr. Cotton was consulted. He replied that he could do no more for me than might be done at Olney, but recommended particular vigilance, lest I should attempt my life:—a caution for which there was the greatest occasion. At the same time that I was convinced of Mrs. Unwin's aversion to me, I could endure no other companion. The whole management of me consequently devolved upon her, and a terrible task she had; she performed it, however, with a cheerfulness hardly ever equalled on such an occasion; and I have often heard her say, that if ever she praised God in her life it was when she found that she was to have all the labour. She performed it accordingly, but, as I hinted once before, very much to the hurt of her own constitution. It will be thirteen years in little more than a week, since this malady seized me. Methinks I hear you ask,—your affection for me will, I know, make you wish to do so,—Is it removed? I reply, in great measure, but not quite. Occasionally I am much distressed, but that distress becomes continually less frequent, and I think less violent I find writing, and especially poetry, my best remedy. Perhaps had I understood music, I had never written verse, but had lived upon fiddle-strings instead. It is better however as it is. A poet may, if he pleases, be of a little use in the world, while a musician, the most skilful, can only divert himself and a few others. I have been emerging gradually from this pit. As soon as I became capable of action, I commenced carpenter, made cupboards, boxes, stools. I grew weary of this in about a twelvemonth, and addressed myself to the making of birdcages. To this employment succeeded that of gardening, which I intermingled with that of drawing, but finding that the latter occupation injured my eyes, I renounced it, and commenced poet. I have given you, my dear, a little history in shorthand ; I know that it will touch your feelings, but do not let it interest them too much. *In the year when I wrote the Task*, (for it occupied me about a year,) *I was very often most supremely unhappy*, and am under God indebted in good part to that work for not having been much worse. You did not know what a clever fellow I am, and how I can turn my hand to any thing.

I perceive that this time I shall make you pay double postage, and there is no help for it. Unless I write myself out now, I shall forget half of what I have to say. Now therefore for the interruptions at which I hinted.—There came a lady into this country, by name and title Lady Austen, the widow of the late Sir Robert Austen. At first she lived with her sister, about a mile from Olney ; but in a few weeks took lodgings at the vicarage here. Between the vicarage and the back of our house are interposed, our garden, an orchard, and the garden belonging to the vicarage. She had lived much in France, was very sensible, and had infinite vivacity. She took a great liking to us, and we to her. She had been used to a great deal of company, and we, fearing that she would find such a transition into silent retirement irksome, contrived to give her our agreeable company often. Becoming continually more and more intimate, a practice obtained at length of our dining with each other alternately every day, Sundays excepted. In order to facilitate our communication, we made doors in the two garden-walls above-said, by which means we considerably shortened the way from one house to the other, and could meet when we pleased without entering the town at all, a measure the rather expedient, because in winter the town is abominably dirty, and she kept no carriage. On her first settlement in our neighbourhood, I made it my particular business, (for at that time I was not employed in writing, having published my first volume, and not begun my second,) to pay my devoirs to her ladyship every morning at eleven. Customs very soon become laws. I began the "Task,"—for she was the lady who gave me the Sofa for a subject. Being once engaged in the work, I began to feel the inconvenience of my morning attendance. We had seldom breakfasted ourselves till ten, and the intervening hour was all the time that I could find in the whole day for writing; and occasionally it would happen that the half of that hour was all that I could secure for the purpose. But there was no remedy: long usage had made that which at first was optional, a point of good manners, and consequently of necessity, and I was forced to neglect the Task to attend upon the Muse who had inspired the subject. But she had ill health, and before I quite finished the work was obliged to repair to Bristol. Thus, as I told you, my dear, the cause of the many interruptions that I mentioned, was removed, and now, except the Bull that I spoke of, we have seldom any company at all. After all that I have said upon this matter, you will not completely understand me perhaps, unless I account for the remainder of the day. I will add therefore, that having paid my morning visit, I walked; returning from my walk, I dressed; we then met and dined, and parted not till between ten and eleven at night.

The little item that you inserted in your cover, concerning a review of a certain author's work, in the Gentleman's Magazine, excited Mrs. Unwin's curiosity to see it in a moment. In vain did I expostulate with her on the vanity of all things here below, especially of human praise, telling her what perhaps indeed she had heard before, but what on such an occasion I thought it not amiss to remind her of, that at the best it is but as the idle wind that whistles as it passes by, and that a little attention to the dictates of reason would presently give her the victory over all the curiosity that she felt so troublesome. For a short time, indeed, I prevailed, but the next day the fit returned upon her with more violence than before. She would see it,—she was resolved that she would see it that moment. You must know, my dear, that a watchmaker lives within two or three doors of us, who takes in the said Magazine for a gentleman at some distance, and, as it happened, it had not been sent to its proper owner. Accordingly the messenger that the lady dispatched, returned with it, and she was gratified. As to myself, I read the article indeed, and read it to her; but I do not concern myself much you may suppose about such matters, and shall only make two or three cursory remarks, and so conclude. In the first place therefore, I observe that it is enough to craze a poor poet to see his verses so miserably misprinted, and which is worse if possible, his very praises in a manner annihilated, by a jumble of the lines out of their places, so that in two instances, the end of the period takes the lead of the beginning of it. The said poet has still the more reason to be crazed, because the said Magazine is in general singularly correct. But at Christmas, no doubt your printer will get drunk as well as another man. It is astonishing to me that they know so exactly how much I translated of Voltaire. My recollection refreshed by them tells me that they are right in the number of the books that they affirm to have been translated by me, but till they brought the fact again to my mind, I myself had forgotten that part of the business entirely. My brother had twenty guineas for eight books of English Henriade, and I furnished him with four of them. They are not equally accurate in the affair of the Tame Mouse. That I kept one is certain, and that I kept it as they say, in my bureau,—but not in the Temple. It was while I was at Westminster. I kept it till it produced six young ones, and my transports when I first discovered them cannot easily be conceived,—any more than my mortification, when going again to visit my little family, I found that mouse herself had eaten them!

I turned her loose, in indignation, and vowed never to keep a mouse again. Who the writer of this article can be, I am not able to imagine, nor where he had his information of these particulars. But they know all the world and every thing that belongs to it. The mistake that has occasioned the mention of Unwin's name in the margin would be ludicrous if it were not, inadvertently indeed, and innocently on their part, profane. I should have thought it impossible that when I spoke of One who had been wounded in the hands and in the side, any reader in a Christian land could have been for a moment at a loss for the person intended.

Adieu, my dear cousin; I intended that one of these should have served as a case for the other, but before I was aware of it, I filled both sheets completely. However, as your money burns in your pocket, there is no harm done. I shall not add a syllable more except that I am and, while I breathe, ever shall be most truly yours,

WM. COWPER.

Yes; one syllable more. Having just finished the Iliad, I was determined to have a deal of talk with you.

TO LADY HESKETH.

Olney, Feb. 9, 1786.

MY DEAREST COUSIN—I have been impatient to tell you that I am impatient to see you again. Mrs. Unwin partakes with me in all my feelings upon this subject, and longs also to see you. I should have told you so by the last post, but have been so completely occupied by this tormenting specimen, that it was impossible to do it. I sent the General a letter on Monday, that would distress and alarm him; I sent him another yesterday, that will, I hope, quiet him again. Johnson has apologized very civilly for the multitude of his friend's strictures; and his friend has promised to confine himself in future to a comparison of me with the original, so that, I doubt not, we shall jog on merrily together. And now, my dear, let me tell you once more, that your kindness in promising us a visit has charmed us both. I shall see you again. I shall hear your voice. We shall take walks together. I will show you my prospects, the hovel, the alcove, the Ouse, and its banks, every thing that I have described. I anticipate the pleasure of those days not very far distant, and feel a part of it at this moment. Talk not of an inn ! Mention it not for your life ! We have never had so many visitors, but we could easily accommodate them all ; though we have received Unwin, and his wife, and his sister, and his son all at once. My dear, I will not let you come till the end of May, or beginning of June, because before that time my greenhouse will not be ready to receive us, and it is the only pleasant room belonging to us. When the plants go out, we go in. I line it with mats, and spread the floor with mats ; and there you shall sit with a bed of mignionette at your side, and a hedge of honeysuckles, roses, and jasmine ; and I will make you a bouquet of myrtle every day. Sooner than the time I mention the country will not be in complete beauty. And I will tell you what you shall find at your first entrance. Imprimis, as soon as you have entered the vestibule, if you cast a look on either side of you, you shall see on the right hand a box of my making. It is the box in which have been lodged all my hares, and in which lodges Puss at present : but he, poor fellow, is worn out with age, and promises to die before you can see him. On the right hand stands a cupboard, the work of the same author ; it was once a dove-cage, but I transformed it. Opposite to you stands a table, which I also made : but a merciless servant having scrubbed it until it became paralytic, it serves no purpose now but of ornament ; and all my clean shoes stand under it. On the left hand, at the further end of this superb vestibule, you will find the door of the parlour, into which I will conduct you, and where

I will introduce you to Mrs. Unwin, unless we should meet her before, and where we will be as happy as the day is long. Order yourself, my cousin, to the Swan at Newport, and there you shall find me ready to conduct you to Olney.

My dear, I have told Homer what you say about casks and urns, and have asked him, whether he is sure that it is a cask in which Jupiter keeps his wine. He swears that it is a cask, and that it will never be any thing better than a cask to eternity. So if the god is content with it, we must even wonder at his taste, and be so too.—Adieu! my dearest, dearest cousin, W. C.

TO LADY HESKETH.

Monday, March 20, 1786.

Those mornings that I set apart for writing to you, my dearest cousin, are my holiday mornings. At those times I give myself a dispensation from all poetical employments, and as soon as I cease to converse with you, betake myself to a walk in the garden. You will observe therefore that my health cannot possibly suffer by such a procedure, but is rather likely to be benefited; for finding it easy as well as pleasant to write when I write to you, I consequently spend less time at my desk than when Homer lies before me, and have more opportunity of taking exercise and air. Though you *seem* to be so, you are not *in fact* beforehand with me in what you say of my letters, for it has long been an agreed point between me and Mrs. Unwin that yours are the best in the world. You will say—"that is impossible, for I always write what comes uppermost, and never trouble myself either about method or expression." And for that very reason, my dear, they are what they are, so good that they could not be better. As to expression, you have no need to study it; yours is sure to be such as it ought; and as to method, you know as well as I, that it is never more out of its place than in a letter. I have only to add on this subject, that not a word of all this is designed as a compliment to you, but merely as a justification of our opinion.

I begin heartily to wish that Signor Fuseli had accomplished his critique of what now lies before him. You have twice been disagreeably constrained to apologize to Mr. Burrows for the delay, and I am very unwilling that you should be a third time reduced to that necessity. I shall be obliged when it comes to my hands again to bestow on it perhaps two or three sittings, in order to accommodate the copy to his remarks, and to give it such further improvements of my own as it shall appear to me to be still susceptible of: which done, I shall remit it instantly to you. Should you have occasion any time to send your Samuel city-ward, I shall be glad if you will charge him with my poetry-box for Johnson, that he may pack the papers in it. This however is not necessary, for they will probably come equally safe under any such cover as he will give them. I bestowed two mornings in the last week, on the extirpation of elisions only. And from all that part of the second book, which you have not seen, and from the third and fourth completely, have so effectually weeded them out, that in all those quarters you cannot find above three; and those not only pardonable on account of necessity, but such as you would yourself approve, I believe, rather than the vacuity that would be occasioned by their removal. I displaced, I suppose, not less than thirty, some of them horrible creatures, and such as even I myself was glad to be rid of. The same care I shall take throughout the whole translation. I am also a very good boy in another respect: I use all possible diligence to give a graceful gait and movement to such lines as rather hobbled a little before, with this reserve however, that when the sense requires it, or when for the sake of avoiding a monotonous cadence of the lines, of which there is always danger in so long a work, it shall appear to be prudent, I still leave a verse behind me that has some uneasiness in its formation. It is not possible to read Paradise Lost, with an ear for harmony, without being sensible of the great advantage which Milton drew from such a management. One line only occurs to me at present as an instance of what I mean, and I cannot stop to recollect more ; but rumbling and rough as it is, it is in my mind, considering the subjects, one of the finest that ever was composed. He is describing hell ; and as if the contemplation of such a scene had scared him out of all his poetical wits, he finishes the terrible picture thus,—

> *Abominable, unutterable, and worse*
> Than fancy yet had formed, or fear conceived,
> Gorgons and hydras and chimæras dire.

Agree with me, my dear, that the deformity of the first of these three lines is the greatest beauty imaginable. This, however, is only an instance of uncouthness where the *sense* recommends it. Had I the book before me, I could soon fill my sheet with quotations of irregular lines taken from the most beautiful parts of his poem, which he used partly as foils to the rest, and partly to relieve the ear, as I said, from the tedium of an unvaried and perpetual smoothness. This I understand to be one of the great secrets of verse-writing in a piece of great length. Uncritical readers find that they perform a long journey through several hundred pages perhaps without weariness ; they find the numbers harmonious, but are not aware of the art by which that harmony is brought to pass, much less suspect that a violation of all harmony on some occasions, is the very thing to which they are not a little indebted for their gratification. Half-strained critics are disgusted ; they discover that this line and that line limps, but cannot enter into the poet's reasons for making it do so ; and critics indeed, who have a well-formed ear and a true classical taste are pleased, and know how to account for it. I know, my beloved cousin, that you will not allow yourself to be of the last-mentioned order. You disdain all intelligence in these matters, and I have no doubt of the sincerity with which you do it. But you must pardon me if I estimate your judgement in poetry at a much higher rate than yourself. Of this, at least I am sure, that of all the remarks you have made upon mine not one has bespoke any deficiency of taste or judgement in the maker. On the contrary, I have seen good reason to acquiesce in them all, the *cask* excepted, which is a word that the Greek makes necessary, and the "*gently away*," which I do not pretend to be no blemish, but an excusable one.

Than the broad Hellespont in all his parts,

—so it shall stand, my dear, in the volume, you may rest assured; for though I have in my own mind stickled much for the insertion of the word *whole*, as in that place emphatical, I am become now a convert to your opinion, and judge the line mended by the change: smoother it is, no doubt, and sufficiently emphatical into the bargain.

Many thanks for Mr. Hornby's note, (whom, by the way, I before called Stanley, not being able to read his name, even in his own handwriting,) every such piece of information is a clap on the back, the effect of which I feel instantly in my head, and write the better for it. The Task has succeeded beyond my utmost expectations; if Homer succeed as well,—and it shall not fail through any negligence of mine, I shall account my fortune, as a poet, made for ever.

You must not think too highly of my loyalty. A true Whig always loves a good king. But this by way of parenthesis.—I was going to observe that the day puts me in mind of June,—clear sun and soft air. Mrs. Unwin never walks in the garden without looking at the borders to consider which of all the flowers will be blown in June. She has my fear of strangers, but she has no fear of *you*. *Au contraire*, she, as well as somebody else, most heartily loves and longs to see you.—Adieu, my dear coz, ever yours, W. C.

TO JOSEPH HILL, ESQ.

Olney, June 19, 1786.

My dear cousin's arrival has, as it could not fail to do, made us happier than we ever were at Olney. Her great kindness in giving us her company is a cordial that I shall feel the effect of, not only while she is here, but while I live.

Olney will not be much longer the place of our habitation. At a village two miles distant we have hired a house of Mr. Throckmorton, a much better than we occupy at present, and yet not more expensive. It is situated very near to our most agreeable landlord, and his agreeable pleasure grounds. In him, and in his wife, we shall find such companions as will always make the time pass pleasantly while they are in the country, and his grounds will afford us good air, and good walking room in the winter; two advantages which we have not enjoyed at Olney, where I have no neighbour with whom I can converse, and where, seven months in the year, I have been imprisoned by dirty and impassable ways, till both my health and Mrs. Unwin's have suffered materially.

Homer is ever importunate, and will not suffer me to spend half the time with my distant friends that I would gladly give them.

W. C.

TO THE REV. JOHN NEWTON.

Aug. 5, 1786.

My dear Friend—I am neither idle nor forgetful; on the contrary I think of you often, and my thoughts would more frequently find their way to my pen, were I not of necessity every day occupied in Homer. This long business engrosses all my mornings, and when the days grow shorter will have all my evenings too; at present they are devoted to walking, an exercise to me as necessary as my food.

You have heard of our intended removal. The house that is to receive us is in a state of preparation, and, when finished, will be both smarter and more commodious than our present abode. But the circumstance that recommends it chiefly is its situation. Long confinement in the winter, and indeed for the most part in the autumn too, has hurt us both. A gravel walk, thirty yards long, affords but indifferent scope to the locomotive faculty : yet it is all that we have had to move in for eight months in the year, during thirteen years that I have been a prisoner. Had I been confined in the Tower, the battlements of it would have furnished me with a larger space. You say well, that there was a time when I was happy at Olney ; and I am now as happy at Olney as I expect to be any where without the presence of God. Change of situation is with me no otherwise an object than as both Mrs. Unwin's health and mine may happen to be concerned in it. A fever of the slow and spirit-oppressing kind seems to belong to all, except the natives, who have dwelt in Olney many years ; and the natives have putrid fevers. Both they and we, I believe, are immediately indebted for our respective maladies to an atmosphere encumbered with raw vapours issuing from flooded meadows ; and we in particular, perhaps, have fared the worse, for sitting so often, and sometimes for months, over a cellar filled with water. These ills we shall escape in the uplands ; and as we may reasonably hope, of course, their consequences. But as for happiness, he that has once had communion with his Maker must be more frantic than ever I was yet, if he can dream of finding it at a distance from Him. I no more expect happiness at Westón than here, or than I should expect it, in company with felons and outlaws, in the hold of a ballast-lighter. Animal spirits, however, have their value, and are especially desirable to him who is condemned to carry a burthen, which at any rate will tire him, but which, without their aid, cannot fail to crush him. The dealings of God with me are to myself utterly unintelligible. I have never met, either in books or in conversation, with an experience at all similar to my own. More than a twelvemonth has passed since I began to hope that, having walked the whole breadth of the bottom of this Red Sea, I was beginning to climb the opposite shore, and I prepared to sing the song of Moses. But I have been disappointed: those hopes have been blasted; those comforts have been wrested from me. I could not be so duped, even by the arch-enemy himself, as to be made to question the divine nature of them; but I have been made to believe, (which, you will say, is being duped still more,) that God gave them to me in derision, and took them away in vengeance. Such, however, is, and has been my persuasion many a long day; and when I shall think on that subject more comfortably, or, as you will be inclined to tell me, more rationally and scripturally, I know not. In the mean time, I embrace with alacrity every alleviation of my case, and with the more alacrity, because, whatsoever proves a relief of my distress, is a cordial to Mrs. Unwin, whose sympathy with me, through the whole of it, has been such, that, despair excepted, her burthen has been as heavy as mine. Lady Hesketh, by her affectionate behaviour, the cheerfulness of her conversation, and the constant sweetness of her temper, has cheered us both; and Mrs. Unwin not less than me. By her help we get change of air and of scene, though still resident at Olney; and by her means, have intercourse with some families in this country, with whom, but for her, we could never have been acquainted. Her presence here would, at any time, even in my happiest days, have been a comfort to me; but, in the present day, I am doubly sensible of its value. She leaves nothing unsaid, nothing undone, that she thinks will be conducive to our well-being; and, so far as she is concerned, I have nothing to wish, but that I could believe her sent hither in mercy to myself,—then I should be thankful.

I understand that Mr. Bull is in town. If you should see him and happen to remember it, be so good as to tell him that we called at his door yesterday evening. All were well, but Mrs. B. and Mr. Greatheed were both abroad.

I am, my dear friend, with Mrs. Unwin's love to Mrs. N. and yourself, hers and yours, as ever, W. C.

TO LADY HESKETH.

The Lodge, Dec. 24, 1786.

You must by no means, my dearest coz, pursue the plan that has suggested itself to you on the supposed loss of your letter. In the first place I choose that my Sundays, like the Sundays of other people, shall be distinguished by something that shall make me look forward to them with agreeable expectation, and for that reason desire that they may always bring me a letter from you. In the next place, if I know when to *expect* a letter, I know likewise when to *enquire after* a letter, if it happens not to come; a circumstance of some importance, considering how excessively careless they are at the Swan, where letters are sometimes overlooked, and do not arrive at their destination, if no inquiry be made, till some days have passed after their arrival at Olney. It has happened frequently to me to receive a letter long after all the rest have been delivered, and the Padre assured me that Mr. Throckmorton has sent notes three several times to Mrs. Marriot, complaining of this neglect. For these reasons, my dear, thou must write still on Saturdays, and as often on other days as thou pleasest.

The screens came safe, and one of them is at this moment interposed between me and the fire, much to the comfort of my peepers. The other of them being fitted up with a screw that was useless, I have consigned to proper hands, that it may be made as serviceable as its brother. They are very neat, and I account them a great acquisition. Our carpenter assures me that the lameness of the chairs was not owing to any injury received in their journey, but that the maker never properly finished them. They were not high when they came, and in order to reduce them to a level, we have lowered them an inch. Thou knowest, child, that the short foot could not be lengthened, for which reason we shortened the long ones. The box containing the plate and the brooms reached us yesterday, and nothing had suffered the least damage by the way. Every thing is smart, every thing is elegant, and we admire them all. The short candlesticks are short enough. I am now writing with those upon the table; Mrs. U. is reading opposite, and they suit us both exactly. With the money that you have in hand, you may purchase, my dear, at your most convenient time, a tea-urn; that which we have at present having never been handsome, and being now old and patched. A parson once, as he walked across the parlour, pushed it down with his belly, and it never perfectly recovered itself. We want likewise a tea-waiter, meaning, if you please, such a one as you may remember to have seen at the Hall, a wooden one. To which you may add, from the same fund, three or four yards of yard-wide muslin, wherewithal to make neckcloths for my worship. If after all these disbursements any thing should be left in the bottom of the purse, we shall be obliged to you if you will expend it in the purchase of silk pocket-handkerchiefs. There, my precious—I think I have charged thee with commissions in plenty.

You neither must nor shall deny us the pleasure of sending to you such small matters as we do. As to the partridges, you may recollect possibly, when I remind you of it, that I never eat them; they refuse to pass my stomach; and Mrs. Unwin rejoiced in receiving them only because she could pack them away to you—therefore never lay us under any embargoes of this kind, for I tell you beforehand, that we are both incorrigible. My beloved cousin, the first thing I open my eyes upon in a morning, is it not the bed in which you have laid me? Did you not, in our old dismal parlour at Olney, give me the tea on which I breakfast?—the chocolate that I drink at noon, and the table at which I dine?—the every thing, in short, that I possess in the shape of convenience, is it not all from you? and is it possible, think you, that we should either of us overlook an opportunity of making such a tiny acknowledgement of your kindness? Assure yourself that never, while my name is Giles Gingerbread, will I dishonour my glorious ancestry, and my illustrious appellation, by so unworthy a conduct. I love you at my heart, and so does Mrs. U., and we must say thank you, and send you a peppercorn when we can. So thank you, my dear, for the brawn and the chine, and for all the good things that you announce, and at present I will, for your sake, say no more of thanksgiving.

I have answered the Welshman's letter, and have a hope that I shall hear no more of him. He desired my advice, whether to publish or not. In answer, I congratulated him on the possession of a poetical talent, with which he might always amuse himself when fatigued with the weightier matters of the law. As to publication, I recommended it to him by all means, as the principal incentive to exertion. And with regard to his probability of success, I told him that, as he had, I understood, already made the experiment by appearing in print, he could judge how that matter stood, better than I or any man could do it for him. What could I say, my dear? I was really unwilling to mortify a brother bard, and yet could not avoid it but at the expense of common honesty.

The Padre is to dine with us on Thursday next. I am highly pleased with him, and intend to make all possible advances to a nearer acquaintance. Why he is so silent in company I know not. Perhaps he is reserved, like some other people: or perhaps he holds it unsuitable to his function to be forward in mixed conversation. Certain it is, that he has enough to say when he and I are together. He has transcribed the ninth book for me, and is now transcribing the twelfth, which Mrs. Throckmorton left unfinished. Poor Teedon has dined with us once, and it did me good to stuff him.

We have heard from the poor widow, after whom you so kindly enquire. She answered a letter of Mrs. Unwin's about a week since. Her answer was affectionate, tender, and melancholy to a great degree, but not without expressions of hope and confidence in God. We understand that she has suffered much in her health, as well as in her mind. It could not be otherwise, for she was attached to her husband in the extreme. We have learned by a sidewind, since I mentioned her last, that Billy left every thing, or almost every thing, to the children. But she has at present one hundred pounds a year, and will have another hundred hereafter, if she outlives Mrs. U., being jointured in her estate. In the mean time, her sister lives with her, who has, I believe determined never to marry, from which circumstance she must doubtless derive advantage. She spent some time at Clapham, after her return from Winchester, is now with Mr. John Unwin at Croydon, and goes soon to her gloomy mansion, as she calls it, in Essex. We asked her hither, in hope that a little time spent at Weston might be of use to her, but her affairs would not suffer her to come. She is greatly to be pitied ; and whether she will ever recover the stroke is, I think, very uncertain.

I had some time since a very clever letter from Henry C. which I answered as well as I could, but not in kind. I seem to myself immoderately stupid on epistolary occasions, and especially when I wish to shine. Such I seem now, and such to have been ever since I began. So much the worse for you. Pray, my dear, send me a bit of Indian glue, and an almanack.

It gives me true pleasure to learn that the General at least says he is better, but it would give me much more to hear others say the same. Thank your sister for her instructions concerning the lamp, which shall be exactly followed.—I am, my dearest, your most Gingerbread Giles, &c.,

WM. COWPER.

TO SAMUEL ROSE, ESQ.

Weston, Oct. 19, 1787.

Dear Sir,—A summons from Johnson, which I received yesterday, calls my attention once more to the business of translation. Before I begin I am willing to catch though but a short opportunity to acknowledge your last favour. The necessity of applying myself with all diligence to a long work that has been but too long interrupted, will make my opportunities of writing rare in future.

Air and exercise are necessary to all men, but particularly so to the man whose mind labours; and to him who has been all his life accustomed to much of both, they are necessary in the extreme. My time since we parted, has been devoted entirely to the recovery of health and strength for this service, and I am willing to hope with good effect. Ten months have passed since I discontinued my poetical efforts; I do not expect to find the same readiness as before, till exercise of the neglected faculty, such as it is, shall have restored it to me.

You find yourself, I hope, by this time as comfortably situated in your new abode, as in a new abode one can be. I enter perfectly into all your feelings on occasion of the change. A sensible mind cannot do violence even to a local attachment without much pain. When my father died I was young, too young to have reflected much. He was Rector of Berkhampstead, and there I was born. It had never occurred to me that a parson has no fee-simple in the house and glebe he occupies. There was neither tree, nor gate, nor stile, in all that country, to which I did not feel a relation, and the house itself I preferred to a palace. I was sent for from London to attend him in his last illness, and he died just before I arrived. Then, and not till then, I felt for the first time that I and my native place were disunited for ever. I sighed a long adieu to fields and woods, from which I once thought I should never be parted, and was at no time so sensible of their beauties, as just when I left them all behind me, to return no more. W. C.

TO LADY HESKETH.

The Lodge, Nov. 27, 1787.

IT is the part of wisdom, my dearest cousin, to sit down contented under the demands of necessity, because they are such. I am sensible that you cannot in my uncle's present infirm state, and of which it is not possible to expect any considerable amendment, indulge either us, or yourself, with a journey to Weston. Yourself I say, both because I know it will give you pleasure to see *Causidice mi* once more, especially in the comfortable abode where you have placed him, and because after so long an imprisonment in London, you who love the country and have a taste for it, would of course be glad to return to it. For my own part, to me it is ever new, and though I have now been an inhabitant of this village a twelvemonth, and have during the half of that time been at liberty to expatiate, and to make discoveries, I am daily finding out fresh scenes and walks, which you would never be satisfied with enjoying;—some of them are unapproachable by you either on foot or in your carriage. Had you twenty toes (whereas I suppose you have but ten) you could not reach them; and coach wheels have never been seen there since the flood. Before it indeed, (as Burnet says that the earth was then perfectly free from all inequalities in its surface,) they might have been seen there every day. We have other walks both upon hill tops and in valleys beneath, some of which by the help of your carriage, and many of them without its help, would be always at your command.

On Monday morning last, Sam brought me word that there was a man in the kitchen who desired to speak with me. I ordered him in. A plain, decent, elderly figure made its appearance, and being desired to sit, spoke as follows: "Sir, I am clerk of the parish of All-Saints, in Northampton; brother of Mr. Cox the upholsterer. It is customary for the person in my office to annex to a bill of mortality, which he publishes at Christmas, a copy of verses. You would do me a great favour, Sir, if you would furnish me with one." To this I replied, "Mr. Cox, you have several men of genius in your town, why have you not applied to some of them? There is a namesake of yours in particular, Cox the statuary, who, every body knows, is a first-rate maker of verses. He surely is the man of all the world for your purpose."—"Alas! Sir, I have heretofore borrowed help from him, but he is a gentleman of so much reading, that the people of our town cannot understand him." I confess to you, my dear, I felt all the force of the compliment implied in this speech, and was almost ready to answer, Perhaps, my good friend, they may find me unintelligible too for the same reason. But on asking him whether he had walked over to Weston on purpose to implore the assistance of my Muse, and on his replying in the affirmative, I felt my mortified vanity a little consoled, and pitying the poor man's distress which appeared to be considerable, promised to supply him. The waggon has accordingly gone this day to Northampton loaded in part with my effusions in the mortuary style. A fig for poets who write epitaphs upon individuals! I have written *one*, that serves *two hundred* persons.

A few days since, I received a second very obliging letter from Mr. Mackenzie. He tells me that his own papers, which are by far, he is sorry to say it, the most numerous, are marked V. I. Z. Accordingly, my dear, I am happy to find that I am engaged in a correspondence with Mr. Viz, a gentleman for whom I have always entertained the profoundest veneration. But the serious fact is, that the papers distinguished by those signatures have ever pleased me most, and struck me as the work of a sensible man, who knows the world well, and has more of Addison's delicate humour than any body.

A poor man begged food at the Hall lately. The cook gave him some vermicelli soup. He ladled it about sometime with the spoon, and then returned it to her, saying, "I am a poor man it is true, and I am very hungry, but yet I cannot eat broth with maggots in it." Once more, my dear, a thousand thanks for your box full of good things, useful things, and beautiful things.—Yours ever, W. C.

TO LADY HESKETH.

The Lodge, Dec. 10, 1787.

I THANK you for the snip of cloth, commonly called a pattern. At present I have two coats, and but one back. If at any time hereafter I should find myself possessed of fewer coats, or more backs, it will be of use to me.

Even as you suspect, my dear, so it proved. The ball was prepared for, the ball was held, and the ball passed, and we had nothing to do with it. Mrs. Throckmorton, knowing our trim, did not give us the pain of an invitation, for a pain it would have been. And why? as Sternhold says,—because, as Hopkins answers, we must have refused it. But it fell out singularly enough, that this ball was held, of all days in the year, on my birth day—and so I told them—but not till it was all over.

Though I have thought proper never to take any notice of the arrival of my MSS. together with the *other good things* in the box, yet certain it is, that I received them. I have furbished up the tenth book till it is as bright as silver, and am now occupied in bestowing the same labour upon the eleventh. The twelfth and thirteenth are in the hands of ——, and the fourteenth and fifteenth are ready to succeed them. This notable job is the delight of my heart, and how sorry shall I be when it is ended.

The smith and the carpenter, my dear, are both in the room, hanging a bell; if I therefore make a thousand blunders, let the said intruders answer for them all.

I thank you, my dear, for your history of the G—s. What changes in that family! And how many thousand families have in the same time experienced changes as violent as theirs! The course of a rapid river is the justest of all emblems, to express the variableness of our scene below. Shakspeare says none ever bathed himself twice in the same stream, and it is equally true that the world upon which we close our eyes at night is never the same with that on which we open them in the morning.

I do not always say, give my love to my uncle, because he knows that I always love him. I do not always present Mrs. Unwin's love to you, partly for the same reason, (Deuce take the smith and the carpenter!) and partly because I forget it. But to present my own I forget never, for I always have to finish my letter, which I know not how to do, my dearest coz, without telling you that I am ever yours, W. C.

TO LADY HESKETH.

Dec. 19, 1787 (in Post mark).

Saturday, my dearest cousin, was a day of receipts. In the morning I received a box filled with an abundant variety of stationery ware, containing, in particular, a quantity of paper sufficient, well covered with good writing, to immortalize any man. I have nothing to do, therefore, but to cover it as aforesaid, and my name will never die. In the evening I received a smaller box, but still more welcome on account of its contents. It contained an almanack in red morocco, a pencil of a new invention, called an everlasting pencil, and a noble purse, with a noble gift in it, called a Bank note for twenty-five pounds. I need use no arguments to assure you, my cousin, that by the help of ditto note, we shall be able to fadge very comfortably till Christmas is turned, without having the least occasion to draw upon you. By the post yesterday—that is, Sunday morning—I received also a letter from Anonymous, giving me advice of the kind present which I have just particularized; in which letter allusion is made to a certain piece by me composed, entitled, I believe, the Drop of Ink. The only copy I ever gave of that piece, I gave to yourself. It is *possible*, therefore, that between you and *Anonymous* there may be some communication. If that should be the case, I will beg you just to signify to him, as opportunity may occur, the safe arrival of his most acceptable present, and my most grateful sense of it.

My toothache is in a great measure, that is to say, almost entirely removed; not by snipping my ears, as poor Lady Strange's ears were snipped, nor by any other chirurgical operation, except such as I could perform myself. The manner of it was as follows: we dined last Thursday at the Hall; I sat down to table, trembling lest the tooth, of which I told you in my last, should not only refuse its own office, but hinder all the rest. Accordingly, in less than five minutes, by a hideous dislocation of it, I found myself not only in great pain, but under an absolute prohibition not only to eat, but to speak another word. Great emergencies sometimes meet the most effectual remedies. I resolved, if it were possible, then and there to draw it. This I effected so dexterously by a sudden twitch, and afterwards so dexterously conveyed it into my pocket, that no creature present, not even Mrs. Unwin, who sat facing me, was sensible either of my distress, or of the manner of my deliverance from it. I am poorer by one tooth than I was, but richer by the unimpeded use of all the rest.

When I lived in the Temple, I was rather intimate with a son of the late Admiral Rowley and a younger brother of the present Admiral. Since I wrote to you last, I received a letter from him, in a very friendly and affectionate style. It accompanied half a dozen books, which I had lent him five and twenty years ago, and which he apologized for having kept so long, telling me that they had been sent to him at Dublin by mistake; for at Dublin, it seems, he now resides. Reading my poems, he felt, he said, his friendship for me revive, and wrote accordingly. I have now, therefore, a correspondent in Ireland, another in Scotland, and a third in Wales. All this would be very diverting, had I a little more time to spare to them.

My dog, my dear, is a spaniel. Till Miss Gunning begged him, he was the property of a farmer, and while he was their property had been accustomed to lie in the chimney corner, among the embers, till the hair was singed from his back, and till nothing was left of his tail but the gristle. Allowing for these disadvantages, he is really handsome; and when nature shall have furnished him with a new coat, a gift which, in consideration of the ragged condition of his old one, it is hoped she will not long delay, he will then be unrivalled in personal endowments by any dog in this country. He and my cat are excessively fond of each other, and play a thousand gambols together that it is impossible not to admire.

Know thou, that from this time forth, the post comes daily to Weston. This improvement is effected by an annual subscription of ten shillings. The Throcks invited us to the measure, and we have acceded to it. Their servant will manage this concern for us at the Olney post office, and the subscription is to pay a man for stumping three times a week from Olney to Newport Pagnel, and back again.

Returning from my walk to-day, while I was passing by some small closes at the back of the town, I heard the voices of some persons extremely merry at the top of the hill. Advancing into the large field behind our house, I there met Mr. Throck, wife, and brother George. Combine in your imagination as large proportions as you can of earth and water intermingled so as to constitute what is commonly called mud, and you will have but an imperfect conception of the quantity that had attached itself to her petticoats: but she had half-boots, and laughed at her own figure. She told me that she had this morning transcribed sixteen pages of my Homer. I observed in reply, that to write so much, and to gather all that dirt, was no bad morning's work, considering the shortness of the days at this season.—Yours, my dear, W. C.

TO LADY HESKETH.

The Lodge, March 3, 1788.

One day last week, Mrs. Unwin and I, having taken our morning walk and returning homeward through the wilderness, met the Throckmortons. A minute after we had met them, we heard the cry of hounds at no great distance, and mounting the broad stump of an elm which had been felled, and by the aid of which we were enabled to look over the wall, we saw them. They were all at that time in our orchard; presently we heard a terrier, belonging to Mrs. Throckmorton, which you may remember by the name of Fury, yelping with much vehemence, and saw her running through the thickets within a few yards of us at her utmost speed, as if in pursuit of something which we doubted not was the fox. Before we could reach the other end of the wilderness, the hounds entered also; and when we arrived at the gate which opens into the grove, there we found the whole weary cavalcade assembled. The huntsman dismounting, begged leave to follow his hounds on foot, for he was sure, he said, that they had killed him: a conclusion which I suppose he drew from their profound silence. He was accordingly admitted, and with a sagacity that would not have dishonoured the best hound in the world, pursuing precisely the same track which the fox and the dogs had taken, though he had never had a glimpse of either after their first entrance through the rails, arrived where he found the slaughtered prey. He soon produced dead reynard, and rejoined us in the grove with all his dogs about him. Having an opportunity to see a ceremony, which I was pretty sure would never fall in my way again, I determined to stay and to notice all that passed with the most minute attention. The huntsman having by the aid of a pitchfork lodged reynard on the arm of an elm, at the height of about nine feet from the ground, there left him for a considerable time. The gentlemen sat on their horses contemplating the fox, for which they had toiled so hard; and the hounds assembled at the foot of the tree, with faces not less expressive of the most rational delight, contemplated the same object. The huntsman remounted; cut off a foot, and threw it to the hounds;—one of them swallowed it whole like a bolus. He then once more alighted, and drawing down the fox by the hinder legs, desired the people, who were by this time rather numerous, to open a lane for him to the right and left. He was instantly obeyed, when throwing the fox to the distance of some yards, and screaming like a fiend, "tear him to pieces"—at least six times repeatedly, he consigned him over absolutely to the pack, who in a few minutes devoured him completely. Thus, my dear, as Virgil says, what none of the gods could have ventured to promise me, time itself, pursuing its accustomed course, has of its own accord presented me with. I have been in at the death of a fox, and you now know as much of the matter as I, who am as well informed as any sportsman in England.—Yours,

W. C.

TO MRS. KING.

Weston Underwood, March 3, 1788.

I owe you many acknowledgments, dear madam, for that unreserved communication, both of your history and of your sentiments, with which you favoured me in your last. It gives me great pleasure to learn that you are so happily circumstanced, both in respect of situation and frame of mind. With your view of religious subjects, you could not indeed, speaking properly, be pronounced unhappy in any circumstances; but to have received from above not only that faith which reconciles the heart to affliction, but many outward comforts also, and especially that greatest of all earthly comforts, a comfortable home, is happiness indeed. May you long enjoy it! As to health or sickness, you have learned already their true value, and know well that the former is no blessing, unless it be sanctified, and that the latter is one of the greatest we can receive, when we are enabled to make a proper use of it.

There is nothing in my story that can possibly be worth your knowledge; yet, lest I should seem to treat you with a reserve which, at your hands, I have not experienced, such as it is, I will relate it.—I was bred to the law; a profession to which I was never much inclined, and in which I engaged rather because I was desirous to gratify a most indulgent father, than because I had any hopes of success in it myself. I spent twelve years in the Temple, where I made no progress in that science, to cultivate which I was sent thither. During this time my father died. Not long after him, died my mother-in-law; and at the expiration of it, a melancholy seized me, which obliged me to quit London, and consequently to renounce the bar. I lived some time at St. Alban's. After having suffered in that place long and extreme affliction, the storm was suddenly dispelled, and the same day-spring from on high which has arisen upon you, arose on me also. I spent eight years in the enjoyment of it; and have ever since the expiration of those eight years, been occasionally the prey of the same melancholy as at first. In the depths of it I wrote the Task, and the volume which preceded it; and in the same deeps am now translating Homer. But to return to Saint Alban's. I abode there a year and half. Thence I went to Cambridge, where I spent a short time with my brother, in whose neighbourhood I determined, if possible, to pass the remainder of my days. He soon found a lodging for me at Huntingdon. At that place I had not resided long, when I was led to an intimate connexion with a family of the name of Unwin. I soon quitted my lodging, and took up my abode with them. I had not lived long under their roof, when Mr. Unwin, as he was riding one Sunday morning to his cure at Gravely, was thrown from his horse; of which fall he died. Mrs. Unwin having the same views of the gospel as myself, and being desirous of attending a purer ministration of it than was to be found at Huntingdon, removed to Olney, where Mr. Newton was at that time the preacher, and I with her. There we continued till Mr. Newton, whose family was the only one in the place with which we could have a connexion, and with whom we lived always on the most intimate terms, left it. After his departure, finding the situation no longer desirable, and our house threatening to fall upon our heads, we removed hither. Here we have a good house, in a most beautiful village, and, for the greatest part of the year, a most agreeable neighbourhood. Like you, madam, I stay much at home, and have not travelled twenty miles from this place and its environs, more than once these twenty years.

All this I have written, not for the singularity of the matter, as you will perceive, but partly for the reason which I gave at the outset, and partly that, seeing we are become correspondents, we may know as much of each other as we can, and that as soon as possible.

I beg, madam, that you will present my best respects to Mr. King, whom, together with yourself, should you at any time hereafter take wing for a longer flight than usual, we shall be happy to receive at Weston; and believe me, dear Madam, his and your obliged and affectionate,

W. C.

TO LADY HESKETH.

The Lodge, July 28, 1788.

It is in vain that you tell me you have no talent at description, while in fact you describe better than any body. You have given me a most complete idea of your mansion and its situation; and I doubt not that with your letter in my hand by way of map, could I be set down on the spot in a moment, I should find myself qualified to take my walks and my pastime in whatever quarter of your paradise it should please me the most to visit. We also, as you know, have scenes at Weston worthy of description; but because you know them well, I will only say that one of them has, within these few days, been much improved; I mean the lime walk. By the help of the axe and the woodbill, which have of late been constantly employed in cutting out all straggling branches that intercepted the arch, Mr. Throckmorton has now defined it with such exactness, that no cathedral in the world can show one of more magnificence or beauty. I bless myself that I live so near it; for were it distant several miles, it would be well worth while to visit it, merely as an object of taste; not to mention the refreshment of such a gloom both to the eyes and spirits. And these are the things which our modern improvers of parks and pleasure grounds have displaced without mercy, because, forsooth, they are rectilinear! It is a wonder they do not quarrel with the sunbeams for the same reason.

Have you seen the account of five hundred celebrated authors now living? I am one of them; but stand charged with the high crimé and misdemeanor of totally neglecting method; an accusation which, if the gentleman would take the pains to read me, he would find sufficiently refuted. I am conscious at least myself of having laboured much in the arrangement of my matter, and of having given to the several parts of my book of the Task, as well as to each poem in the first volume, that sort of slight connexion which poetry demands, for in poetry, (except professedly of the didactic kind) a logical precision would be stiff, pedantic, and ridiculous. But there is no pleasing some critics; the comfort is, that I am contented, whether they be pleased or not. At the same time, to my honour be it spoken, the chronicler of us five hundred prodigies bestows on me, for aught I know, more commendations than on any other of my confraternity. May he live to write the histories of as many thousand poets, and find me the very best among them! Amen!

I join with you, my dearest coz, in wishing that I owned the fee simple of all the beautiful scenes around you, but such emoluments were never designed for poets. Am I not happier than ever poet was, in having thee for my cousin, and in the expectation of thy arrival here whenever Strawberry Hill shall lose thee?—Ever thine, W. C.

TO MRS. KING.

Weston Underwood, Oct. 11, 1788.

My Dear Madam,—You are perfectly secure from all danger of being overwhelmed with presents from me. It is not much that a poet can possibly have it in his power to give. When he has presented his own works, he may be supposed to have exhausted all means of donation. They are his only superfluity. There was a time, but that time was before I commenced writer for the press, when I amused myself in a way somewhat similar to yours; allowing, I mean, for the difference between masculine and female operations. The scissors and the needle are your chief implements; mine were the chisel and the saw. In those days you might have been in some danger of too plentiful a return for your favours. Tables, such as they were, and joint-stools such as never were, might have travelled to Pertenhall in most inconvenient abundance. But I have long since discontinued this practice, and many others which

I found it necessary to adopt, that I might escape the worst of all evils, both in itself and in its consequences—an idle life. Many arts I have exercised with this view, for which nature never designed me; though among them were some in which I arrived at considerable proficiency, by mere dint of the most heroic perseverance. There is not a 'squire in all this country who can boast of having made better squirrel-houses, hutches for rabbits, or bird-cages, than myself; and in the article of cabbage-nets, I had no superior. I even had the hardiness to take in hand the pencil, and studied a whole year the art of drawing. Many figures were the fruit of my labours, which had, at least, the merit of being unparalleled by any production either of art or nature. But before the year was ended, I had occasion to wonder at the progress that may be made, in despite of natural deficiency, by dint alone of practice; for I actually produced three landscapes, which a lady thought worthy to be framed and glazed. I then judged it high time to exchange this occupation for another, lest, by any subsequent productions of inferior merit, I should forfeit the honour I had so fortunately acquired. But gardening was, of all employments, that in which I succeeded best; though even in this I did not suddenly attain perfection. I began with lettuces and cauliflowers: from them I proceeded to cucumbers; next to melons. I then purchased an orange-tree, to which, in due time, I added two or three myrtles. These served me day and night with employment during a whole severe winter. To defend them from the frost, in a situation that exposed them to its severity, caused me much ingenuity and much attendance. I contrived to give them a fire heat; and have waded night after night through the snow, with the bellows under my arm, just before going to bed, to give the latest possible puff to the embers, lest the frost should seize them before morning. Very minute beginnings have sometimes important consequences. From nursing two or three little evergreens, I became ambitious of a greenhouse, and accordingly built one; which, verse excepted, afforded me amusement for a longer time than any expedient of all the many to which I have fled for refuge from the misery of having nothing to do. When I left Olney for Weston, I could no longer have a greenhouse of my own; but in a neighbour's garden I find a better, of which the sole management is consigned to me.

I had need take care, when I begin a letter, that the subject with which I set off be of some importance; for before I can exhaust it, be it what it may, I have generally filled my paper. But self is a subject inexhaustible, which is the reason that though I have said little, and nothing, I am afraid, worth your hearing, I have only room to add, that I am, my dear Madam, most truly yours, W. C.

TO SAMUEL ROSE, ESQ.

Weston, Aug. 8, 1789.

MY DEAR FRIEND,—Come when you will, or when you can, you cannot come at a wrong time, but we shall expect you on the day mentioned.

If you have any book that you think will make pleasant evening reading, bring it with you. I now read Mrs. Piozzi's Travels to the ladies after supper, and shall probably have finished them before we shall have the pleasure of seeing you. It is the fashion, I understand, to condemn them. But we who make books ourselves are more merciful to book-makers. I would that every fastidious judge of authors were himself obliged to write; there goes more to the composition of a volume than many critics imagine. I have often wondered that the same poet who wrote the Dunciad should have written these lines,

> The mercy I to others show,
> That mercy show to me.

Alas! for Pope, if the mercy he showed to others was the measure of the mercy he received! he was the less pardonable too, because experienced in all the difficulties of composition.

I scratch this between dinner and tea; a time when I cannot write much without disordering my noddle, and bringing a flush into my face. You will excuse me therefore if, through respect for the two important considerations of health and beauty, I conclude myself, ever yours,

W. C.

TO MRS. BODHAM.

Weston, February 27, 1790.

My dearest Rose—Whom I thought withered and fallen from the stalk, but whom I find still alive: nothing could give me greater pleasure than to know it, and to learn it from yourself. I loved you dearly when you were a child, and love you not a jot the less for having ceased to be so. Every creature that bears any affinity to my mother is dear to me, and you, the daughter of her brother, are but one remove distant from her: I love you, therefore, and love you much, both for her sake and for your own. The world could not have furnished you with a present so acceptable to me as the picture which you have so kindly sent me. I received it the night before last, and viewed it with a trepidation of nerves and spirits somewhat akin to what I should have felt had the dear original presented herself to my embraces. I kissed it, and hung it where it is the last object that I see at night, and of course the first on which I open my eyes in the morning. She died when I had completed my sixth year; yet I remember her well, and am an ocular witness of the great fidelity of the copy. I remember, too, a multitude of the maternal tendernesses which I received from her, and which have endeared her memory to me beyond expression. There is in me, I believe, more of the Donne than of the Cowper; and though I love all of both names, and have a thousand reasons to love those of my own name, yet I feel the bond of nature draw me vehemently to your side. I was thought in the days of my childhood much to resemble my mother, and in my natural temper, of which at the age of fifty-eight I must be supposed a competent judge, can trace both her, and my late uncle, your father. Somewhat of his irritability, and a little I would hope both of his and of her ——, I know not what to call it without seeming to praise myself, which is not my intention, but speaking to *you*, I will even speak out, and say *good nature*. Add to all this, I deal much in poetry, as did our venerable ancestor, the Dean of St. Paul's, and I think I shall have proved myself a Donne at all points. The truth is, that whatever I am, I love you all.

I account it a happy event that brought the dear boy, your nephew, to my knowledge, and that, breaking through all the restraints which his natural bashfulness imposed on him, he determined to find me out. He is amiable to a degree that I have seldom seen, and I often long with impatience to see him again.

My dearest cousin, what shall I say in answer to your affectionate invitation? I *must* say this: I cannot come now, nor soon, and I wish with all my heart I could. But I will tell you what may be done perhaps, and it will answer to us just as well: you and Mr. Bodham can come to Weston, can you not? The summer is at hand, there are roads and wheels to bring you, and you are neither of you translating Homer. I am crazed that I cannot ask you all together for want of house-room; but for Mr. Bodham and yourself we have good room, and equally good for any third, in the shape of a Donne, whether named Hewitt, Bodham, Balls, or Johnson, or by whatever name distinguished. Mrs. Hewitt has particular claims upon me; she was my playfellow at Berkhampstead, and has a share in my warmest affections. Pray tell her so. Neither do I at all forget my cousin Harriet. She and I have been many a time merry at Catfield, and have made the parsonage ring with laughter. Give my love to her. Assure yourself, my dearest cousin, that I shall receive you as if you were my sister; and Mrs. Unwin is, for my sake, prepared to do the same. When she has seen you she will love you for your own.

I am much obliged to Mr. Bodham, for his kindness to my Homer, and with my love to you all, and with Mrs. Unwin's kind respects, am, my dear, dear Rose, ever yours,

W. C.

P.S.—I mourn the death of your poor brother Castres, whom I should have seen had he lived, and should have seen with the greatest pleasure. He was an amiable boy, and I was very fond of him.

Still another P.S.—I find, on consulting Mrs. Unwin, that I have underrated our capabilities, and that we have not only room for you and Mr. Bodham, but for two of your sex, and even for your nephew into the bargain. We shall be happy to have it all so occupied. Your nephew tells me that his sister, in the qualities of the mind, resembles you; that is enough to make her dear to me, and I beg you will assure her that she is so. Let it not be long before I hear from you.

TO JOHN JOHNSON, ESQ.

Weston, March 23, 1790.

YOUR MSS. arrived safe in New Norfolk Street, and I am much obliged to you for your labours. Were you now at Weston I could furnish you with employment for some weeks, and shall perhaps be equally able to do it in summer, for I have lost my best amanuensis in this place, Mr. George Throckmorton, who is gone to Bath.

You are a man to be envied, who have never read the

Odyssey, which is one of the most amusing story-books in the world. There is also much of the finest poetry in the world to be found in it, notwithstanding all that Longinus has insinuated to the contrary. His comparison of the Iliad and Odyssey to the meridian, and to the declining sun, is pretty, but I am persuaded, not just. The prettiness of it seduced him; he was otherwise too judicious a reader of Homer to have made it. I can find in the latter no symptoms of impaired ability, none of the effects of age; on the contrary, it seems to me a certainty, that Homer, had he written the Odyssey in his youth, could not have written it better: and if the Iliad in his old age, that he would have written it just as well. A critic would tell me, that instead of *written*, I should have said *composed*. Very likely;—but I am not writing to one of that snarling generation.

My boy, I long to see thee again. It has happened some way or other, that Mrs. Unwin and I have conceived a great affection for thee. That I should, is the less to be wondered at, (because thou art a shred of my own mother;) neither is the wonder great that she should fall into the same predicament: for she loves every thing that I love. You will observe, that your own personal right to be beloved makes no part of the consideration. There is nothing that I touch with so much tenderness as the vanity of a young man, because I know how extremely susceptible he is of impressions that might hurt him in that particular part of his composition. If you should ever prove a coxcomb, from which character you stand just now at a greater distance than any young man I know, it shall never be said that I have made you one; no, you will gain nothing by me but the honour of being much valued by a poor poet, who can do you no good while he lives, and has nothing to leave you when he dies. If you can be contented to be dear to me on these conditions, so you shall; but other terms more advantageous than these, or more inviting, none have I to propose.

Farewell. Puzzle not yourself about a subject when you write to either of us; every thing is subject enough from those we love. W. C.

TO MRS. THROCKMORTON.

The Lodge, May 10, 1790.

My dear Mrs. Frog—You have by this time, I presume, heard from the Doctor, whom I desired to present to you our best affections, and to tell you that we are well. He sent an urchin, (I do not mean a hedge-hog, commonly called an urchin in old times, but a boy, commonly so called at present,) expecting that he would find you at Bucklands, whither he supposed you gone on Thursday. He sent him charged with divers articles, and among others with letters, or at least with a letter; which I mention, that if the boy should be lost, together with his dispatches, past all possibility of recovery, you may yet know that the Doctor stands acquitted of not writing. That he is utterly lost, (that is to say, the boy, for the Doctor being the last antecedent, as the grammarians say, you might otherwise suppose that he was intended,) is the more probable, because he was never four miles from his home before, having only travelled at the side of a plough-team; and when the Doctor gave him his direction to Bucklands, he asked, very naturally, if that place was in England. So what has become of him Heaven knows!

I do not know that any adventures have presented themselves since your departure worth mentioning, except that the rabbit, that infested your wilderness, has been shot for devouring your carnations; and that I myself have been in some danger of being devoured in like manner by a great dog, viz. Pearson's. But I wrote him a letter on Friday, (I mean a letter to Pearson, not to his dog, which I mention to prevent mistakes—for the said last antecedent might occasion them in this place also,) informing him, that unless he tied up his great mastiff in the day-time, I would send him a worse thing, commonly called and known by the name of an attorney. When I go forth to ramble in the fields, I do not sally like Don Quixote, with a purpose of encountering monsters, if any such can be found ; but am a peaceable poor gentleman, and a poet, who mean nobody any harm,—the foxhunters and the two universities of this land excepted.

I cannot learn from any creature whether the Turnpike Bill is alive or dead ;—so ignorant am I, and by such ignoramuses surrounded. But if I know little else, this at least I know, that I love you, and Mr. Frog ; that I long for your return, and that I am, with Mrs. Unwin's best affections, ever yours, W. C.

TO LADY HESKETH.

The Lodge, May 28, 1790.

My dearest Coz—I thank thee for the offer of thy best services on this occasion. But Heaven guard my brows from the wreath you mention, whatever wreath beside may hereafter adorn them! It would be a leaden extinguisher clapped on all the fire of my genius, and I should never more produce a line worth reading. To speak seriously, it would make me miserable, and therefore I am sure that thou, of all my friends, wouldst least wish me to wear it.—Adieu, ever thine—in Homer-hurry, W. C.

TO JOHN JOHNSON, ESQ.

Weston, July 31, 1790.

You have by this time, I presume, answered Lady Hesketh's letter. If not, answer it without delay ; and this injunction I give you, judging that it may not be entirely unnecessary ; for though I have seen you but once, and only for two or three days, I have found out that you are a scatter-brain. I made the discovery perhaps the sooner, because in this you very much resemble myself, who in the course of my life have, through mere carelessness and inattention, lost many advantages; an insuperable shyness has also deprived me of many. And here again there is a resemblance between us. You will do well to guard against both, for of both, I believe, you have a considerable share as well as myself.

We long to see you again, and are only concerned at the short stay you propose to make with us. If time should seem to you as short at Weston, as it seems to us, your visit here will be gone "as a dream when one awaketh, or as a watch in the night."

It is a life of dreams, but the pleasantest one naturally wishes longest.

I shall find employment for you, having made already some part of the fair copy of the Odyssey a foul one. I am revising it for the last time, and spare nothing that I can mend. The Iliad is finished.

If you have Donne's poems, bring them with you, for I have not seen them many years and should like to look them over.

You may treat us too, if you please, with a little of your music, for I seldom hear any, and delight much in it. You need not fear a rival, for we have but two fiddles in the neighbourhood,—one a gardener's, the other a tailor's: terrible performers both! W. C.

TO MR. JOHNSON [PRINTER].

I DID not write the line that has been tampered with hastily, or without due attention to the construction of it; and what appeared to me its only merit is, in its present state, entirely annihilated.

I know that the ears of modern verse writers are delicate

to an excess, and their readers are troubled with the same squeamishness as themselves. So that if a line do not run as smooth as quicksilver, they are offended. A critic of the present day serves a poem as a cook does a dead turkey, when she fastens the legs of it to a post and draws out all the sinews. For this we may thank Pope: but unless we could imitate him in the closeness and compactness of his expression, as well as in the smoothness of his numbers, we had better drop the imitation, which serves no other purpose than to emasculate and weaken all we write. Give me a manly rough line, with a deal of meaning in it, rather than a whole poem full of musical periods, that have nothing but their oily smoothness to recommend them!

I have said thus much, as I hinted in the beginning, because I have just finished a much longer poem than the last, which our common friend will receive by the same messenger that has the charge of this letter. In that poem there are many lines which an ear so nice as the gentleman's who made the above-mentioned alteration would undoubtedly condemn; and yet (if I may be permitted to say it) they cannot be made smoother without being the worse for it. There is a roughness on a plum which nobody that understands fruit would rub off, though the plum would be much more polished without it. But, lest I tire you, I will only add that I wish you to guard me from all such meddling; assuring you that I always write as smoothly as I can; but that I never did, never will, sacrifice the spirit or sense of a passage to the sound of it.

TO THE REV. MR. BUCHANAN.

Weston, May 11, 1791.

My dear Sir—You have sent me a beautiful poem, wanting nothing but metre. I would to Heaven that you would give it that requisite yourself; for he who could make the sketch, cannot but be well qualified to finish. But if you will not, I will; provided always nevertheless, that God gives me ability, for it will require no common share to do justice to your conceptions.—I am much yours, W. C.

Your little messenger vanished before I could catch him.

TO LADY HESKETH.

The Lodge, May 18, 1791.

My dearest Coz—Has another of thy letters fallen short of its destination; or wherefore is it, that thou writest not? One letter in five weeks is a poor allowance for your friends at Weston. One that I received two or three days since from Mrs. Frog, has not at all enlightened me on this head. But I wander in a wilderness of vain conjecture.

I have had a letter lately from New York, from a Dr. Cogswell of that place, to thank me for my fine verses, and to tell me, which pleased me particularly, that after having read the Task, my first volume fell into his hands, which he read also, and was equally pleased with. This is the only instance I can recollect of a reader who has done justice to my first effusions: for I am sure, that in point of expression they do not fall a jot below my second, and that in point of subject they are for the most part superior. But enough, and too much of this. The Task he tells me has been reprinted in that city.

Adieu! my dearest coz.

We have blooming scenes under wintry skies, and with icy blasts to fan them.—Ever thine, W. C.

TO THE REV. MR. HURDIS.

Weston, June 13, 1791.

My dear Sir—I am glad to find that your amusements have been so similar to mine; for in this instance too I seemed to have need of somebody to keep me in countenance, especially in my attention and attachment to animals. All the notice that we lords of the creation vouchsafe to bestow on the creatures, is generally to abuse them; it is well therefore that here and there a man should be found a little womanish, or perhaps a little childish in this matter, who will make some amends, by kissing, and coaxing, and laying them in one's bosom. You remember the little ewe lamb, mentioned by the prophet Nathan; the prophet perhaps invented the tale for the sake of its application to David's conscience; but it is more probable that God inspired him with it for that purpose. If he did, it amounts to a proof that he does not overlook, but on the contrary much notices such little partialities and kindness to his *dumb* creatures, as we, because we articulate, are pleased to call them.

Your sisters are fitter to judge than I, whether assembly rooms are the places of all others, in which the ladies may be studied to most advantage. I am an old fellow, but I had once my dancing days, as you have now; yet I could never find that I had learned half so much of a woman's real character by dancing with her, as by conversing with her at home, where I could observe her behaviour at the table, at the fireside, and in all the trying circumstances of domestic life. We are all good when we are pleased; but she is the good woman, who wants not a fiddle to sweeten her. If I am wrong, the young ladies will set me right; in the mean time I will not tease you with graver arguments on the subject, especially as I have a hope that years, and the study of the Scripture, and His Spirit whose word it is, will in due time bring you to my way of thinking. I am not one of those sages, who require that young men should be as old as themselves before they have had time to be so.—With my love to your fair sisters, I remain, dear Sir, most truly yours,

W. C.

TO LADY HESKETH.

The Lodge, July 11, 1791.

MY DEAREST COZ—Your draft is safe in our possession, and will soon be out of it, that is to say, will soon be negotiated. Many thanks for that, and still more for your kindness in bidding me draw yet again, should I have occasion. None I hope will offer. I have a purse at Johnson's, to which, if need should arise, I can recur at pleasure. The present is rather an expensive time with us, and will probably cause the consumption of some part of my loose cash in the hands of my bookseller.

I am not much better pleased with that dealer in authors than yourself. His first proposal, which was to pay me with my own money, or in other words to get my copy for nothing, not only dissatisfied but hurt me, implying, as I thought, the meanest opinion possible of my labours. For that for which an intelligent man will give nothing, can be worth nothing. The consequence was that my spirits sank considerably below par, and have but just begun to recover themselves. His second offer, which is, to pay all expenses, and to give me a thousand pounds next midsummer, leaving the copyright still in my hands, is more liberal. With this offer I have closed, and Mr. Rose will to-morrow clench the bargain. Josephus understands that Johnson will gain two hundred pounds by it, but I apprehend that he is mistaken, and that Mr. Rose is right, who estimates his gains at one. Mr Hill's mistake, if he be mistaken, arises from his rating the expenses of the press at only five hundred pounds, whereas Johnson rates them at six. Be that as it may, I am contented. If he gains two, I shall not grudge, and if he gains but one, considering all things, I think he will gain enough.

As to Sephus' scheme of signing the seven hundred copies in order to prevent a clandestine multiplication of them, at the same time that I feel the wisdom of it, I feel also an unsurmountable dislike of it. It would be calling Johnson a knave, and telling the public that I think him one. Now, though I do not perhaps think so highly of his liberality as some people do, and I was once myself disposed to think, yet I have no reason at present to charge him with dishonesty. I must even take my chance, as other poets do, and if I am wronged, must comfort myself with what somebody has said,—that authors are the natural prey of booksellers.

You judge right in supposing that I pity the King and Queen of France. I can truly say, that, except the late melancholy circumstances of our own, (when our sovereign had lost his senses, and his wife was almost worried out of hers,) no royal distresses have ever moved me so much. And still I pity them, prisoners as they are now for life, and since their late unsuccessful attempt, likely to be treated more scurvily than ever. Heaven help them, for in their case, all other help seems vain.

The establishment of our guests at Weston is given up; not for any impediment thrown in the way by Mrs. Bodham, for she consented with the utmost disinterestedness, to the measure, but because on surveying accurately the house in which they must have dwelt, it was found to be so mere a ruin that it would have cost its value to make it habitable. They could only take it from year to year, for which reason the landlord would do nothing.

Many thanks for the Mediterranean hint; but unless I were a better historian than I am, there would be no proportion between the theme and my ability. It seems indeed not to be so properly a subject for one poem as for a dozen.

I was pleased with Bouillie's letter, or to say truth, rather with the principles by which it was dictated. The letter itself seems too much the language of passion, and can only be cleared of the charge of extravagance by the accomplishment of its denunciations,—an event, I apprehend, not much to be expected.

We are all well except poor Catharine, who yesterday consulted Dr. Kerr, and to-day is sick of his prescription. Our affectionate hearts all lay themselves at your pettitoes, and with Mrs. Unwin's best remembrances, I remain, for my own peculiar, most entirely thine, WM. COWPER.

The Frogs are expected here on Wednesday.

TO THE REV. WALTER BAGOT.

Weston, Aug. 2, 1791.

MY DEAR FRIEND—I was much obliged, and still feel myself much obliged to Lady Bagot, for the visit with which she favoured me. Had it been possible that I could have seen Lord Bagot too, I should have been completely happy. For, as it happened, I was that morning in better spirits than usual; and though I arrived late, and after a long walk, and extremely hot, which is a circumstance very apt to disconcert me, yet I was not disconcerted half so much as I generally am at the sight of a stranger, especially of a stranger lady, and more especially at the sight of a stranger lady of quality. When the servant told me that Lady Bagot was in the parlour, I felt my spirits sink ten degrees; but the moment I saw her, at least when I had been a minute in her company, I felt them rise again, and they soon rose even above their former pitch. I know two ladies of fashion now, whose manners have this effect upon me. The Lady in question, and the Lady Spencer. I am a shy animal, and want much kindness to make me easy. Such I shall be to my dying day.

Here sit *I*, calling myself *shy*, yet have just published by the *by*, two great volumes of poe*try*.

This reminds me of Ranger's observation in the Suspicious Husband, who says to somebody, I forget whom—"*There is a degree of assurance in you modest men, that we impudent fellows can never arrive at!*"—Assurance indeed! Have you seen 'em? What do you think they are? Nothing less I can tell you than a translation of Homer. Of the sublimest poet in the world. That's all. Can I ever have the impudence to call myself shy again?

You live, I think, in the neighbourhood of Birmingham? What must you not have felt on the late alarming occasion! You I suppose could see the fires from your windows. We, who only heard the news of them, have trembled. Never sure was religious zeal more terribly manifested, or more to the prejudice of its own cause.

Adieu, my dear friend.—I am, with Mrs. Unwin's best compliments, ever yours, W. C.

TO CLOTWORTHY ROWLEY, ESQ.

Weston Underwood, Oct. 22, 1791.

My dear Rowley—How often am I to be mortified by hearing that you have been within sixty miles of me, and have taken your flight again to an immeasurable distance? Will you never in one of these excursions to England, (three of which at least you have made since we have had intercourse by letter,)—will you never find your way to Weston? Consider that we are neither of us immortal, and that if we do not contrive to meet before we are fifty years older, our meeting in this world at least will be an affair altogether hopeless; for by that time your travelling days will be over, as mine have been these many years.

I have to tell you in answer to your question, what I am doing,—that I am preparing to appear in a new character, not as an author, but as an editor;—editor of Milton's Poetical Works, which are about to be published in a more splendid style than ever yet. My part of the business is to translate the Latin and Italian pieces, to settle the text, to select notes from others, and to write notes of my own. At present the translation employs me; when that shall be finished, I must begin to read all the books that I can scrape together, of which either Milton or his works are the subject; and that done shall proceed to my commentary. Few people have studied Milton more, or are more familiar with his poetry, than myself; but I never looked into him yet with the eyes of an annotator: therefore whether I may expect much or little difficulty, I know no more than you do, but I shall be occupied in the business, no doubt, these two years. Fuseli is to be the painter, and will furnish thirty capital pictures to the engraver.

I have little poems in plenty, but nothing that I can send to Ireland, unless you could put me into a way of conveying them thither at free cost, for should you be obliged to pay for them, *le jeu ne vaudra pas les chandelles.*

I rejoice that your family are all well, and in every thing that conduces to your happiness. Adieu, my good, old, and valued friend; permit me to thank you once more for your kind services in the matter of my subscription, and believe me most truly yours, WM. COWPER.

TO SAMUEL ROSE, ESQ.

The Lodge, Dec. 21, 1791.

MY DEAR FRIEND—It grieves me, after having indulged a little hope that I might see you in the holidays, to be obliged to disappoint myself. The occasion too is such as will ensure me your sympathy.

On Saturday last, while I was at my desk near the window, and Mrs. Unwin at the fireside, opposite to it, I heard her suddenly exclaim, "Oh! Mr. Cowper, don't let me fall! I turned and saw her actually falling, together with her chair, and started to her side just in time to prevent her. She was seized with a violent giddiness, which lasted, though with some abatement, the whole day, and was attended too with some other very, very alarming symptoms. At present however she is relieved from the vertigo, and seems in all respects better.

She has been my faithful and affectionate nurse for many years, and consequently has a claim on all my attentions. She has them, and will have them as long as she wants them; which will probably be, at the best, a considerable time to come. I feel the shock, as you may suppose, in every nerve. God grant that there may be no repetition of it. Another such a stroke upon her would, I think, overset me completely; but at present I hold up bravely. W. C.

TO MR. JOSEPH JOHNSON, ST. PAUL'S CHURCHYARD, LONDON.

Weston Underwood, July 8, 1792.

DEAR SIR—

Truditur dies die,
Novæque pergunt interire lunæ.

Days, weeks, and months escape me, and nothing is done, nor is it possible for me to do any thing that demands study and attention in the present state of our family. I am the electrician; I am the escort into the garden; I am wanted, in short, on a hundred little occasions that occur every day in Mrs. Unwin's present state of infirmity; and I see no probability that I shall be less occupied in the same indispensable duties for a long time to come. The time fixed in your proposals for publication meanwhile steals on; and I have lately felt my engagement for Milton bear upon my spirits with a pressure which, added to the pressure of some other private concerns, is almost more than they are equal to. Tell me if you expect to be punctual to your assignation with the public, and that the artists will be ready with their part of the business so soon as the spring of 94? I cannot bear to be waited for, neither shall I be able to perform my part of the work with any success if I am hunted; and I ask this question thus early lest my own distress should increase, and should ultimately prove a distress to you. My translations are finished, and when I have finished also the revisal of them, will be, I believe, tolerably well executed. They shall be heartily at your service, if by this unhappy interception my time should be so shortened as to forbid my doing more.

Your speedy answer will oblige yours affectionately.

Wm. Cowper.

TO THE REV. MR. GREATHEED.

Eartham, Aug. 6, 1792.

My dear Sir—Having first thanked you for your affectionate and acceptable letter, I will proceed, as well as I can, to answer your equally affectionate request that I would send you early news of our arrival at Eartham. Here we are in the most elegant mansion that I have ever inhabited, and surrounded by the most delightful pleasure grounds that I have ever seen; but which, dissipated as my powers of thought are at present, I will not undertake to describe. It shall suffice me to say that they occupy three sides of a hill, which in Buckinghamshire might well pass for a mountain, and from the summit of which is beheld a most magnificent landscape bounded by the sea, and in one part of it by the Isle of Wight, which may also be seen plainly from the window of the library in which I am writing.

It pleased God to carry us both through the journey with far less difficulty and inconvenience than I expected. I began it indeed with a thousand fears, and when we arrived the first evening at Barnet, found myself oppressed in spirit to a degree that could hardly be exceeded. I saw Mrs. Unwin weary, as she might well be, and heard such a variety of noises, both within the house and without, that I concluded she would get no rest. But I was mercifully disappointed. She rested, though not well, yet sufficiently;

and when we finished our next day's journey at Ripley, we were both in better condition, both of body and mind, than on the day preceding. At Ripley we found a quiet inn, that housed, as it happened, that night, no company but ourselves. There we slept well, and rose perfectly refreshed. And except some terrors that I felt at passing over the Sussex hills by moonlight, met with little to complain of till we arrived about ten o'clock at Eartham. Here we are as happy as it is in the power of terrestrial good to make us. It is almost a Paradise in which we dwell; and our reception has been the kindest that it was possible for friendship and hospitality to contrive. Our host mentions you with great respect, and bids me tell you that he esteems you highly. Mrs. Unwin, who is, I think, in some points, already the better for her excursion, unites with mine her best compliments both to yourself and Mrs. Greatheed. I have much to see and enjoy before I can be perfectly apprised of all the delights of Eartham, and will therefore now subscribe myself, yours my dear sir, with great sincerity, W. C.

TO MRS. COURTENAY, WESTON UNDERWOOD.

Eartham, Sept. 10, 1792.

MY DEAR CATHARINA—I am not so uncourteous a knight as to leave your last kind letter, and the last I hope that I shall receive for a long time to come, without an attempt, at least, to acknowledge and to send you something in the shape of an answer to it; but having been obliged to dose myself last night with laudanum, on account of a little nervous fever, to which I am always subject, and for which I find it the best remedy, I feel myself this morning particularly under the influence of Lethean vapours, and, consequently, in danger of being uncommonly stupid!

You could hardly have sent me intelligence that would have gratified me more than that of my two dear friends,

Sir John and Lady Throckmorton, having departed from Paris two days before the terrible 10th of August. I have had many anxious thoughts on their account; and am truly happy to learn that they have sought a more peaceful region, while it was yet permitted them to do so. They will not, I trust, revisit those scenes of tumult and horror while they shall continue to merit that description. We are here all of one mind respecting the cause in which the Parisians are engaged; wish them a free people, and as happy as they can wish themselves. But their conduct has not always pleased us: we are shocked at their sanguinary proceedings, and begin to fear, myself in particular, that they will prove themselves unworthy, because incapable of enjoying it, of the inestimable blessings of liberty. My daily toast is, Sobriety and Freedom to the French; for they seem as destitute of the former, as they are eager to secure the latter.

We still hold our purpose of leaving Eartham on the 17th; and again my fears on Mrs. Unwin's account begin to trouble me; but they are now not quite so reasonable as in the first instance. If she could bear the fatigue of travelling then, she is more equal to it at present; and supposing that nothing happens to alarm her, which is very probable, may be expected to reach Weston in much better condition than when she left it. Her improvement, however, is chiefly in her looks, and in the articles of speaking and walking; for she can neither rise from her chair without help, nor walk without a support; nor read, nor use her needles. Give my love to the good Doctor, and make him acquainted with the state of his patient, since he, of all men, seems to have the best right to know it.

I am proud that you are pleased with the Epitaph I sent you, and shall be still prouder to see it perpetuated by the chisel. It is all that I have done since here I came, and all that I have been able to do. I wished, indeed, to have requited Romney for his well-drawn copy of me, in rhyme; and have more than once or twice attempted it; but I find, like the man in the fable, who could leap only at Rhodes, that verse is almost impossible to me except at Weston.—Tell my friend George that I am every day mindful of him, and always love him; and bid him by no means to vex himself about the tardiness of Andrews. Remember me affectionately to William, and to Pitcairn, whom I shall hope to find with you at my return; and should you see Mr. Buchanan, to him also.—I have now charged you with commissions enow, and having added Mrs. Unwin's best compliments and told you that I long to see you again, will conclude myself, my dear Catharina, most truly yours,

Wm. Cowper.

TO THE REV. JOHN NEWTON.

Oct. 18, 1792.

My dear Friend—I thought that the wonder had been all on my side, having been employed in wondering at your silence, as long as you at mine. Soon after our arrival at Eartham, I received a letter from you, which I answered, if not by the return of the post, at least in a day or two. Not that I should have insisted on the ceremonial of letter for letter, during so long a period, could I have found leisure to double your debt; but while there, I had no opportunity for writing, except now and then a short one; for we breakfasted early, studied Milton as soon as breakfast was over, and continued in that employment till Mrs. Unwin came forth from her chamber, to whom all the rest of my time was necessarily devoted. Our return to Weston was on the 19th of last month, according to your information. You will naturally think that, in the interval, I must have had sufficient leisure to give you notice of our safe arrival. But the fact has been otherwise. I have neither been well myself, nor is Mrs. Unwin, though better, so much improved in her health, as not still to require my continual assistance. My disorder has been the old one, to which I have been subject so many years, and especially about this season,—a nervous fever; not, indeed, so oppressive as it has sometimes proved, but sufficiently alarming both to Mrs. Unwin and myself, and such as made it neither easy nor proper for me to make much use of my pen while it continued. At present I am tolerably free from it,—a blessing for which I believe myself partly indebted to the use of James's powder, in small quantities; and partly to a small quantity of laudanum, taken every night; but chiefly to a manifestation of God's presence vouchsafed to me a few days since; transient, indeed, and dimly seen, through a mist of many fears and troubles, but sufficient to convince me, at least while the enemy's power is a little restrained, that He has not cast me off for ever.

Our visit was a pleasant one,—as pleasant as Mrs. Unwin's weakness, and the state of my spirits, never very good, would allow. As to my own health, I never expected that it would be much improved by the journey; nor have I found it so. Some benefit, indeed, I hoped, and perhaps a little more than I found. But the season was, after the first fortnight, extremely unfavourable,—stormy and wet; and the prospects, though grand and magnificent, yet rather of a melancholy cast, and consequently not very propitious to me. The cultivated appearance of Weston suits my frame of mind far better than wild hills that aspire to be mountains, covered with vast unfrequented woods, and here and there affording a peep between their summits at the distant ocean. Within doors all was hospitality and kindness, but the scenery *would* have its effect; and though delightful in the extreme to those who had spirits to bear it, was too gloomy for me.

Mrs. Unwin performed the journey, both going and returning, better than I had hoped she could. With an arm to lean upon she walks pretty well, though still with a step that totters when she turns; neither can she yet read without poring more than is good for her, or use her needles. But her looks are greatly improved, and her speech, especially in the earlier part of the day, is as strong and articulate as ever.

We are glad that the ducks arrived safe. A couple were likewise sent a little before our departure for Sussex, which we hope arrived safe also. I must now to breakfast;—and with Mrs. Unwin's affectionate remembrances and thanks for your kind mention of her in your letter, conclude myself yours, my dear friend, most sincerely, W. C.

TO THE REV. MR. HURDIS.

Weston, Feb. 23, 1793.

My dear Sir—My eyes, which have long been inflamed, will hardly serve me for Homer, and oblige me to make all my letters short. You have obliged me much, by sending me so speedily the remainder of your notes. I have begun with them again, and find them, as before, very much to the purpose. More to the purpose they could not have been, had you been Poetry Professor already. I rejoice sincerely in the prospect you have of that office, which, whatever may be your own thoughts of the matter, I am sure you will fill with great sufficiency. Would that my interest and power to serve you were greater! One string to my bow I have, and one only, which shall not be idle for want of my exertions. I thank you likewise for your very entertaining notices and remarks in the natural way. The hurry in which I write would not suffer me to send you many in return, had I many to send, but only two or three present themselves.

Frogs will feed on worms. I saw a frog gathering into his gullet an earth-worm as long as himself; it cost him time and labour, but at last he succeeded.

Mrs. Unwin and I, crossing a brook, saw from the foot-bridge somewhat at the bottom of the water which had the appearance of a flower. Observing it attentively, we found that it consisted of a circular assemblage of minnows; their heads all met in a centre; and their tails diverging at equal distances, and being elevated above their heads, gave them the appearance of a flower half blown. One was longer than the rest; and as often as a straggler came in sight, he quitted his place to pursue him, and having driven him away, he returned to it again, no other minnow offering to take it in his absence. This we saw him do several times. The object that had attached them all was a dead minnow, which they seemed to be devouring.

After a very rainy day, I saw on one of the flower borders what seemed a long hair, but it had a waving, twining motion. Considering more nearly, I found it alive, and endued with spontaneity, but could not discover at the ends of it either head or tail, or any distinction of parts. I carried it into the house, when the air of a warm room dried and killed it presently.

W. C.

TO WILLIAM HAYLEY, ESQ.

Weston, Feb. 24, 1793.

Your letter (so full of kindness, and so exactly in unison with my own feelings for you) should have had, as it deserved to have, an earlier answer, had I not been perpetually tormented with inflamed eyes, which are a sad hindrance to me in every thing. But to make amends, if I do not send you an early answer, I send you at least a speedy one, being obliged to write as fast as my pen can trot, that I may shorten the time of poring upon paper as much as possible. Homer too has been another hindrance, for always when I can see, which is only about two hours every morning, and not at all by candlelight, I devote myself to him, being in haste to send him a second time to the press, that nothing may stand in the way of Milton. By the way, where are my dear Tom's remarks, which I long to have, and must have soon, or they will come too late?

Oh! you rogue! what would you give to have such a dream about Milton, as I had about a week since? I dreamed that being in a house in the city, and with much company, looking towards the lower end of the room from the upper end of it, I descried a figure which I immediately knew to be Milton's. He was very gravely, but very neatly attired in the fashion of his day, and had a countenance which filled me with those feelings that an affectionate child has for a beloved father, such, for instance, as Tom has for you. My first thought was wonder, where he could have been concealed so many years; my second, a transport of joy to find him still alive; my third, another transport to find myself in his company; and my fourth, a resolution to accost him. I did so, and he received me with a complacence, in which I saw equal sweetness and dignity. I spoke of his Paradise Lost, as every man must, who is worthy to speak of it at all, and told him a long story of the manner in which it affected me, when I first discovered it, being at that time a schoolboy. He answered me by a smile and a gentle inclination of his head. He then grasped my hand affectionately, and with a smile that charmed me, said, "Well, you for your part will do well also;" at last recollecting his great age, (for I understood him to be two hundred years old,) I feared that I might fatigue him by much talking, I took my leave, and he took his, with an air of the most perfect good breeding. His person, his features, his manner, were all so perfectly characteristic, that I am persuaded an apparition of him could not represent him more completely. This may be said to have been one of the dreams of Pindus, may it not?

With Mary's kind love, I must now conclude myself, my dear brother, ever yours, LIPPUS.

TO LADY HESKETH.

The Lodge, May 7, 1793.

MY DEAREST COZ—You have thought me long silent, and so have many others. In fact I have not for many months written punctually to any but yourself and Hayley. My time, the little I have, is so engrossed by Homer, that I have at this moment a bundle of unanswered letters by me, and letters likely to be so. Thou knowest, I dare say, what it is to have a head weary with thinking. Mine is so fatigued by breakfast time, three days out of four, I am utterly incapable of sitting down to my desk again for any purpose whatever.

I am glad I have convinced thee at last that thou art a Tory. Your friend's definition of Whig and Tory may be just for aught I know, as far as the latter are concerned; but respecting the former, I think him mistaken. There is no TRUE Whig who wishes all power in the hands of his own party. The division of it, which the lawyers call tripartite, is exactly what he desires; and he would have neither Kings, Lords, nor Commons unequally trusted, or in the smallest degree predominant. Such a Whig am I, and such Whigs are the true friends of the constitution.

Adieu! my dear, I am dead with weariness. W. C.

TO THOMAS PARK, ESQ.

W. U. July 15, 1793.

Dear Sir—Within these few days I have received, by favour of Miss Knapps, your acceptable present of Chapman's translation of the Iliad. I know not whether the book be a rarity, but a curiosity it certainly is. I have as yet seen but little of it, enough however to make me wonder that any man, with so little taste for Homer, or apprehension of his manner, should think it worth while to undertake the laborious task of translating him; the hope of pecuniary advantage may perhaps account for it. His information, I fear, was not much better than his verse, for I have consulted him in one passage of some difficulty, and find him giving a sense of his own, not at all warranted by the words of Homer. Pope sometimes does this, and sometimes omits the difficult part entirely. I can boast of having done neither, though it has cost me infinite pains to exempt myself from the necessity.

I have seen a translation by Hobbes, which I prefer for its greater clumsiness. Many years have passed since I saw it, but it made me laugh immoderately. Poetry that is not good can only make amends for that deficiency by being ridiculous; and, because the translation of Hobbes has at least this recommendation, I shall be obliged to you, should it happen to fall in your way, if you would be so kind as to procure it for me. The only edition of it I ever saw (and perhaps there never was another,) was a very thick 12mo., both print and paper bad, a sort of book that would be sought in vain, perhaps, anywhere but on a stall.

When you saw Lady Hesketh, you saw the relation of mine with whom I have been more intimate, even from childhood, than any other. She has seen much of the world, understands it well, and, having great natural vivacity, is of course one of the most agreeable companions.

I have now arrived almost at the close of my labours on the Iliad, and have left nothing behind me, I believe, which I shall wish to alter on any future occasion. In about a fortnight or three weeks I shall begin to do the same for the Odyssey, and hope to be able to perform it while the Iliad is in printing. Then Milton will demand all my attention, and when I shall find opportunity either to revise your MSS. or to write a poem of my own, which I have in contemplation, I can hardly say. Certainly not till both these tasks are accomplished.—I remain, dear sir, with many thanks for your kind present, sincerely yours, WM. COWPER.

TO MRS. CHARLOTTE SMITH.

Weston, July 25, 1793.

MY DEAR MADAM—Many reasons concurred to make me impatient for the arrival of your most acceptable present, and among them was the fear lest you should perhaps suspect me of tardiness in acknowledging so great a favour; a fear that, as often as it prevailed, distressed me exceedingly. At length I have received it, and my little bookseller assures me that he sent it the very day he got it; by some mistake however the waggon brought it instead of the coach, which occasioned a delay that I could ill afford.

It came this morning about an hour ago; consequently I have not had time to peruse the poem, though you may be sure I have found enough for the perusal of the Dedication. I have in fact given it three readings, and in each have found increasing pleasure.

I am a whimsical creature; when I write for the public I write of course with a desire to please, in other words to acquire fame, and I labour accordingly, but when I find that I have succeeded, feel myself alarmed, and ready to shrink from the acquisition.

This I have felt more than once, and when I saw my name at the head of your Dedication, I felt it again; but the consummate delicacy of your praise soon convinced me that I might spare my blushes, and that the demand was less upon my modesty than my gratitude. Of that be assured, dear Madam, and of the truest esteem and respect of your most obliged and affectionate, humble servant. W. C.

P.S.—I should have been much grieved to have let slip this opportunity of thanking you for your charming sonnets, and my two most agreeable old friends, Monimia and Orlando.

TO THE REV. MR. BUCHANAN.

Mundsley, September 5, 1795.

"——— to interpose a little ease,
Let my frail thoughts dally with false surmise!"

I WILL forget for a moment that to whomsoever I may address myself, a letter from me can no otherwise be welcome than as a curiosity. To you, sir, I address this; urged to it by extreme penury of employment, and the desire I feel to learn something of what is doing, and has been done, at Weston (my beloved Weston !) since I left it.

The coldness of these blasts, even in the hottest days, has been such that, added to the irritation of the salt spray with which they are always charged, they have occasioned me an inflammation in the eyelids, which threatened a few days since to confine me entirely; but by absenting myself as much as possible from the beach, and guarding my face with an umbrella, that inconvenience is in some degree abated. My chamber commands a very near view of the ocean, and the ships at high water approach the coast so closely that a man furnished with better eyes than mine might, I doubt not, discern the sailors from the window. No situation—at least when the weather is clear and bright—can be pleasanter; which you will easily credit when I add that it imparts something a little resembling pleasure even to me. Gratify me with news of Weston ! If Mr. Gregson and your neighbours the Courtenays are there, mention me to them in such terms as you see good. Tell me if my poor birds are living ! I never see the herbs I used to give them without a recollection of them, and sometimes am ready to gather them, forgetting that I am not at home. Pardon this intrusion.

Mrs. Unwin continues much as usual.

TO LADY HESKETH.

Mundsley, Oct. 13, 1798.

Dear Cousin—You describe delightful scenes, but you describe them to one who, if he even saw them, could receive no delight from them; who has a faint recollection, and so faint as to be like an almost forgotten dream, that once he was susceptible of pleasure from such causes. The country that you have had in prospect has been always famed for its beauties; but the wretch who can derive no gratification from a view of Nature, even under the disadvantage of her most ordinary dress, will have no eyes to admire her in any.

In one day—in one minute, I should rather have said—she became an universal blank to me; and, though from a different cause, yet with an effect as difficult to remove as blindness itself. In this country, if there are not mountains there are hills; if not broad and deep rivers, yet such as are sufficient to embellish a prospect; and an object still more magnificent than any river, the ocean itself, is almost immediately under the window. Why is scenery like this, I had almost said, why is the very scene which many years since I could not contemplate without rapture, now become, at the best, an insipid wilderness? It neighbours nearly, and as nearly resembles, the scenery of Catfield; but with what different perceptions does it present me! The reason is obvious. My state of mind is a medium through which the beauties of Paradise itself could not be communicated with any effect but a painful one.

There is a wide interval between us, which it would be far easier for you than for me to pass. Yet I should in vain invite you. We shall meet no more. I know not what Mr. Johnson said of me in the long letter he addressed to you yesterday, but nothing, I am sure, that could make such an event seem probable.—I remain, as usual, dear cousin, yours,

Wm. Cowper.

NOTES.

Page 1. To Mrs. Cowper. For notices of Cowper's correspondents, see *Introduction.* This letter was addressed to her at the Park House, Hartford, or Hertford, in whose neighbourhood, at Hertingfordbury. she lived.

l. 1. **Charles's.** Major (afterwards General) Cowper.

l. 3. **epidemical,** general, affecting a (whole) people; Gk. *ἐπί*, among, and *δῆμος*, people.

l. 4. **country,** region.

l. 5. **almost to suffocation,** almost extending to or producing suffocation.

not that, it is not the case that.

l. 6. **blessed be God,** *i.e.* I give thanks to God for it.

our family, the family of the Unwins, with whom Cowper was now living.

l. 11. **the world,** worldly, as opposed to religious, people.

the place, indeed, swarms with them. Cf. *To Hill*, July 3, 1765: "Here is a card-assembly, and a dancing-assembly, and a horse-race, and a club, and a bowling-green, so that I am well off, you perceive, in point of diversions; especially as I shall go to 'em just as much as I should if I lived a thousand miles off." And cf. p. 67, l. 6, and note.

l. 12. **cards and dancing.** Cowper repeatedly attacks the passion for card-playing that was rife in his day; cf. *Task*, i. 472-477. What he loved were "fireside enjoyments, homeborn happiness," not the theatre or the card-party. Cf. *Task,* iv. 307-210:—

"Cards were superfluous here, with all the tricks
That idleness had ever yet contrived
To fill the void of an unfurnished brain," *et seq.*

Cowper possessed a card-table, which, however, he tells us,

"serves all purposes except the only one for which it was originally designed" (*To Newton*, March 19, 1785). While disapproving of dancing, Cowper writes with much tolerance on the subject to Hurdis (see p. 121, l. 16 *et seq.*).

l. 13. **gentle inhabitants**, people in good society, those above the trading classes; cf. *gentleman, gentlefolk.*

l. 14. **to be accessories to**, to give countenance to, to aid and abet; as in 'to be accessory to a crime.'

l. 15. **murdering**, misspending, misusing; cf. 'to murder the Queen's English,' *i.e.* to talk ungrammatically; 'to murder a tune,' *i.e.* to play or sing it badly.

l. 16. **Methodists.** The members of the religious sect founded by John and Charles Wesley in 1727 were, from the strict *method* of their lives, called *Methodists.* The name, like *Teetotaller*, given originally in derision, has been adopted by the Wesleyans. In Cowper's day, however, it was used generally to designate the Evangelical or Low Church party. *Occiduus* (Latin for 'western'), the "pastor of renown," whom Cowper satirizes in *The Progress of Error* (124-141), and to whose "sabbatical concerts" he refers in a letter to Newton (Sept. 9, 1781), has been supposed by some to be Charles Wesley; but more probably a clergyman near Olney is alluded to. See *Introduction*, p. xviii.

l. 19. **the Scripture**, the Bible.

faithful, true.

l. 20. **those holy mysteries**, the redemption of mankind revealed in the Bible; cf. 1 *Cor.* iv. 1, where St. Paul speaks of himself as a steward of "the mysteries of God."

l. 21. **twice every day.** The Rev. Isaac Nicholson, says Cowper (*To Lady Hesketh*, Sept. 14, 1765), "reads prayers here twice a day, all the year round." This was done in compliance with the terms of a bequest of £70 per annum, left by one George Sayer for that purpose.

l. 23. **read.** Cowper does not seem to have been a great reader in private, though he did a good deal of reading aloud (see below, p. 2, l. 13; p. 42, l. 11; p. 111, l. 19). Writing to Hill (Nov. 23, 1783), he says: "My reading is pretty much circumscribed, both by want of books and the influence of particular reasons. Politics are my abhorrence. Philosophy—I should have said natural philosophy, ... does not suit me. ... Poetry, English poetry, I never touch." See also note on "work in the garden" below. Books of voyages and travels were what interested him most.

Page 2, l. 1. **ride.** Cowper visited his brother John at Cambridge every alternate week, and generally went on horseback. "My distance," he writes (*To Major Cowper*, Oct. 18, 1768), "from Cambridge has made a horseman of me at last, or at least is likely to do so." And though elsewhere he speaks of himself as "a professed horseman," in May, 1781 he tells Unwin that Nature "did not design me for a horseman, and that if all men were of my mind, there would be an end of all jockeyship for ever." It seems probable that Cowper had his own horsemanship in his mind when he wrote *John Gilpin.*

work in the garden. Cowper loved "the garden with its many cares" (*Task,* iii. 397), and was proud of his walls well-spread with fruit-trees (*ib.* 408). "I am become a great florist and shrub-doctor," he tells Mrs. Cowper (March 14, 1767); and on May 14, 1767, he writes to Hill: "Having commenced gardener, I study the arts of pruning, sowing, and planting; and enterprise every thing in that way, from melons down to cabbages." Cf. also *To Park,* March 10, 1792: "From thirty-three to sixty I have spent my time in the country, where my reading has been only an apology for idleness, and where, when I had not either a magazine or a review in my hand, I was sometimes a carpenter, at others a bird-cage maker, or a gardener, or a drawer of landscapes." And see p. 110, l. 21 *et seq.*

we seldom sit, etc., *i.e.* we rest for an hour after dinner, and then usually go out.

l. 2. **adjourn.** The group breaks up in the house and reunites in the garden. *Adjourn* is properly 'to postpone (a meeting) to another day' (Fr. *jour,* Lat. *diurnus,* from *dies,* a day).

l. 3. **her son,** William Cawthorne Unwin; see *Introduction,* p. xl.

l. 6. **Martin's collection,** a collection of hymns made by the Rev. Martin Madan, Cowper's cousin, and a prominent Evangelical clergyman of the time.

l. 7. **harpsichord,** an old harp-shaped musical instrument. The still older *spinet* developed into the harpsichord, and that into the modern piano. All three instruments had a keyboard, but in the two former the strings were *plucked* instead of being *struck,* as in the last. *Harpsichord* is compounded of Old Fr. *harpe,* a harp, and *chorde,* a string. The *s* seems to have been introduced for ease of pronunciation. For the connecting vowel ('harp-s-*i*-chord'), cf. 'hand-*i*-craft,' 'black-*a*-moor,' 'per-*i*-wig.'

l. 8. **our hearts,** etc., *i.e.* we sing not merely with musical voices, but—what is more important—with sincerely pious feelings.

l. 16. **I need not tell you.** Mrs. Cowper was herself strongly Evangelical, and therefore did not need to be assured of the cheerfulness of such a life. To ordinary people this round of religious observances seems excessive; but probably the regular exercise and the domestic love that surrounded him prevented this overstrained piety from having prejudicial effects upon Cowper's mind.

l. 18. **dwell together in unity.** Cf. Bible, *Psalms*, cxxxiii. 1: "Behold how good and how pleasant it is for brethren to dwell together in unity!"

l. 21. **God of our salvation,** God that saves or redeems us. The phrase occurs several times in the Bible; see 1 *Chron.* xvi. 35; *Psalms*, lxv. 5, lxxix. 9.

l. 24. **taking orders,** taking holy orders, becoming a clergyman.

l. 25. **every new convert,** etc. Persons newly converted to religion think that God has called them to the office of clergyman.

l. 27. **to give me full,** etc., to make it quite clear to me that I am right in declining it.

ll. 29, 30. **the dread of public exhibitions.** On being made Clerk of the Journals of the House of Lords, an appointment entailing an examination at the bar of the House as to his qualifications for the post, Cowper wrote: "They whose spirits are formed like mine, to whom a public exhibition of themselves on any occasion is mortal poison, may have some idea of the situation; others can have none."

l. 32. **the truth,** *i.e.* religious truth; belief in Christ.

l. 34. **Had I the zeal,** etc. When God bade Moses go to Pharaoh, King of Egypt, to deliver the Israelites from bondage, and Moses represented that he was "slow of speech," God commanded him to take with him Aaron his brother, who could "speak well," and who should "be his spokesman unto the people." See Bible, *Exodus*, iv. 10-16.

l. 35. **spokesman.** In the *Ayenbite of Inwyt* (1340) we find *spekeman*, formed like *watchman*. Later the Perfect *spoke* took the place of the Present, and *s* was inserted on the analogy of compounds like *kinsman*, *sportsman*, etc.

Page 3. This and the following letters down to p. 93 were written from Olney.

l. 2. **South Sea Voyages,** narratives of voyages in the South Seas, a name then given to the South Pacific Ocean. Cowper's letters contain frequent references to books of travel. See p. 42, l. 12 *et seq.*, and cf. *To Newton*, Oct. 6, 1783: "I am much obliged to you for the voyages, which I received and began to read last night"; and *To the same*, June 21, 1784: "I charged him with a petition to Lord Dartmouth, to send me Cook's last voyage, which I have a great curiosity to see." Cf. also *Task*, iv. 114-117:—

> "He travels, and I too. I tread his deck,
> Ascend his topmast, through his peering eyes
> Discover countries, and with kindred heart
> Suffer his woes, and share in his escapes."

ll. 2, 3. **Lord Dartmouth.** William Legge, second Earl of Dartmouth, was born in 1731, the same year as Cowper, and was his fellow-student at Westminster School. He visited Olney on the 9th of June, 1777, as one of a committee to inspect and report on the ruinous state of its bridge. There he saw Cowper, and conversed with him on Cook's South Sea Voyages, which were then engaging public attention, and was shown over his garden. Cf. p. 44, l. 18. The poet alludes to Lord Dartmouth in *Truth*, 377, 378 :—

> "We boast some rich ones whom the Gospel sways,
> And one who wears a coronet and prays."

l. 4. **Cook's.** Probably the narrative of Cook's first voyage. Captain James Cook, born 1728, made his first voyage in 1768, when he discovered the Society Isles and reached Australia, arriving home June, 1771. On his second voyage in 1772 he visited New Zealand, explored the Friendly Isles, and rounded Cape Horn, returning July, 1774. He set out on his third voyage in 1776, discovered the Sandwich Islands, and explored the western coast of North America. He was murdered by the natives at Owhyhee, one of the Sandwich group, on Feb. 14, 1779.

l. 5. **Forster's.** Johann Reinhold Forster, born 1729, accompanied Captain Cook in his second voyage round the world, as naturalist to the expedition, and took his son with him, who published a narrative of the voyage. He died in 1798.

'Tis well for the poor natives, etc. It is a good thing for the natives that there is nothing in these islands to tempt the national greed. Cf. *Task*, i. 672-677 (where Cowper apostrophizes Omai, a native of Otaheite, who was brought to England by Cook in 1775, and became one of the "lions" of London) :—

> "We found no bait
> To tempt us in thy country. Doing good,
> Disinterested good, is not our trade.
> We travel far, 'tis true, but not for naught;
> And must be bribed to compass earth again
> By other hopes and richer fruits than yours."

l. 7. **yams and bananas.** The yam (Port. *inhame*) is a root resembling the potato. The banana (a Spanish word of West Indian origin) is the plantain, a tropical fruit.

Curiosity, etc. Cf. *Task*, i. 633-636 (of Omai) :—

> "Thee, gentle savage! whom no love of thee
> Or thine, but curiosity perhaps
> Or else vain-glory, prompted us to draw
> Forth from thy native bowers."

l. 10. **Baker.** Henry Baker (born 1698, died 1774) obtained in 1744 the Copley Medal of the Royal Society for his microscopical experiments. He wrote *The Microscope made Easy*, etc.

l. 11. **Vincent Bourne** was assistant-master at Westminster School in Cowper's time, and published one or two volumes of Latin poems, twenty-seven of which Cowper translated into English verse. He died in 1747. See p. 13, l. 13; pp. 15, 16; p. 38, l. 7.

l. 16. **the vacation.** Hill was a lawyer, and the law vacation was now coming to a close.

l. 20. **the pamphlet of that name.** This pamphlet is a skit written by Richard Tickell and published anonymously under the title of "Anticipation: containing the substance of His M——y's most gracious speech to both H——s of P——t, on the opening of the approaching session, together with a full and authentic account of the debate which will take place in the H——e of C—— s, on the motion for the address, and the amendment; with notes"; *Dublin*, 1778. 8vo, pp. 74.

l. 22. **the Review,** *The Monthly Review*, a Whig periodical started by Dr. Ralph Griffiths in 1749. It expired in 1842. Cf. p. 22, l. 30. Goldsmith wrote some critiques for it.

ll. 24, 25. **the Jamaica fleet.** England was at this time at war with France and Spain, as well as with her American Colonies, so that her merchant ships sailed under the convoy of men-of-war.

l. 25. **imports**, etc. He hopes that the fleet is bringing him some pine-apple plants for his garden. See note to p. 2, l. 1. Cowper took to rearing pine-apples in 1778, when "Mr. Wright's gardener presented him with six fruiting pines, which he put into a bark bed" (*To Unwin*, Dec. 3).

l. 26. **frame,** *i.e.* a glass frame to shelter these tropical plants from the cold. In a letter to Unwin (May 26, 1779) Cowper says he "wants as much (glass) as will serve for a large frame."

l. 27. **a fable.** His poem entitled *The Pine-apple and the Bee.* The bee, eager to get at the fragrant pine-apple, in vain "search'd for crannies in the frame." In the same way "to joys forbidden man aspires," and

"Our dear delights are often such,
Exposed to view but not to touch;
The sight our foolish heart inflames,
We long for pine-apples in frames."

makes a figure, is a prominent feature.

l. 28. **Two pair of soles.** Cowper calls himself "the most ichthyophagous (fish-eating) of Protestants," and his letters bear out the statement.

Page 4, l. 1. Arion was a famous poet and musician, who, having obtained great wealth in Italy by his profession, was returning with it to Lesbos, when the sailors resolved to murder him for his wealth. Arion gained permission to play a last tune on his lyre, and then threw himself into the sea; whereupon one of a number of dolphins that had been attracted round the ship by the sweetness of his music, bore him safely ashore.

l. 3. **to fiddle you**, etc. Cowper means to say that he does not send his poem with a view to getting another present of fish in return for it. At the same time, if Hill thinks his poetry deserves such a gift, he shall thank his poetical genius for its help, as Arion did his.

l. 7. **attend**, *i.e.* I send them to her.

She has put, etc. Mrs. Hill had sent Cowper "fifty sorts of stove plant seeds," which he had presented to Mr. George Wright, who had a country-seat, Gayhurst, about four miles from Olney (*To Unwin*, Dec. 3, 1778, and Sept. 21, 1779).

l. 17. **Johnson's biography**, Dr. Samuel Johnson's *Lives of the Poets*. The edition of the Poets to which Johnson contributed these biographical and critical prefaces was issued 1779-1781. In a letter to Unwin, May 26 of this year, Cowper thanks him for sending him some volumes of the work. For further references to the *Lives*, see p. 23, l. 1; p. 44, l. 31; p. 66, l. 8.

ll. 18, 19. **a swinging one**, 'an important one.' The word is usually written *swingeing* (from *swinge*, to beat), to distinguish it from *swinging* (from *swing*, to sway). *Swinge* is the causal form of swing; cf. *fall*, *fell*; *sit*, *set*.

l. 21. **to the last degree**, to the greatest extent.

A pensioner. Johnson received a pension of £300 a year from the Crown in 1762. Cowper means that one who has received the royal favour is likely to be hard upon a republican like Milton. He himself was granted a pension of £300 by the Crown, July 5, 1794.

l. 23. **his royal patron**, George III., who had granted him the pension, and who gave him an interview in the royal library in 1765.

l. 25. **As a man**, 'as regards his (Milton's) character and actions.' The phrase is opposed to "as a poet" below.

l. 26. **Churlishness**, etc., *i.e.* Johnson's delineation of Milton is made up of two characteristics: a surly demeanour in his private life, and a bitter hatred of royalty in his public life. Cf. Johnson's *Life of Milton*: "Milton's republicanism was, I am afraid, founded in an envious hatred of greatness. ... He hated monarchs in the state, and prelates in the church. ... What we know of

Milton's character, in domestick relations, is, that he was severe and arbitrary."

Page 5, l. 4. **has plucked**, etc., *i.e.* he has passed a strongly adverse criticism upon several of Milton's poems. See p. 45, ll. 17, 18.

ll. 8, 9. **the childish prattlement**, etc. Johnson says: "Its (the *Lycidas's*) form is that of a pastoral, easy, familiar, and therefore disgusting. ... We know that they never drove afield, and that they had no flocks to batten," etc. On the pastoral form of poetry Professor Masson remarks: "Defensible or not originally, desirable or not among ourselves, as we may think this artifice of pastoralism, this device for poets of an imaginary removal of themselves into an Arcadian land in order to think under Arcadian conditions, it is gross ignorance not to know how largely it once prevailed, and what a wealth of old poetry we owe to it. From the youth of Spenser, himself the pastoralist-in-chief, on through the lives of the next generation, or from 1580 to 1640, much of the finest English poetry is in the pastoral form. During that period the word 'shepherd' was an accepted synonym in England for the word 'poet.'" Cf. note to p. 24, l. 1.

l. 11. **the sweetness of the numbers**, the harmony of the rhythm. Cowper could appreciate the wonderful music of the *Lycidas*. Johnson says: "The diction (of *Lycidas*) is harsh, the rhymes uncertain, and the numbers unpleasing." *Numbers* (Lat. *numeri*, verses; *numerus*, musical measure) for poetry or poetic rhythm, was a common word in Pope's and after Pope's time, who wrote of himself:—

"I lisp'd in numbers, for the numbers came."

ll. 11, 12. **the classical spirit**, etc. Johnson does not spare this feature of the poem. "Among the flocks, and copses, and flowers (he writes), appear the heathen deities; Jove and Phœbus, Neptune and Æolus, with a long train of mythological imagery, such as a College easily supplies."

l. 14. **stopped by**, etc. "Against" is to be taken with "stopped," not with "prejudice."

l. 15. **Was there ever**, etc. Cowper was a great admirer of Milton, and there are many reminiscences of his style and manner in the *Task*. In 1791 he undertook an edition of Milton, and translated his Latin and Italian poems, but annotated only two books of the *Paradise Lost*. Cf. *To Unwin*, Jan. 17, 1782: "You did not mention Milton's Allegro and Penseroso, which I remember being so charmed with when I was a boy that I was never weary of them"; and pp. 134, 135, below.

l. 17. **organ**. Similarly Tennyson (*Alciacs*) calls Milton "God-gifted organ-voice of England."

l. 18. **the Dorian flute.** Of the three primitive Greek musical modes or scales, the Lydian, the Phrygian, and the Dorian, the last was the most grave and solemn. Perhaps Cowper had Milton's lines (*Par. Lost*, i. 549-551) in his mind :—

"Anon they move
In perfect phalanx to the Dorian mood
Of flutes and soft recorders."

l. 19. **Virgil**, the famous Roman poet of Augustan times, author of the *Æneid.*

l. 21. **talks something**, etc. Johnson says: "Poetry may subsist without rhyme, but English poetry will not often please; nor can rhyme ever be safely spared but where the subject is able to support itself." And again: "The variety of pauses, so much boasted by the lovers of blank verse, changes the measures of an English poet to the periods of a declaimer; and there are only a few skilful and happy readers of Milton, who enable their audience to perceive where the lines end or begin."

l. 24. **his pension.** See note to "pensioner" above, p. 4, l. 21.

l. 26. **no room**, *i.e.* in the single sheet allowed (for one postage) by the Post Office regulations. See *Introduction*, p. xxxviii.

l. 27. **Miss Shuttleworth**, Unwin's sister-in-law.

l. 28. **the two miniature pictures**, portraits on a small scale, *i.e.* Unwin's two children. We now speak of 'a miniature' rather than 'a miniature picture.'

l. 32. **testify**, 'declare'; lit. 'bear witness to.'

Page 6, l. 1. **I seldom send one**, etc. See *Introduction*, pp. xxv., xxvi.

l. 2. **This is not to be understood**, etc. He wishes his correspondent to understand that his depreciation of his letters is not intended as a slur upon Unwin's taste in liking to receive them, but as a commendation of his own modesty. *Encomium* is Gk. ἐγκώμιον, a laudatory ode; from ἐν, in, and κῶμος, revelry.

l. 5. **just**, true, appropriate.

ll. 5, 6. **Sir Joshua Reynolds**, the celebrated English portrait painter (born 1723, died 1792). He was a member of the celebrated club to which Johnson, Garrick, and Burke belonged, and published his *Discourses on Painting* in 1781.

l. 11. **sense of perfection**, etc., *i.e.* men of true genius place before themselves a high ideal which they are unable to attain to in their performances.

l. 13. **Your servant**, etc. Cowper playfully makes his bôw to Sir Joshua, as if the painter had "popped in" on a visit. "Your servant" = "I am your servant," a polite form of greeting.

l. 17. **the Modern Patriot.** Cowper's verses with this title are to be found among his poetry. The "Patriots," as they called themselves, came into existence as a "popular" or anti-Court party during Walpole's administration (1721-1742), and claimed to be the champions of the cause of honesty and freedom against ministerial corruption and royal ascendancy. Cf. *Friendship*, 127-129:—

> "Courtier and Patriot cannot mix
> Their heterogeneous politics
> Without an effervescence."

Cowper uses the term ironically in the title of his poem, which is a satire on politicians of the "Opposition" school, who supported the "rebellion" of the American Colonies, and encouraged "lawless mobs" in "insulting the court." Cowper was an "old Whig," moderate, constitutional, and anti-democratic. Cf. p. 89, ll. 26, 27; p. 136, ll. 10-16.

l. 19. **Burke's speech.** Burke (b. 1729, d. 1797) entered Parliament in 1765, and in the present year (1780) brought in his bill for economical reform, which was lost in the following year on the second reading by 233 to 190.

l. 27. **commences his own judge**, begins to exercise the functions of judge of himself. *Commence* is technically used at the Universities, where to 'commence M.A.,' etc., means to take the full degree of Master of Arts. Cf. Johnson, *Life of Milton:* "Cromwell had now dismissed the Parliament ... and commenced monarch himself." Cf. also p. 80, l. 34; p. 109, l. 22.

l. 29. **has laid his leaf-gold**, etc. As a man, when he tries to gild decayed wood, finds that it crumbles away under his fingers, so an author applies his talents or poetical skill to a subject which loses all its point and interest before he has done with it. We now usually say "gold-leaf." *Touch* in "touchwood" is a corruption of M. E. *tache*, tinder.

l. 34. **I must do with it**, etc. A touching indication of the poet's natural gaiety of disposition, which cannot be wholly repressed and caged by his state of health and his gloomy theology.

my linnet. For Cowper's fondness for animals, see *Introduction*, p. xxi.

l. 36. **whisk**, 'move quickly'; properly *wisk*, the Scandinavian *viske*, to wipe, rub; related to *wash*.

Page 7, ll. 1, 2. **the following**, viz., his poem entitled *The Nightingale and the Glowworm.* Its "subject" or moral is that "brother should not war with brother," but should

> "Sing and shine by sweet consent
> Till life's poor transient night is spent,

Respecting in each other's case
The gifts of nature and of grace."

The "manner" of the poem is light and unpretending.

l. 4. **sterling,** 'of genuine worth.' *Sterling* was originally a noun, meaning a coin of true weight, so named from the *Esterlings* or Easterlings, the Hanse merchants, who were the first money-dealers in England.

l. 5. **philosophical,** 'scientific.' Writers of Cowper's day used "philosophy" where we should say "science." Cf. p. 39, l. 30; p. 43, l. 6; and the first quotation in note to p. 40, l. 30; and *To Unwin*, Dec., 1873: "The endeavour (to fill the balloon) was, I believe, very philosophically made:" and *Task*, iii. 229, "philosophic tube" (telescope); and 243:—

"Philosophy, baptised
In the pure fountain of eternal love,
Has eyes indeed."

Also Campbell, *To the Rainbow*:—

"I ask not proud Philosophy
To teach me what thou art."

the Register, "The Annual Register," a summary of the history of each year, first issued in 1758.

l. 6. **the glow-worm is,** etc. In the poem the nightingale "thinks to put him in his crop," when he is "harangued" by the worm and induced to spare him. *Nightingale* is O. E. *nihtegale*, 'singer of the night.'

l. 8. **quartered,** placed in quarters, lodged.

l. 11. **One vice may swallow,** etc. One vice may take the place of another and so put an end to it, but no vice has ever put an end to itself by over-indulgence leading to satiety. It is the coroner's duty to hold an inquest in cases of sudden death, by accident, suicide, etc., and pronounce the verdict resulting from the investigation. In cases of wilful suicide the verdict is *felo de se*, which is Law Latin for "a felon of himself," *i.e.* one who commits felony by suicide.

ll. 15, 16. **the biography,** Dr. Johnson's; see above, p. 4. l. 17.

l. 18. **franks,** franked sheets of letter paper. See *Introduction*, p. xxxviii.

l. 20. **latitude of excursion,** liberty to wander away from the subject and write of different matters.

l. 22. **boluses.** *Bolus* (Gk. βῶλος, a clod, lump) is a medicinal preparation in a large, soft mass, to be divided into pills. Here "boluses" is equivalent to "pills," which were gilded to hide their nauseousness. The sense is: 'I am obliged to you for thinking that the pleasant style of my composition so well disguises the unimportance of the subject-matter, that you can read my letters without disgust.'

l. 23. **verily believe**, etc. I really think that no one in the world but myself could dress up such subjects so as to make them inviting to a man of your taste.

l. 25. **I wish**, etc. I wish I could make the style of my letters brighter than it is, so that the outward expression at all events should be more pleasing, even if the subject-matter were not.

l. 27. **but my leaf-gold**, etc. But my power of writing brilliantly has been so impaired by the gloom which always envelops my mind, that I think you read my letters rather out of affection for me than because you enjoy them.

Page 8, l. 1. **longwinded.** Primarily applied to tedious speakers, who do not easily lose their breath; then to their discourses. Here it means 'long-drawn-out,' 'with the comparison carried into minute particulars.'

l. 2. **halt**, 'limp,' *i.e.* become inapplicable or confused.

so do mine. The metaphor of the gilding of the pill becoming tinged or tarnished by the vapours that hang over his mind is rather complicated.

l. 3. **I deal much in ink.** I use ink, not for writing but for drawing. In February of this year Cowper commenced drawing, and commissioned Unwin to buy him some Indian ink and a few brushes and pencils. Writing to Unwin, April 6, 1780, he says: "The necessity of amusement ... has lately taught me to draw, and to draw too with such surprising proficiency in the art, considering my total ignorance of it two months ago, that when I show your mother my productions, she is all admiration and applause." See also p. 81, ll. 1-3; p. 110, ll. 10-21. It appears that the poet took lessons from a local artist and sculptor, named James Andrews, whom he calls his "Michael Angelo" (*To Newton*, May 10, 1780).

l. 5. **guilty of no deceptions**, etc. A writer may vitiate the taste or injure the morals of his readers, but an artist deals in illusions that do no harm to anyone.

l. 7. **dab-chicks.** *Dabchick*, properly *dapchick*, 'the diving bird' (*dap* being another form of *dip*) or didapper. It is a small water-bird that frequently dives in search of food.

l. 10. **O! I could spend**, etc. For Cowper's love of Nature, see *Introduction*, p. xxii.

ll. 12, 13. **think ... as I have done**, have the same religious views as I have had; could reflect, as I have done, on his sinful state.

l. 14. **miserable.** On account of their sins or through despair of pardon.

l. 15. **unawakened.** Used in a religious sense :—'unconscious of one's state as a sinner.' Cf. Bible, 1 *Cor.* xv. 34 : "Awake to righteousness, and sin not."

l. 17. **to their advantage.** They are happier than I am in their enjoyment of trifles, because they have no suspicion that they are trifles.

l. 18. **rested in,** etc. The earth, the planets, and the sun are but trifles, if we merely regard them as interesting in themselves, without looking beyond them to God who made them.

ll. 29, 30. **a frame of four lights,** a frame-work containing four sets of (glass) plates. See above, p. 3, ll. 25, 26.

l. 31. **a greenhouse.** See note to p. 20, l. 17.

l. 32. **Lord Bute's gardener.** The Marquis of Bute lived at Luton, not far from Olney. He was a favourite courtier of George III., and by him appointed Prime Minister in 1762. Frightened by his unpopularity, he resigned in the following year.

Page 9. l. 1. Mr. Newton, etc. In this letter Cowper playfully imagines himself as paying a visit to Mrs. Cowper at her house in London to meet Newton.

l. 5. **What was brown,** etc. My hair, which was once brown, has turned gray.

ll. 6, 7. **Green fruit must rot,** etc. Cowper means that his intellectual faculties have had no chance of developing in consequence of the melancholy that overspreads his mind.

l. 9. **steal away silently.** They bring little change or infirmity to me, to draw my attention to their flight.

l. 10. **as poor mad King Lear,** etc. Cf. Shaks., *King Lear*, IV. vi. 188-191 :—

> "It were a delicate stratagem, to shoe
> A troop of horse with felt : I'll put 't in proof ;
> And when I have stol'n upon these sons-in-law,
> Then, kill, kill, kill, kill, kill, kill !"

l. 13. **always listening to their flight.** A pathetic touch. It was characteristic of Cowper's theology to be always dwelling upon the shortness of life and the need of preparation for death.

l. 18. **corresponding,** etc. None of my correspondents care for good-for-nothing topics.

l. 28. **a coxcomb,** 'a conceited fellow.' A corruption of *cock's comb*, the crest of a cock, used for a fool's cap in Shakspere, and hence a fool. Cf. p. 115, l. 27. Similarly *small-pox=small-pocks.*

l. 31. **late scene of riot.** The Gordon riots ; see *Introduction*, p. xv.

Page 10. l. 2. The law was, etc. See *Introduction*, p. xv.

l. 7. **three visits,** *i.e.* three letters; see note to p. 9, l. 1.

my taciturnity. Cf. *Introduction*, p. xx.

l. 10. **make my bow,** etc. In keeping with the notion that he is paying a visit.

l. 12. This letter is a striking instance of Cowper's faculty of making the most trivial occurrence interesting and humorous by his manner of describing it. See *Introduction*, p. xxxi, and note, p. 38, ll. 18, 19.

l. 16. **back parlour.** A house has often two parlours or sitting-rooms, one in the front part and the other behind.

one of the hares. The poet kept three tame hares, named Puss, Tiney, and Bess, and built them boxes to sleep in. In the evening they were often allowed to gambol in his parlour, and in the daytime were let out into the hall. Hence, when the hares were out, visitors had to enter by the back door (see p. 47, ll. 21-24).

l. 22. **lattice-work,** a net-work of crossed laths. From French *lattis*, lath-work; Germ. *latte*, a lath.

l. 26. **redoubtable.** This word (like 'doughty') is nowadays used mock-heroically, in humorous satire on its old serious meaning of 'formidable.'

Thomas Freeman, the Olney ginger-bread baker.

ll. 30, 31. **Richard Coleman,** the son of a drunken cobbler at St. Albans, of whom Cowper charitably undertook the charge when he left that place for Huntingdon. Dick Coleman (as he was generally called) lived at this time next door to his benefactor.

ll. 31, 32. **carrying less weight,** not being so stout and heavy as Thomas. In horse-racing, horses of superior stamp are made to carry heavier weights than the other competitors, so as to equalize the chances of victory. Cf. *John Gilpin*, 115, 116:—

" 'He carries weight!' 'He rides a race!'
'Tis for a thousand pound!' "

Page 11, l. 5. **hunt,** hunting party; people in pursuit of the hare.

l. 7. **the race,** etc., *i.e.* only he and Puss were left running.

l. 10. **got the start,** got in front.

pushed for, ran in the direction of.

l. 12. **tanyard,** a piece of ground where hides are tanned into leather. The hides are soaked in pits of water, between layers of bark, with lime.

l. 25. **presuming upon,** etc., trusting that the interest I know you take in the most unimportant event that concerns me, will serve to make even this trivial letter acceptable.

l. 27. **Terence.** Publius Terentius Afer (*i.e.* the *African*, since he was born at Carthage), the famous Roman comic dramatist, six of whose plays have come down to us.

Nihil mei, etc., 'Nothing that concerns me do you deem a matter of indifference to you.' Cf. Terence, *Heauton Timoroumenos* ('The Self-tormentor'), I. i. 25: "Homo sum: humani nil a me alienum puto," 'I am a man, and nothing that concerns man do I deem a matter of indifference to me.' Cowper varies Terence's words again in a letter to Newton, May 28, 1781: "I can say it in Latin, and Mrs. Unwin in English—*Nihil tui a me alienum puto.*"

l. 29. **I must write, and must.** The first *must* is a verb, the second is a noun. The meaning is that when a person says you must do a thing, it is useless to put forward excuses.

Page 12, l. 3. **overruled,** rejected, declared insufficient. 'To overrule a plea' is a law term.

l. 4. **irrefragable,** 'that cannot be refuted'; lit. 'that cannot be broken back' (Lat. *re-*, back, *frangere*, to break).

l. 7. **Lady Anne,** a humorous name for Mrs. William Unwin. Cowper's "pet name" for Lady Austen was "*Sister* Anne."

l. 8. **like a true knight.** One of the laws of chivalry was devotion and obedience to ladies. Cf. p. 129, l. 20.

l. 10. **I do not love,** etc., I am not fond of recurring to topics that may be thought unpleasant.

ll. 15, 16. **a certain nomination,** *i.e.* to a vacancy on the foundation of Christ's Hospital, called also the Bluecoat School, one of the great London schools; established by Edward VI. in 1553.

l. 19. **long blue petticoat.** The garb of Christ's Hospital boys is a long flowing blue coat and yellow stockings. They wear no head-gear.

l. 21. **In the press,** etc. He quotes, as it were, the formal advertisement of his coming book, which was eventually published on March 1, 1782. The volume consisted of the four poems mentioned below and some minor pieces, to which were subsequently added *Hope*, *Charity*, *Conversation*, and *Retirement.*

l. 29. **sprung up,** 'came into being, was composed,' with a hint at the quickness of their production.

l. 34. **writes a Preface.** This Preface is dated Feb. 18., 1782, but was first prefixed to the fifth edition, 1790; the publisher fearing that its distinctly evangelical tone would injure the sale of the book. *Writes* = is to write.

Johnson. See *Introduction*, p. xlii.

l. 36. **I never mentioned to you.** Unwin, we find, felt somewhat hurt at being so long kept in the dark.

Page 13, ll. 1, 2. **if that Mr. All-the-world**, etc., *i.e.* if the public whom I have mentioned should think my book worth buying and reading.

l. 5. **underwriters**, lit. 'those who write their names under,' and so agree to accept, the conditions on which property is insured; insurance agents. The term is generally applied to insurers of ships and cargoes.

l. 6. **them**, my poems. The remark is a playful one.

l. 7. **even upon the credit**, etc. Cowper says that he is not rich enough to take the risk, even when he is supported by a confidence in his own talents.

ll. 9, 10. **to subject himself to an ambiguity**, to accept a doubtful chance (of being able to sell a sufficient number of copies).

ll. 11, 12. **all peradventures**, all contingencies. *Peradventure* is a noun here, as the second *must* is above, p. 11, l. 29.

l. 14. **Vincent Bourne.** See note, p. 3, l. 11. For "frank," see *Introduction*, p. xxxviii. Here "frank" is equivalent to "letter."

My Muse, etc., *i.e.* my book shall be presented to you as soon as it is published. Cf. ll. 18, 19 below.

l. 20. **my trumpeter**, an announcement of my merits. Cf. the phrase "to blow one's own trumpet," *i.e.* to praise oneself. Also *To Unwin*, April 1, 1782: "I could not have found a better trumpeter. ... Methinks I see you with the long tube in your mouth, proclaiming to your numerous connexions my poetical merits," etc. And see p. 21, l. 24.

l. 23. **blast.** Keeping up the metaphor of the "trumpeter."

l. 28. **season of publication.** The two publishing seasons are the early spring and the beginning of winter.

l. 29. **the town is going into the country.** People of fashion were leaving their town for their country houses. The "London season" apparently terminated earlier in Cowper's day than it does now.

Page 14, l. 3. **the press**, the proofs of my book for the press.

ll. 5, 6. **knock out the brains**, spoil the sense.

l. 9. **a presumptuous intermeddler.** Cowper found reason to complain of this meddling; see the letter to Mr. Johnson, p. 118.

ll. 11, 12. **cobbling, and tinkering**, introducing emendations (as cobblers mend shoes, and tinkers pots and pans).

ll. 12, 13. **a shred of his own**, a bit of his own composition.

l. 21. **double or treble letters**, *i.e.* two or even three sheets. See *Introduction*, p. xxxviii.

ll. 23, 24. **inconvenient to me**, too expensive; "not convenient to a purse like mine" (p. 13, l. 6).

ll. 24, 25. **to live by my wits**, to make money out of my authorship. The phrase, playfully employed here by Cowper, is generally used in the invidious sense of 'to make a living by skill in deceiving or defrauding others.'

l. 25. **to him, who**, etc., *i.e.* to my publisher, who hopes to make a little money out of the book.

l. 27. **totidem**, the same number.

l. 30. **stocks.** The "stock" was a kind of stiff collar, of silk or some similar material, fastened round the neck by a buckle. The "neckcloth" was tied.

l. 33. **stock-buckle.** This silver stock-buckle still exists among the Cowper relics. It was purchased at Olney, Sept. 27, 1837, of Thomas Kitchener, assistant to Mr. Wilson, Cowper's barber, and is now in the possession of Mrs. Welton of Olney. Cf. note to p. 46, l. 33.

Page 15, l. 1. **Bourne.** See note to p. 3, l. 11.

l. 8. **the turn**, the point or piquancy; aptness of expression.

l. 9. **expensive**, laborious, difficult.

l. 14. **the Jackdaw**, Cowper's translation of Bourne's *Cornicula*. The "point" he "sharpened" perhaps is in his translation of the last two lines, in which Cowper's "And such a head between 'em" is an addition to the original.

l. 17. **Vinny**, familiar for "Vincent."

ll. 18, 19. **Tibullus, Propertius, Ausonius.** The two former are famous Roman elegiac poets of the Augustan age; the last flourished under the Emperor Gratian in the fourth century.

l. 19. **in his way**, *i.e.* as writers of light, elegant pieces.

l. 20. **Ovid.** A Roman poet of much elegance and versatility, who lived in the time of Augustus.

l. 21. **with a love of partiality**, *i.e.* with a love that favours him above others; with a special affection.

usher, assistant-master.

l, 25. **trusted to his genius**, etc. He seemed to trust that people would overlook his slovenliness in consideration of his genius.

l. 28. **a magpie or a cat.** Cf. the "Jackdaw" above, and "Familiarity Dangerous" (verses on a "Youthful Tabby"), another of Cowper's translations of Bourne.

l. 32. **rational**, as in the "Jackdaw."

religious, as in the "Invitation to the Redbreast":—

> "Thus music must needs be confess'd
> To flow from a fountain above"; etc.

Page 16, l. 2. **classical**, pure in his style and language.

l. 3. **the classics**, the best Latin and Greek authors.

l. 10. **one, which, if ever finished**, etc. Cowper's *Hope*, a poem of 771 lines.

l. 11. **But this must make part**, etc. As has been seen above (note to p. 12, l. 21), this poem was included in Cowper's first published volume.

l. 15. **stand no chance**, *i.e.* of acceptance with the public.

l. 16. **will go down**, will be tolerated, will satisfy the public; lit. 'will be swallowed.'

l. 17. **franks.** See *Introduction*, p. xxxviii.

ll. 20, 21. **blowing as it does from the east.** Cf. *To Mrs. Newton*, June, 1780: "I have had several indifferent nights, and the wind is easterly; two circumstances so unfavourable to me in all my occupations," etc. And *To Lady Hesketh*, June 3, 1788: "Then came an east wind, baneful to me at all times." Also *Task*, iv. 363, 364:—

"The unhealthful east,
That breathes the spleen."

l. 30. **your safe arrival.** Newton's arrival at his home in London, after a visit paid by himself and Mrs. Newton to Cowper at Olney.

Page 17, l. 3. **an article**, 'an item,' 'a particular statement'; as we speak of the 'articles' of a treaty; cf. p. 55, l. 1. The meaning is: 'The question of our meeting can be settled only by reference to the table of events fixed by Divine Providence for the year then current.'

ll. 7, 8. **agreeables**, 'pleasures.' Notice the adjective turned into a noun; similar forms are *eatables*, *explosives*, *combustibles*, *valuables*, *moveables*, etc. Cf. *To Hill*, Nov. 11, 1782: "All these are so many *insuperables* in the way." Lamb (*Letters*, ii.) has: "In this world 'tis better not to think too much of pleasant *possibles*, that we may not be out of humour with present *insipids*."

l. 11. **dash it**, 'spoil the pleasure'; cf. 'to dash (*i.e.* frustrate) one's hopes.'

l. 14. **Lady Austen.** See *Introduction*, pp. xii., xiii. Shortly before this, Cowper had noticed Lady Austen with her sister Mrs. Jones from his window, and got Mrs. Unwin to invite the ladies to tea.

waving all forms, 'not keeping to the rules of etiquette' (which provide that the residents of a town or district make the first call on a new-comer). *Waving* is for *waiving*: Cowper, like other writers, confuses these two distinct words; cf. *To Newton*, Jan. 13, 1787: "As to fame, and honour, and glory .. I would cheerfully wave (*i.e.* waive) them all." In several instances, however, he writes *waive* correctly; cf. p. 61, l. 10, and *To Newton*, April 19 and June 5, 1788.

l. 16. **handsome,** 'ample, unstinted'; cf. 'a handsome subscription.'

ll. 16, 17. **returned the visit.** To Mrs. Jones's at Clifton Reynes (in the neighbourhood of Olney), a place of which Mr. Jones was the clergyman.

l. 21. **I had rather,** etc. Cowper means that he had rather have any faults in his verses pointed out to him before publication, than have them stigmatized by the critics afterwards.

l. 22. **Johnson.** See *Introduction*, p. xlii. In a later letter (Aug. 25) Cowper says that Johnson "uses the discretion my poetship has allowed him, with much discernment," and has "marked several defective passages, which I have corrected, much to the advantage of the poems."

l. 23. **a marginal Q.** A "Q," or ?, in the margin denotes "Query," expressing a doubt as to the correctness of the passage so marked.

l. 29. **fritter it,** 'break it up' (uselessly). A *fritter* (from Lat. *frictus*, 'fried') is a slice for frying; hence 'to fritter' is 'to reduce to slices,' and so 'to waste,' as in 'to fritter one's time away.'

l. 33. **the sheets,** *i.e.* the proof sheets of his poems.

Page 18, l. 3. Memorandum-book, etc. See *The Progress of Error*, ll. 373, 374.

l. 6. **"down derry down."** Words, musical but meaningless, used as the chorus or burden to a song. Scott (*Ivanhoe*, Cap. xvii.) says that "the chorus of 'derry down' is supposed to be as ancient as the times of the Druids." Cf. the XVIth century song of "The Three Ravens":—

'There were three ravens sat on a tree,
Down a down, hey-down, hey-down;
They were as black as they might be,
With a down.
And one of them said to his make
'Where shall we our breakfast take'?
With a down derry, derry, derry down, down."

ll. 6, 7. **the word being made to rhyme to itself.** Milton once and Spenser occasionally make a word rhyme with itself, but only when used in differing senses. Cf. Milton, *Sonnets*, iv. 5, 8: "Ruth" (the name) and "ruth" (compassion); Spenser, *Faerie Queene*, I. i. 39, 4, 7: "steepe" (abrupt) and "steepe" (soak).

l. 12. **Charity.** See note to p. 12, l. 21.

l. 15. **Hope.** See notes to p. 16, ll. 10, 11. Faith, Hope, Charity, the three Christian graces, are linked together by St. Paul, 1 *Cor.* xiii. 13.

l. 18. **diligence,** 'coach'; a French term.

l. 20. **my phiz,** 'my face,' 'my likeness.' *Phiz* is a cant abbreviation of *physiognomy;* cf. *biz* (for *business*), *nob* (for *nobleman*), *sov* (for *sovereign*), etc. A silhouette or profile of Cowper was taken in 1791, and in 1792 his portrait was taken twice, first in oils by Abbot, and a second time in crayons by Romney. In 1793 a sketch of him was made by Lawrence. Cf. p. 130, l. 35.

l. 23. **Autolycus,** a son of Mercury, notorious for his crafty thefts. Shakspere gives this name to the rogue in *Winter's Tale,* the "snapper-up of unconsidered trifles."

ll. 24, 25. **at a venture,** on the chance of its resembling me.

l. 29. **the thing,** the correct thing; a true likeness.

l. 30. **cast,** mould, form, character. Cf. p. 53, l. 6; p. 132, l. 22.

ll. 32, 33. **just the man,** Cowper exactly; a perfect likeness of him.

l. 35. **as yours,** etc. Cowper writes with reference to a portrait which Newton had recently had taken of himself.

Page 19, l. 3. **Euphrosyne,** Miss Catlett, Newton's niece, a girl of twelve, who had accompanied the Newtons on their visit to Olney (see note to p. 16, l. 30). On account of her high spirits Cowper had dubbed her "Euphrosyne," one of the three Graces,

> "In Heaven yclep'd Euphrosyne,
> And by men, heart-easing Mirth."
> Milton, *L'Allegro,* 12, 13.

l. 5. **My very dear Friend.** This kind of jingling composition ("hop o' my thumb lines" Cowper calls them in a subsequent letter) was rather a favourite with Thackeray.

ll. 5, 6. **what, when you have read,** *i.e.* the present rhyming letter.

l. 8. **by the tune and the time,** judging from the rhyme and the measure.

l. 10. **The thought,** *i.e.* of writing this rhyming epistle.

l. 11. **Madam,** Mrs. Unwin. Weston Park lay within easy walk of Olney, somewhat nearer to it than Weston Underwood.

l. 12. **with spreading sails,** 'at our best speed'; a jocose comparison of themselves to ships flying before the wind.

l. 13. **Charity.** See note to p. 12, l. 21.

l. 15. **wears Methodist shoes.** Cowper represents the reviewer as saying that his poetry is Evangelical in its tone. For the "Methodists," see note to p. 1, l. 16.

l. 16. **her pace**, the style of the poem.

grace, divine grace, the favour of God.

l. 18. **hoidening play**, 'rude, rough amusements'; such, perhaps, as bear-baiting and cock-fighting. *Hoiden* or *hoyden* is the Old Dutch *heyden*, a 'heathen,' and meant a clownish fellow. It is now used in the meaning of an ill-bred, romping girl.

l. 19. **assume a borrowed plume**, etc., *i.e.* though the poem sometimes adopts the style of the lighter class of poetry and is humorous in its tone. The *Monthly Review*, in criticizing Cowper's first volume, wrote: "His very religion has a smile that is arch, and his sallies of humour an air that is religious."

ll. 21, 22. **on a new construction.** The "new construction" is the mixture of religion and humour, piety and sarcasm.

l. 22. **She has baited**, etc., *i.e.* the aim of the poem is by amusing the reader to allure him to read what may profit him. Cf. p. 60, ll. 15-17; and *Epistle to Lady Austen*, 19-22:—

"I, who scribble rhyme
To catch the triflers of the time,
And tell them truths divine and clear,
Which, couched in prose, they will not hear;
Who labour hard to allure and draw
The loiterers I never saw," etc.

ll. 28, 29. **to the end of my sense**, though I have often been at my wit's end to find a suitable rhyme.

l. 29. **by hook or crook**, by some means or other. Under the old forest laws the villagers were not allowed to *cut* wood; they might take only what withered boughs they could collect by employing *hooks* and *crooks*.

Page 20, ll. 3, 4. **a minuet pace.** As soon as you entered, the floor moved up and down and made you dance a minuet (a graceful dance, with short steps; Lat. *minutus*, small).

Swimming. *i.e.* moving with slow, graceful action.

l. 7. **what will make you dance.** He compares his jingling letter to the floor laid on springs, because it will keep Newton's brain on the dance while he reads it.

l. 10. **Madam**, Mrs. Newton.

l. 15. **what I said of Scott.** In an omitted passage of this letter Cowper had mentioned that Mr. Scott had not come to see them. The Rev. Thomas Scott (b. 1747, d. 1821) was at this time curate of Weston Underwood, near Olney. He was a friend of Newton's, and afterwards became curate of Olney. His *Commentary on the Bible* is well-known. Cf. p. 44, l. 10; p. 48, l. 35; p. 68, l. 19.

l. 17. **has visited we.** *We* is put jocosely for *us*, to make a rhyme, as "himself and he" is put for "he." Cf. *John Gilpin*, 15, 16 :—

"Myself and children three
Will fill the chaise; so you must ride
On horseback after we."

The Greenhouse. The greenhouse, from which this letter is dated, was of Cowper's own building, and in the extremely hot summer of this year (1781) he tells Newton (Aug. 16) that he had "converted it into a summer parlour. The walls hung with garden mats, and the floor covered with a carpet, the sun too in a great measure excluded by an awning of mats,... it affords us by far the pleasantest retreat in Olney." Again writing to Unwin (June 8, 1783) he says: "I find myself seated in my favourite recess, the greenhouse." See p. 32, ll. 4, 26, and note to p. 32, ll. 6, 7; p. 38, l. 18; p. 85, ll. 15-21; p. 110, l. 36. Cf. also *To Newton*, Sept. 18, 1784: "My greenhouse is never so pleasant as when we are just upon the point of being turned out of it."

l. 18. **your preface.** See note to p. 12, l. 34.

l. 23. **my interlineation**, my proposed amendment, written between the lines of the original.

l. 30. **in the world**, at all, in the least.

Page 21, l. 1. **Dr. Johnson.** See note to p. 4, l. 17.

l. 6. **animadversions**, 'censures.' To 'animadvert' is lit. 'to turn the mind to' (Lat. *animus*, the mind; *ad*, to; *vertere* to turn).

Dr. Watts (b. 1674, d. 1748), was a Nonconformist divine and poet. He wrote the *Horæ Lyricæ*, a Logic, and *The Improvement of the Mind*, but is most celebrated as a hymn-writer. Johnson's criticism of his poetry is on the whole rather favourable, and cannot, at any rate, be characterized as "severe."

l. 11. **execution**, the style or language in which he clothed his "conceptions."

Pope. The celebrated English poet, born 1688, died 1744. *The Dunciad* is a poetical satire, in heroic verse, on certain poets and writers of Pope's day. The first three books were published in 1728, and the fourth in 1742.

l. 14. **somebody's blockhead**, 'some stupid fellow.' *Blockhead* means first 'a stupid head' (cf. *wooden-head*), and then 'a stupid-headed person, a dullard.' The latter is its usual present meaning. Cf. *Dunciad*, i. 145-147 :—

"A Gothic library! of Greece and Rome
Well purged, and worthy Settle, *Banks*, and Broome."

In the first edition the latter line ran :—

> "Well purged, and worthy W——y, *W——s* (*i.e.* Watts), and Bl——."

l. 18. **I never suffer a line to pass,** etc. Cf. *To Bagot*, May 20, 1786 (on his translation of the *Iliad*) : "The rigour that I exercised upon the first book, I intend to exercise upon all that follow, and have now actually advanced into the middle of the seventh, nowhere admitting more than one line in fifty of the first translation." And see p. 17, l. 32.

l. 19. **my doctrines,** 'my religious beliefs.' Cowper was a Low-Church Whig, Johnson was a High-Church Tory.

l. 21. **numbers.** See note to p. 5, l. 11.

l. 24. **trumpeters,** 'advertisers of my merits.' Cf. p. 13, l. 20, and note.

ll. 25, 26. **Sir Richard Blackmore** (b. 1650, d. 1729) produced no fewer than six epic poems, comprising some 58 books; by which he earned for himself and his "endless line" a niche in the *Dunciad* (ii. 267, 268) :—

> "All hail him victor in both gifts of song,
> Who sings so loudly and who sings so long."

His *Creation*, a philosophical poem, in seven books, was published in 1712, on which Johnson (*Life of Blackmore*) remarks : "This poem, if he had written nothing else, would have transmitted him to posterity among the first favourites of the English Muse." Addison praised it in the *Spectator* (No. 339), but it is now neglected.

l. 29. **about your pipe.** Cowper strongly objected to tobacco smoking, and had condemned the practice in his *Conversation*, 251 *et seq.* :—

> "Pernicious weed ! whose scent the fair annoys,
> Unfriendly to society's chief joys,
> Thy worst effect is banishing for hours
> The sex whose presence civilizes ours ;
>
> . . . .
>
> "They dare not wait the riotous abuse
> Thy thirst-creating steams at length produce,
> When wine has given indecent language birth,
> And forced the floodgates of licentious mirth."

l. 33. **it hardly falls,** etc., 'it can hardly be included under the censure I have pronounced against smoking' (in the lines quoted above). Cowper was equally lenient to the practice in the case of his friend Bull; see the letter to him on p. 32. But see also p. 33, ll. 30, 31.

ll. 34, 35. **You never fumigate,** etc., **nor do you use it,** etc.

These are the two special charges Cowper brings agaiust the practice in the verses from *Conversation* above.

Page 22, l. 2. **it leads you**, etc. Not to annoy others, Newton would retire, in the winter to his study, in the summer to his garden, to enjoy his smoke.

l. 6. **Hawkins Browne** (b.1706, d. 1760) is the author of *Design and Beauty* and *The Immortality of the Soul*, a Latin poem. His poem in praise of smoking is entitled *The Pipe of Tobacco.*

l. 8. **Retirement.** See note to p. 12, l. 21.

l. 14. **Johnson.** His publisher; see *Introduction*, p. xlii.

l. 22. **penury of matter**, lack of topics to write about.

l. 23. **hatching.** Jocosely for "composing."

l. 30. **Review.** Probably *The Monthly Review* (see note to p. 3, l. 22), which Cowper seems to have seen pretty regularly, rather than *The Critical Review*, which was set up in opposition to it by Archibald Hamilton in 1756.

Page 23, l. 1. **Johnson's critique.** In his *Lives*; see note to p. 4, l. 17. Cf. p. 45, l. 18 *et seq.*

Prior. Matthew Prior, the poet (b. 1664, d. 1721). He writes with ease and vivacity, and is the author of *Alma*, a clever, burlesque poem, *The City Mouse and the Town Mouse*, *Solomon*, etc.

l. 4. **Dryden**, a celebrated English poet (b. 1631, d. 1700); author of *Astræa Redux*, *Annus Mirabilis*, *Mac Flecknoe*, *The Hind and the Panther*, etc., together with numerous dramas.

ll. 6, 7. **a mechanical maker of verses.** Cf. *Table Talk*, 654, 655: "He (Pope)—

Made poetry a mere mechanic art,
And every warbler has his tune by heart."

l. 10. **phlegmatic**, 'dull, sluggish.' According to the old physiology, there were four *humours* which were supposed to make up human dispositions, and which may be thus tabulated, with their corresponding *elements*:—

(1) *blood*	(2) *phlegm*	(3) *choler* (*i.e.* bile)	(4) *gall*
sanguine	phlegmatic	choleric	melancholic
moist	cold	hot	dry
air	water	fire	earth

Phlegm (Gk. *φλέγμα*, from *φλέγειν*, to burn), contrary to its etymology, signified a cold, viscous humour. Cf. Milton, *Par. Lost*, xi. 542-545:—

"For the air of youth,
Hopeful and cheerful, in thy blood will reign
A melancholy damp of cold and dry
To weigh thy spirits down."

l. 13. **Flemish.** The most famous painters of the Flemish School were Vandyck (1599), Snyders (1579), Hobbima (1611), and Teniers jun. (1610).

l. 18. **a laziness and carelessness.** Cf. Johnson, *Life of Dryden:* "His faults of negligence are beyond recital. Such is the unevenness of his compositions, that ten lines are seldom found together without something of which the reader is ashamed. ... He was no lover of labour. What he thought sufficient, he did not stop to make better."

l. 23. **subscribe to,** agree to, give my support to.

l. 25. **I do not recollect,** etc. Cowper's memory *did* fail him, for Johnson did take notice of *Solomon,* which he speaks of as "having infused into it much knowledge and much thought; often polished to elegance, often dignified with splendour, and sometimes heightened to sublimity"; but as labouring under "the most fatal of all faults," tediousness.

l. 26. **Solomon.** *Solomon on the Vanity of the World* is a poem in three books, the first of which treats of *Knowledge*, the second of *Pleasure*, and the third of *Power.* It is written in the heroic couplet, and was published in 1718.

the best poem. So Prior himself thought.

l. 28. **he condemns him for,** etc. Johnson says that Prior's amorous effusions "are not dictated by nature or by passion," but are "the dull exercises of a skilful versifier, resolved at all adventures to write something about Chloe, and trying to be amorous by dint of study. His fictions therefore are mythological. Venus ... asks when she was seen 'naked and bathing.' Then Cupid is 'mistaken'; then Cupid is 'disarmed,'" etc. Johnson similarly found fault with *Lycidas* for its pastoral machinery; see p. 5, ll. 8, 9, and note.

l. 34. **Tibullus.** See note to p. 15, l. 18.

l. 36. **the prince of all poetical inamoratos,** the chief of all writers of love-poems.

Page 24, l. 1. **There is a fashion,** etc. As in the case of pastoral imagery, the machinery of classical mythology was a device of the poets who used it "for distancing themselves from the ordinary and prosaic, and enabling them to live and move mentally in a more poetic air" (Masson).

l. 3. **his old fusty-rusty remarks.** Johnson calls it "a dull and tedious dialogue, which excites neither esteem for the man, nor tenderness for the woman. The example of Emma, who resolves to follow an outlawed murderer wherever fear and guilt shall drive him, deserves no imitation; and the experiment by which Henry tries the lady's constancy, is such as must end either in infamy to her, or in disappointment to himself." *Fusty-rusty* means 'effete, antiquated.'

ll. 3, 4. **Henry and Emma.** Prior's poem is founded on the model of the old fifteenth century ballad of *The Nut-brown Maid.*

l. 13. **how that enchanting piece has bewitched them.** Lady Mary Wortley Montagu (b. 1690, d. 1762) says in one of her letters: "I was so much charmed at fourteen with the dialogue of Henry and Emma, I can say it by heart to this day—without reflecting on the monstrous folly of the story in plain prose. ... This senseless tale is, however, so well varnished with melody of words and pomp of sentiments, I am convinced it has hurt more girls than ever were injured by the worst poems extant."

l. 17. **a burthen,** 'wearisome,' 'irksome.' This spelling (instead of the more usual *burden*) serves to distinguish the word from *burden,* 'the refrain of a song,' which has a different derivation.

l. 18. **as the Bacchanals served Orpheus.** Orpheus, the famous poet and musician of Greek mythology, was attacked by the Thracian women while they were celebrating the orgies of Bacchus. They tore his body to pieces, and threw his head into the river Hebrus. *Bacchanals* (more properly *Bacchantes* or *Bacchæ*) were the female attendants of Bacchus, the god of wine, who celebrated his festival with wild fits of madness.

l. 19. **husky, dry,** prosy, unsentimental.

l. 23. **the subject of love.** There is no question that Johnson possessed great powers of *affection;* it is the passion of love that Cowper regards him as devoid of.

l. 29. **honestly printed,** printed without any attempt at spreading the matter over an undue number of pages, by spacing the type, etc.

ll. 29, 30. **public entrée,** public entrance; coming before the public (as an author).

l. 31. **were naught,** were good-for-nothing.

Page 25, l. 1. **The soles.** Cf. note to p. 3, l. 28.

l. 3. **vending,** 'selling,' 'pushing the sale of'; from Lat. *vendere,* to sell.

l. 5. **My authorship.** Jocosely for 'I in my capacity of author.' The word is on the model of 'his lordship,' etc. Similarly Cowper has "my poetship" (note to p. 17, l. 22).

l. 7. **as Horace observed.** See his *Epistles,* I. xvii. 35: *Principibus placuisse viris nos ultima laus est,* "To be approved by the great is the highest praise that I can win."

l. 11. **Many a man,** etc. Cf. *To Unwin,* May 8, 1784, where Cowper says that he was recommended to write a sequel to John

Gilpin, but "having always observed that authors, elated with the success of a first part, have fallen below themselves when they attempted a second, I had more prudence than to take her counsel." As examples of the difficulty of producing a second masterpiece, some have adduced Homer with his *Odyssey* (see p. 115, l. 4 *et seq.*), Milton with his *Paradise Regained*, Bunyan with his *Holy War*, and Defoe with his Second Part of *Robinson Crusoe.*

l. 17. **the advanced price of grain.** This was of course long before the abolition of the Corn Laws (in 1846) gave England her cheap bread.

ll. 18, 19. **feed upon a promise**, find solace, in their need, in God's promises to His people in the Bible.

l. 19. **wrap themselves**, etc., find similar solace in Christ's gospel, by which they are saved from their sins. Cf. Bible, *Isaiah*, lxi. 10: "He (God) hath clothed me with the garments of salvation, he hath covered me with the robe of righteousness."

l. 20. **A good fire-side**, etc., *i.e.* earthly comforts are but little worth apart from the consolations of religion. *Indifferent*, applied to persons, means (1) 'impartial,' and so (2) 'unconcerned'; applied to things, it means (1) 'tolerable' (neither good nor bad), and so (as here) (2) 'poor, inadequate.' Cf. p. 35, l. 30; p. 43, l. 6.

l. 22. **I would gladly**, etc. Cowper, in his state of religious depression, possessed little or no hope as regards the future life.

ll. 24, 25. **weeps tears of joy**, *i.e.* his excess of joy (in religion) finds relief in tears.

l. 27. **One man**, etc. Cf. *Retirement*, 559-562:—

"Anticipated rents, and bills unpaid,
Force many a shining youth into the shade,
Not to redeem his time, but his estate,
And play the fool, but at a cheaper rate."

l. 28. **to travel**, to go abroad.

ll. 30, 31. **wiser than he went.** So, in *The Progress of Error*, 369-437, the young man returning from foreign travel is represented as "teeming with powers he never felt before," and full of "accomplishments," which "have taken Virtue's place."

l. 31. **his follies**, his losses at the gaming-table, which necessitated his going abroad.

l. 33. **in the senate**, in Parliament.

ll. 33, 34. **its minister**, its Prime Minister.

Page 26, l. 1. **by a party**, *i.e.* by his own political party.

l. 3. **The exact contrast**, etc. In *Truth*, 317-336, Cowper has described the character he refers to here, in his sketch of the poor, but pious, Olney lacemaker, who "just earns a scanty pittance," but "knows her Bible true," and

"In that charter reads, with sparkling eyes,
Her title to a treasure in the skies."

ll. 6, 7. **they pray to him in secret ... to reward them openly.** The phraseology is Scriptural; cf. *Matthew*, vi. 6: "When thou prayest, enter into thy closet, and ... pray to thy Father which is in secret; and thy Father ... shall reward thee openly."

l. 7. **the day of recompense**, the time when they shall receive their reward.

l. 10. **a spiritual eye**, religious insight, which enables the possessor to look beyond the present, and understand the mystery of God's dealings with men.

l. 11. **had in abhorrence**, abhorred.

wretch, 'poor creature,' used here in a good sense.

l. 12. **the apple of his eye**, 'the pupil of his eye'—another Biblical phrase; cf. *Psalms*, xvii. 8: "Keep me as the apple of the eye, hide me under the shadow of thy (God's) wings." Also *Deut.* xxxii. 10; *Zech.* ii. 8.

l. 13. **are not in the secret**, are not spiritually-minded, and so do not understand God's ways.

l. 14. **doubt a Providence**, doubt the existence of a Divine Being who watches over His creatures.

ll. 15, 16. **all the real virtue**, all the really virtuous people.

l. 18. **worship.** See above, l. 1.

l. 19. **behind the curtain**, in the spiritual state of existence, which is hidden from us at present. Cf. Tennyson, *In Memoriam*, lvi. 7:—

"O life as futile, then, as frail!
O for thy voice to soothe and bless!
What hope of answer or redress?
Behind the veil, behind the veil."

l. 20. **very little**, etc., *i.e.* the great men of this world will find themselves in a very different position in the future life.

l. 29. **engage**, contend with each other.

l. 33. **chafing of the spirit**, vexation of mind.

l. 34. **come to a right understanding**, come to an agreement; become reconciled to each other.

Page 27, l. 2. **I love my country**, etc. Cf. *Task*, ii. 206, etc.:—

"England, with all thy faults, I love thee still,
My country! . . . .
. . . . And I can feel
Thy follies too."

ll. 3, 4. **scourged in mercy, than judicially hardened.** Cowper says that he had rather that England should be punished by God for her sins (which would be a merciful thing for Him to do, as it might bring about repentance and amendment), than that she should be made callous and unrepentant by prosperity (which would be a severe judgment upon her sins).

l. 9. **box.** These "boxes" are different compartments separated from one another by wooden partitions.

l. 10. **coffee-house.** In the eighteenth century the London coffee-house took the place of the modern club, and formed a meeting-place for men of similar tastes and occupations. Thus the politicians of Addison's time gathered at Will's coffee-house, and the wits at Button's; Child's was much frequented by the clergy; besides which there were St. James's coffee-house and the Rose.

l. 16. **a roaring syllabub**, a tossing and bubbling mass or mixture. *Syllabub*, or *sillabub*, is properly a mess of curdled milk mixed with wine. Wedgwood explains the word as being something that is *slapped up* or *slubbered up*; Low Germ. *slubbern*, 'to sup up soft food.'

This is the nineteenth winter, etc., *i.e.* it is now nineteen years since I was with you at the coffee-house and saw the waiter pour out your tea.

l. 20. **complexion**, character, manner in which they are passed.

l. 22. **from the inside**, etc. The coffee-house would be full of the noisy talk of the periwigged lawyers and others there assembled. *Periwig* (of which *wig* is a curtailed form) = *perwigge* = *perwicke*, from old Dutch *peruyk*, a peruke. The wearing of perukes prevailed in England more or less till about 1810. Cowper of course wore one: see *To Mrs. Throckmorton*, March 21, 1790: "My periwig is arrived, and is the very perfection of all periwigs," etc., and p. 75, ll. 8-14.

ll. 22, 23. **by a domestic fireside.** For a picture of the poet's evening, cf. *Task*, iv. 36-41; 139-193. See also page 42, l. 4 *et seq.*: "I see the winter approaching," etc.

l. 25. **two rustics**, two country-folk, as opposed to Londoners. The two were Mrs. Unwin and Lady Austen.

l. 26. **your humble servant**, *i.e.* of course, Cowper himself.

One of the ladies. Mrs. Unwin; see p. 2, l. 7, and note on *harpsichord*. Lady Austen played on the guitar.

l. 28. **battledore and shuttlecock.** A favourite game about this time. Miss Edgeworth, writing early in the present century, makes it a common schoolboys' game. The battledore, a kind of racket usually covered with parchment, is used to strike the shuttlecock, which is made of cork and feathers. *Battledore* is a corrupted form of Span. *batidor*, a washing-beetle. In *shuttlecock*, 'shuttle' comes from its being *shot* backwards and forwards, like a weaver's shuttle; 'cock' probably from its being stuck with feathers. In addition to this pastime, Cowper exercised himself with dumb-bells, and, later on, with a skipping-rope.

l. 30. **to admiration**, most admirably. For the adverbial phrase, cf. 'Exact *to the letter*' (*i.e.* literally), 'drawn *to the life*.' See p. 65, l. 6.

ll. 30, 31. **This entertainment over.** An absolute clause; *being* is understood.

Page 28, l. 8. **peace is at hand.** England was at war with France and Spain at this time, as well as with her American Colonies. See *Introduction*, p. xiv.

l. 9. **the siege of Gibraltar.** This famous siege was begun in 1779 by the Spaniards and the French, whose repeated attacks had been repulsed by General Elliot. On the 13th Sept. of the present year they opened fire upon the fortress with 142 guns, but in one night their floating batteries were destroyed with red-hot balls with a loss of 1600 men. The siege was continued till the peace in 1783, but only nominally.

ll. 13, 14. **little people**, people of little importance.

l. 15. **speculations**, theories or guesses about events.

l. 17. **a fine cod.** See note to p. 3, l. 28.

ll. 19, 20. **uneasiness in either eye.** As a boy, Cowper was troubled with specks in his eyes, and was placed by his father under the care of an eminent oculist, named Mr. Disney. At the age of thirteen, an attack of small-pox delivered him from these spots, but his eyes were always liable to inflammation. Cf. *To Lady Hesketh*, Jan. 23, 1786: "My eyes, you know, were never strong, and it was in the character of a carpenter that I almost put them out. The strains and the exertions of hard labour distended and relaxed the blood vessels to such a degree that an inflammation ensued so painful that for a year I was in continual torment, and had so far lost the sight of one of them that I could distinguish with it nothing but the light, and very faintly *that*." Cf. p. 134, l. 19.

l. 20. **my Æsculapius**, *i.e.* my doctor, viz., Elliott mentioned above. Æsculapius, son of Apollo, was the god and inventor of medicine, and hence his name is used as equivalent to "physician." Cf. p. 49, ll. 29, 30.

l. 23. **Not to retaliate**, not in order to pay you back for not writing to me.

l. 29. **chateau**, French for "castle," used here jocosely for "house." Lady Austen was at this time established at Olney Vicarage.

l. 30. **wind thread.** Cf. *Task*, iv. 264, 265, where Cowper speaks of devoting his evening hours to

> "twining silken threads round ivory reels,
> When they command whom man was born to please."

See also p. 47, l. 18.

ll. 30, 31. **Thus did Hercules.** This famous Greek hero was at one time married to Omphale, queen of Lydia, of whom he was so enamoured that he held the distaff and spun among her women, while she armed herself with his lion's skin and club.

Samson, the strong Jewish hero, was a slave to the charms of the fair Delilah and other women, and Cowper thinks that probably he, like Hercules, wound or spun thread to please them. See Bible, *Judges*, xiv. 17 ; xvi. 16, 17.

Page 29, l. 3. **killing lions.** The first of Hercules's twelve "labours" (cf. p. 74, l. 28) was the slaughter of the Nemæan lion ; and one of Samson's feats was the killing of a lion that "roared against him." See *Judges*, xiv. 5, 6.

ll. 4, 5. **I should be their humble servant.** Here a polite formula of saying good-bye. See p. 6, l. 13, and note.

l. 6. **Mr. Smith**, a rich banker of Nottingham, afterwards (in 1796) created Lord Carrington, to whom Cowper had made application, through Unwin, in behalf of the poor of Olney. He sent, "under the strictest injunctions of secrecy," considerable sums on several occasions for their relief. He died in 1838. See below, and p. 53, l. 2, and note.

l. 11. **I had done**, *i.e.* I should have done or acted.

l. 19. **Though laid under**, etc., though I have been strictly enjoined to keep the matter secret.

l. 25. **his delicacies on this subject**, *i.e.* his scruples about having his name as donor disclosed.

singular, remarkable, unusual.

l. 27. **this many a day**, for a long time.

ll. 30, 31. **their debts ... clothed.** Two absolute clauses.

l. 33. **it answers**, it answers its end ; it is of use.

Page 30, l. 2. **the barber, the schoolmaster.** The barber was Wilson, to whom there are frequent allusions in the Letters ; the schoolmaster was Teedon, a singular man, who was to exert a great influence upon the poet in later years. Both were noted purveyors of news at Olney. Cf. *To Newton*, Nov. 27, 1781 : "First Mr. Wilson, then Mr. Teedon, and lastly Mr. Whitford, each with a cloud of melancholy on his brow, and with a mouth wide open, have just announced to us this unwelcome intelligence from America."

ll. 3, 4. **the belligerent powers**, etc. The reference is to the Peace of Versailles; see *Introduction*, p. xiv.

l. 5. **at the door**, close at hand, about to be made.

ll. 5, 6. **I saw this morning**, etc. One of Cowper's inimitably humorous pictures.

ll. 8, 9. **a blacksmith's shed**. This shed stood on the Olney Market-place, opposite to Cowper's house.

ll. 14, 15. **nothing transpired**, what they were talking about did not reach me.

l. 20. **to a fine purpose**. Said ironically for 'with very poor results.'

ll. 20, 21. **at length declared independent**. By the treaty of Nov. 30, 1782, England had acknowledged the independence of the United States. See *Introduction*, p. xiv.

l. 21. **if they can**. Cf. *To Newton*, Feb. 24, 1783: "I may be prejudiced against them (the Americans), but I do not think them equal to the task of establishing an empire." See also below, p. 31, ll. 9, 10.

l. 22. **the parties**, etc., *i.e.* England on the one side, and France, Spain, and Holland on the other. The Peace of Versailles was concluded on the basis of mutual restitution.

ll. 26, 27. **carry their heads high**, 'assume a proud bearing'; 'give themselves airs.' They ought, Cowper thought, to hang their heads with shame.

ll. 28, 29. **are not ... of a piece**, do not coincide. The opinion of Newton, who regarded America as "a land of extraordinary evangelical light," was more favourable to the Americans than Cowper's.

Page 31, l. 4. the guilt of parricide. Cf. *To Newton*, Feb. 24, 1783: "As to the Americans, perhaps I do not forgive them as I ought; perhaps I shall always think of them with some resentment as the destroyers,—intentionally the destroyers, of this country."

l. 6. **her worst enemy**, *i.e.* France.

l. 11. **in a meaner light**, 'to have acted more meanly.' In 1780, on board a captured American ship, there was found the plan of an alliance between Holland and America, dated as far back as Sept. 1778. Remonstrances ensued, and on Dec. 20, 1780, war was declared against the Dutch.

l. 13. **led them by the nose**, made them do their bidding; utilized them for their own purposes.

l. 20. **the rest**, the other powers.

l. 22. **scourge**, punishment.

l. 23. **her ruin**, etc., because, in this quarrel, she has justice on her side.

l. 27. **the quidnuncs.** *Quid nunc* is Latin for "What now?" hence *quidnunc* is a satirical name for a person who is always on the hunt for news, and especially for a political busybody. A "Quihye" (*ko'ī hai?* 'Is any one in attendance?'), for an Anglo-Indian, is a similar formation.

l. 30. **The earth is a grain of sand**, etc. The world and its affairs are insignificant, but man's religious welfare is of the very highest importance.

l. 32. **Mr. Bull.** See *Introduction*, p. xl.

l. 33. **an account**, *i.e.* a money account, a bill.

Page 32, l. 4. My greenhouse. See note to p. 20, l. 17; and below, l. 26.

ll. 6, 7. **wants only the fumes of your pipe.** Cf. *To Bull*, 1783: "Is not our greenhouse a cabinet of perfumes? It is at this moment fronted with carnations and balsams, with mignionette and roses, with jessamine and woodbine, and wants nothing but your pipe to make it truly Arabian—a wilderness of sweets!"

l. 7. **Tobacco.** See notes, p. 21, ll. 29, 33.

l. 8. **the golden age.** According to Ovid (*Met.* i. 89 *et seq.*) there were four ages of the world: the golden (*i.e.* the best and happiest) age; the silver age; the brazen or bronze age; and the iron (*i.e.* the worst) age. These legendary ages must be distinguished from the anthropological ages—the age of stone, the age of bronze, and the age of iron, when man made his implements of stone, bronze, and iron respectively.

So much the worse, etc., *i.e.* the want of tobacco was a mark of inferiority in the golden age. Cf. p. 53, l. 12, and note.

l. 9. **This age of iron, or lead**, these degenerate modern times.

l. 13. **The season**, etc. See ll. 23, 24 below: "Our severest winter," etc.; and cf. p. 39, l. 22 *et seq.*

ll. 14, 15. **who am merely animal.** Cowper means to imply that he leads a merely animal existence, and has no spiritual or religious life. It is about this date that he writes to Bull that "he has not even asked a blessing upon his food for these ten years, nor does he expect that he will ever ask it again." Cf. note to p. 92, ll. 1, 2.

l. 16. **to write**, to compose; to write poetry.

l. 17. **fruit**, 'productions.' The time was soon to come; the *Task* was probably commenced in the following month.

l. 18. **that**, *i.e.* the amusement of poetical composition.

l. 22. **these on Peace.** See Cowper's *Song on Peace*, beginning "No longer I follow a sound." He composed one or two other songs for Lady Austen to sing to her guitar.

Page 33, l. 10. **rivals.** The plants and flowers just mentioned.

ll. 12, 13. **Newport,** *i.e.* Newport Pagnell, a town five miles due south of Olney.

ll. 13, 14. **You would regret,** etc., *i.e.* you would be still more sorry that you live at such a distance, because you thus lose not only my society, but also that of Mr. Bull.

l. 16. **A dissenter.** "He is" is understood. A *dissenter* is one who dissents from or does not conform to the doctrines or ceremonial of the Church of England; a Nonconformist.

a liberal one. Not narrow or bigoted in his religious views.

ll. 17, 18. **master of ... not master of it.** The first "master" means "owner," the second means "controller." He is "not master of it," because he cannot keep it under control; it "runs away with him."

l. 20. **fields of speculation,** *i.e.* he indulges himself in all manner of fanciful theories and ideas.

l. 21. **imagination,** imaginative person.

ll. 26-30. **Every scene ... dejection.** A sentence quite in the Johnsonian style. *Scene* = phase, aspect.

ll. 30, 31. **But—he smokes tobacco.** See, however, above, p. 32, ll. 6, 7. On Cowper's dislike of tobacco, see note to p. 21, l. 29.

ll. 32, 33. **Nihil ... beatum.** "Nothing is blessed in every respect." Cf. "Every rose has its thorn." The lines are from Horace, *Odes*, II. xvi. 27, 28.

l. 34. **his cause.** This appears to have been a case brought before the Privy Council, in which Mr. Fytche claimed the right to dismiss a clergyman, on the ground of immorality, from a living to which he had presented him.

l. 35. **voice,** 'vote.' Cf. Addison, *Cato*, ii. 1: "My voice is still for war."

Page 34, l. 1. **conditional presentations,** *i.e.* presentations (by a patron) of a clergyman to a living on condition of good conduct. English landed proprietors often have in their gift ecclesiastical livings or benefices situated on their estates.

were in fashion, were customary.

l. 3. **upon the terms,** etc., on the condition that he should hold it "so long as he shall conduct himself properly." All English judges now hold their offices by this tenure. Down to

1701 they held them only *durante beneplacito*, "during our (the King's) good pleasure."

l. 5. **the Establishment**, the Established Church, the Church of England.

l. 7. **lay patrons**, non-clerical holders of presentations to livings. See note to l. 1 above.

should have their hands tied, should be prevented from exercising discipline (in removing immoral or incompetent clergymen).

l. 8. **your state**, *i.e.* your statement.

l. 11. **they go for nothing**, they have no weight or value.

l. 12. **proved**, turned out to be.

l. 16. **a song**, his poem entitled *The Rose*, commencing

"The rose had been wash'd, just wash'd in a shower,
Which Mary to Anna convey'd,"

Mary being Mrs. Unwin, and Anna, Lady Austen.

l. 25. **those incidents**, etc. An absolute clause.

l. 27. **to me**, as far as I am concerned.

Page 35, ll. 2, 3. **My passion for retirement**. See *Introduction*, p. xxxvi.

l. 6. **considering the condition of my mind**. A mind, like Cowper's, in a state of chronic depression, might be expected to wish for excitement and change of scene rather than a retired life.

ll. 7, 8. **of course**, in the natural course of things. We are naturally guided in our choice by the decision of Divine Providence.

l. 8. **who appoints**, etc., 'who settles our destiny in life for us.' The phrase is from the Bible, *Acts*, xvii. 26: "(God) hath determined the bounds of their (men's) habitation." Cf. below, l. 33.

l. 10. **The world is before me**. Cf. Milton, *Par. Lost*, xii. 646, 647 (of Adam and Eve):—

"The world was all before them, where to choose
Their place of rest."

l. 11. **the Bastille**. A castle in Paris, built 1369-1383, afterwards notorious as the state prison of a despotic government. It was pulled down by the populace at the outbreak of the French Revolution of 1789. The *Bastille* means "*the* Building," from Old Fr. *bastir* (now *bâtir*), to build. Cowper denounces its "horrid towers, the abode of broken hearts," in the *Task*, v. 379-392.

ll. 13, 14. **a local attachment**, a feeling that makes me cling to a certain locality; a fondness for familiar surroundings.

ll. 14, 15. **even to the place of my birth**, cf. p. 97, l. 21 *et seq.*

l. 27. **this incommodious nook.** Orchard Side, the poet's house at Olney, had to Unwin's eyes the appearance of a prison; and Cowper after he had left it for Weston Lodge (*To Newton*, Dec. 16, 1786) speaks of its coldness, dreariness, and dirt. Cf. also p. 91, l. 3.

l. 30. **indifferent.** See note to p. 25, l. 20.

l. 35. **Iste terrarum,** etc. "That corner of the earth has, beyond all others, charms for me." The quotation is from Horace, *Odes*, II. vi. 13, 14, the true reading being *ille*, not *iste*. Cf. note to p. 88, l. 11.

Page 36, l. 17. **as an historian.** The reference is to Newton's *Review of Ecclesiastical History.* In a previous letter (June 13) Cowper had told Newton that the style of this history was, in his judgment, "incomparably better than that of Robertson or Gibbon."

l. 10. **warrant**, vouch for, support, maintain.

l. 12. **Robertson.** William Robertson (b. 1721, d. 1793) produced three great historical works, the *History of Scotland*, the *History of the Reign of Charles V.*, and the *History of the Discovery of America*, which appeared respectively in 1759, 1769, and 1777. He has great merits as a writer, but his style is somewhat artificial and aims too much at effect.

strut, magniloquence. He has been designated as "rather the orator, ambitious of displaying his eloquence, than the simple narrator of past events."

l. 13. **Gibbon.** Edward Gibbon (b. 1737, d. 1794), the great historian of *The Decline and Fall of the Roman Empire*, acquired, through his long residence on the Continent, a strong sympathy with French modes of thought and a highly Latinized style, which is very elaborate and fastidiously elegant.

finical, affectedly fine.

ll. 14, 15. **precision**, exactness, clearness.

l. 16. **set your periods to a tune**, adopt a measured, rhythmical style in the construction of your sentences. Colman speaks of Gibbon's "measured phraseology," and the Rev. S. Brooke has remarked upon his "heavily-laden style and the *monotonous balance of every sentence.*"

discover, show, disclose.

l. 17. **to exhibit**, etc., to show themselves off.

l. 18. **They sing.** See above, l. 16.

l. 26. **is an emetic**, 'is sickening or disgusting'; lit. 'excites vomiting.' Cf. *Task*, ii. 416-418 :—

"In my soul I loathe
All affectation. 'Tis my perfect scorn;
Object of my implacable disgust."

l. 27. **sensibly**, feelingly, deeply.

l. 28. **my productions**, Cowper's first volume, published on March 1st of the previous year.

l. 30. **Johnson.** His publisher; see *Introduction*, xlii. The inquiry would be as to the sale of the book.

Page 37, ll. 5, 6. the spiritual good...scriptural subjects. The tone of Cowper's volume is distinctly religious, and the subjects are in several cases (as *Hope, Charity*) Biblical. Similarly his *Conversation* (ll. 505-536) contains a paraphrase of a Biblical incident.

were, would be.

l. 9. **a dissipated age**, see *Introduction*, p. xvi.

ll. 11, 12. **shake his head, and drop his chin.** Gestures significant of failure and disappointment.

l. 15. **my Latin ode.** The "English dirge" is Cowper's poem *On the Loss of the Royal George*, written in Sept. 1782, of which the "Latin ode" is a translation in an Horatian metre.

l. 16. **The tune.** The dirge is written to the music of the March in *Scipio*, an opera by Handel.

l. 18. **Alexandrines**, hexameter lines of twelve, thirteen, or fourteen syllables, often divided by a pause into two parts between the sixth and the seventh syllable. Thus the last stanza of the dirge, written as a couplet, runs thus :—

"But Kem|penfelt| is gone,|| his vic|tories| are o'er;
And he| and his| eight hundred|| shall plough| the wave| no more."

The Alexandrine metre was so called from the fact that old French poems in praise of Alexander (as *The Gestes of Alisaundre*, etc.) were written in this measure.

ll. 18, 19. **but a French one.** The Alexandrine being originally a French metre; see above.

l. 21. **The ballad**, etc. Cowper passes on to the Ballad, because his dirge is written in the regular old ballad metre, which resembled the Alexandrine. "No country," writes Mr. Shaw, "(excepting Spain) possesses anything similar in kind or comparable in merit to the old ballads of England." The first considerable collection of these ballads was published by Bishop Percy in 1765. See *Introduction*, p. xvii.

l. 25. **moderns**, 'modern writers.' See note to p. 17, l l. 7, 8

l. 27. **many excellent ballads.** Such are, among the Percy collection, *The Battle of Otterburne*, *Chevy Chase*, and *The Death of Douglas.*

l. 33. **my father,** Dr. John Cowper, rector of Berkhampstead.

l. 34. **at a time when,** etc. Cowper was probably thinking of Prior, with his *Henry and Emma* (see p. 24, l. 3), Gay, and perhaps Allan Ramsay.

l. 35. **Gay's ballad.** "'Twas when the seas were roaring" is the first line of a Song introduced by Gay into his dramatic piece entitled *The What d'ye Call it?* John Gay (b. 1688, d. 1732), is the author of *Trivia, Fables, The Beggar's Opera,* etc. He wrote the play *Three Hours after Marriage* in conjunction with Pope.

l. 36. **Swift's,** etc. Jonathan Swift (b. 1667, d. 1745), author of *The Tale of a Tub*, etc., and sundry poems. Dr. John Arbuthnot (b. 1675, d. 1735) and Pope (see note, p. 21, l. 11) were all contemporary with Gay.

Page 38, l. 2. **well informed,** credibly informed, informed on good authority.

l. 6. **puny days,** inferior age, degenerate times.

l. 7. **Bourne.** See note, p. 3, l. 11.

translated, *i.e.* into Latin.

l. 9. **infinitely surpassing,** etc. For Cowper's rather extravagant admiration of Bourne, see p. 15, ll. 18-20.

l. 10. **Ovid or Tibullus.** See notes, p. 15, ll. 18, 20.

l. 13. **worthy.** Said ironically.

l. 18. **the greenhouse.** See note to p. 20, l. 17.

ll. 18, 19. **A few days since,** etc. Here we have another of those trifling incidents of which Cowper is so charming a narrator. See *Introduction*, p. xxxi. For the poet's pets, see *Introduction*, p. xxi.

l. 22. **the fountain,** the vessel for holding the bird's drinking water.

l. 26. **discovered,** 'showed'; see p. 36, l. 16.

Page 39, l. 7. **at a pinch,** when I am at a loss for something to do.

l. 8. **the versification of them.** Cowper versified this incident in his poem entitled *The Faithful Bird.*

l. 13. **epidemic fever.** See note to p. 1, l. 3, where Cowper writes "*epidemical* fever."

l. 18. **emetic tartar.** We now say "tartar emetic." The poet was a good deal addicted to the use of purgative, as well as other medicines. Cf. p. 36, l. 26; p. 49, ll. 24, 25, and note; p. 129, l. 24; p. 132, l. 5 *et seq.*

It is a tax, etc., *i.e.* my health generally compels me to subject myself to this treatment in autumn.

l. 19. **ether,** atmosphere.

l. 22. **rational,** possessed of reason.

l. 23. **animal too.** Cf. p. 32, ll. 14, 15, where Cowper claims to be "merely animal."

l. 28. **for our humiliation,** *i.e.* our inability to cure it is ordained as a means of humiliating our pride.

l. 30. **a philosopher,** 'a natural philosopher, a man of science'; see note to p. 7, l. 5. Cowper's remarks upon the scientific investigators of his time are in a tone of gentle banter.

Page 40, l. 1. **hypotheses,** pre-established theories or principles which the investigator applies to particular facts or phenomena. This "invention of hypotheses" is the philosophical method of *Deduction,* as opposed to the Baconian method of *Induction,* which evolves the theory from the examination of individual facts. Cowper's investigator "employs his reason in support of his hypotheses" by endeavouring to make his facts fit them.

l. 3. **their influence upon himself.** Cf. p. 16, ll. 20, 21, and note.

l. 5. **project,** theory, speculation.

l. 6. **The vortices of Descartes,** the hypothesis that the planets are carried round the sun by a vortex or whirl of a fine and subtle kind of matter, whose motion keeps up theirs. This theory was once very famous, and almost universally received. Descartes (b. 1596, d. 1650) was a celebrated French philosopher, who gave the death-blow to Scholasticism.

ll. 6, 7. **the gravitation of Newton,** the doctrine that the planets in their course round the sun retain their position in virtue of the mutually attractive force of particles of matter. Sir Isaac Newton (b. 1642, d. 1727), the most distinguished natural philosopher of modern times, published his law of gravitation in his *Principia,* in 1687.

ll. 7, 8. **the electrical fluid of a modern.** Cowper is probably thinking of the electrical researches of Beccaria and Æpinus in 1758 and 1759.

l. 9. **your philosopher.** This is the unemphatic, colloquial use of *your*—'the philosopher of which you and I are talking.' See p. 83, l. 21; and cf. Shaks. *Hamlet,* i. 5. 166, 167:—

> "There are more things in heaven and earth, Horatio,
> Than are dreamt of in your philosophy."

ll. 15, 16. **The world gaze.** The collective noun *world* is used here as a plural, because the writer has in view the various units or persons that it comprises; cf. "*their* praises" below, l. 18.

l. 16. **as he does**, 'as he gazes.' *Do* here stands for a preceding verb in order to avoid repeating it. The theory of some grammarians that the dependent infinitive is elided after this *do* (as, "I do not spend so much as he does [spend]") cannot be maintained, as is shown by such a sentence as, "He ran faster than I could have *done*," where no elision is possible.

l. 17. **as little**, *i.e.* as little as he does the new phenomena.

ll. 21, 22. **a century.** *Century* is to be parsed as a noun in the objective case used adverbially to modify "he has been dead," and denoting duration of time.

l. 22. **make shift**, manage or do without them.

l. 26. **currente calamo**, "as my pen ran on"; writing without premeditation.

l. 30. **these air-balloons.** The first balloon, filled with hot air, was constructed by Montgolfier, in which he ascended at Annonay, in France (where the balloon is still preserved), on June 5, 1783, causing immense interest and excitement, The first ascent in England was made by Lunardi at Moorfields. London, on September 15, 1784. Cf. *To Newton*, December 15, 1783: "I know not how it fares with you, at a time when philosophy (*i.e.* science) has just brought forth her most extraordinary production. ... My mind, however, is frequently getting into these balloons, and is busy multiplying speculations as airy as the regions through which they pass." And *To Unwin*, November 10, 1783: "The balloons prosper. ... Thanks to Montgolfier, we shall fly at last." And again, *To Hill*, January 22, 1785: "Long live the inventors and improvers of balloons! It is always clear overhead, and by and by we shall use no other road." Cowper's friend and neighbour, Mr. Throckmorton, used to amuse himself by sending up fire-balloons, and invited the poet to be present at the spectacle; cf. *To Unwin*, 1783: "Balloons are so much in the mode, that even in this country we have attempted a balloon," etc. Among the newspaper items in the *Task* (iv. 85) are "Ætherial journeys," or accounts of balloon ascents.

l. 34. **gravitating to a centre**, drawn by the force of gravitation to the earth's centre.

l. 35. **comparative levity**, the lightness of his own body as compared with other particles of matter.

ll. 35, 36. **the medium exactly in equilibrio with himself**, *i.e.* such atmospheric or other conditions as shall exactly balance his weight; so that he will remain suspended motionless.

Page 41, l. 2. **that purer element**, the "medium" mentioned above.

l. 3. **his aerial contents**, the "inflammable air" with which his stomach is filled.

l. 7. **pennæ non homini datæ**, "wings not granted to man"; quoted from Horace, *Odes*, I. iii. 35, where Dædalus, the first inventor of a flying machine, is referred to.

l. 8. **to be less regretted.** Because the balloon will take their place.

ll. 8, 9. **a flight of academicians**, a flying group of learned men.

l. 9. **a covey.** We say "a covey of partridges" or other game birds. Cowper jocosely applies the term to a company of ladies on the wing.

l. 11. **the public prints**, the newspapers.

l. 19. **experiments upon this machine**, attempts made to improve upon the balloon.

l. 28. **bandbox**, a light box, generally of cardboard, for holding hats, bonnets, etc.

Page 42, l. 3. **sure of my mark**, sure that the letter will reach you.

l. 4. **I see winter approaching**, etc. See note to p. 27, ll. 22, 23.

l. 11. **two ladies to read to.** The ladies were Mrs. Unwin and Lady Austen. The poet was fond of reading aloud in the winter evenings. See note to p. 1, l. 23.

ll. 12, 13. **we are circumnavigating the globe**, we are reading a book of travels round the world. Cf. the quotation from the *Task* in the note to p. 3, l. 2.

l. 16. **Cook's voyage.** This would be the narrative of Cook's second voyage; see note to p. 3, l. 4. For *Foster*, or rather Forster, see note to page 3, l. 5.

l. 19. **I have neither long visits**, etc., *i.e.* living, as I do, a retired life in the country, I have no long calls to pay, nor need to waste my time in listening to ladies' gossip.

l. 23. **station**, situation in life.

l. 25. **Business, or what**, etc., *i.e.* we shall be sure to have some business (if that is not too grand a term to use for what may be really trivial) which will claim our attention as important.

l. 30. **necessities**, necessary occupations.

Page 43, l. 2. **the Antediluvian world**, mankind existing before the Flood (as related in Bible, *Genesis*, vii. 11-24).

l. 3. **almost millenary,** 'lasting almost a thousand years. Several of the Antediluvians lived to the age of over 900 years; see *Genesis*, v.

l. 4. **It is probable,** etc. Here follows a delightful piece of humorous fancy in Cowper's best vein.

l. 6. **indifferently,** 'poorly'; see note to p. 25, l. 20.

l. 7. **philosophical,** 'scientific'; see note to p. 7, l. 5.

l. 11. **resolve,** solve, explain.

l. 13. **before Noah,** etc., *i.e.* long before the Flood, which happened in the time of the patriarch Noah.

l. 15. **good sizeable cakes,** cakes of a good large size.

ll. 26, 27. **the day is far spent,** it is getting late.

l. 33. **slipt through his fingers,** gone before he was aware.

ll. 33, 34. **passed away like a shadow,** 'glided swiftly and silently away.' A common Biblical figure; cf. *Psalms*, cxliv. 4: "His (man's) days are as a shadow that passeth away."

Page 44, l. 1. **pinched in point,** etc., in a difficulty as regards opportunity for doing things.

ll. 2, 3. **four sides of a sheet.** See *Introduction*, p. xxxviii.

l. 5. **the disproportion,** etc., their not having sufficient time for what they wanted to do.

ll. 9, 10. **Mr. Scott.** See note to p. 20, l. 15.

l. 18. **Lord Dartmouth's Mr. Wright.** This Mr. Wright (a different person from the Mr. Wright of p. 4, l. 8) was steward to Lord Dartmouth, for whom see note to p. 3, ll. 2, 3.

l. 24. **the entertainment,** in lending books to Cowper.

l. 26. **selling a good collection.** When Cowper left the Temple for St. Albans, his library (with the exception of a few law books) was dispersed with his other belongings.

l. 27. **in Essex,** *i.e.* he could make use of Unwin's library, who lived at Stock, in Essex, the books being conveyed to him by waggon. See *Introduction*, p. xxxix., and cf. p. 75, l. 21.

ll. 29, 30. **suitable ... for an author.** See note to p. 109, l. 12; and cf. p. 138, l. 5.

l. 31. **Johnson's Prefaces.** See note to p. 4, l. 17.

Page 45, l. 1. **vouchsafed,** condescended.

l. 7. **that tribute,** the tribute or meed of humble admiration.

l. 12. **sentiment,** opinion, judgment.

l. 13. **through affectation,** in order to show off his superior wisdom.

ll. 14, 15. **his narrative ... rather than,** etc., *i.e.* Cowper's praise is meant for Johnson's narrative of the poets' lives, rather than for his criticism of their poetry.

l. 17. **He finds no beauties in Milton's Lycidas.** See p. 5, l. 6 *et seq.* and notes.

l. 18. **He pours contempt upon Prior.** See p. 23, l. 23 *et seq.*, and notes.

l. 21. **capital,** principal, salient.

l. 25. **Alma,** or "the Progress of the Mind," is a metaphysical poem by Prior, written, says Dr. Johnson, "in professed imitation of *Hudibras*, to which it has at least one accidental resemblance: *Hudibras* wants a plan, because it is left imperfect; *Alma* is imperfect, because it seems never to have had a plan." Mr. Gosse (*18th Century Literature*) remarks: "In this poem Prior consciously follows Butler, to whom he pays a fine compliment; but his muse is more graceful, and less wayward. He had more variety and versatility than Butler, and he not unfrequently obtains an effect which is far above the reach of the author of *Hudibras*." *Hudibras* is a humorous poem by Samuel Butler (b. 1600, d. 1680), in iambic tetrameters, written to satirize the Puritans.

l. 33. **These luminaries,** etc., 'these distinguished men seem to have been endowed with exceptional genius, only to draw our attention to their defects.' Astronomical observation has made us familiar with the "spots" discovered in the sun.

Page 46, l. 1. **Pope.** See note to p. 21, l. 11. Pope was notorious for his vanity and the peevishness of his temper, due in some measure to his chronic state of ill-health.

l. 2. **sensible of,** sensitive to.

restless in provocation, 'perpetually provoking others to attack him.' Pope's quarrel with Dennis, his bitter attacks upon Lord Hervey, Lady Montagu, etc., not to mention the victims of *The Dunciad*, are well known.

l. 3. **To what mean artifices,** etc. In 1714 Pope, at that time engaged on his translation of Homer, believed that Addison was inciting his friend Tickell to produce a rival translation. Whether this was so seems to be doubtful, but it is true that in June 1715 Pope and Tickell simultaneously published a first *Iliad;* and, though Tickell immediately withdrew, Pope continued to believe that Addison had been scheming against him and had himself translated the book. Joseph Addison (b. 1672, d. 1719) is more famous as the essayist of the *Spectator* than as a poet.

l. 4. **Savage.** Richard Savage (b. 1698, d. 1743) wrote the tragedy of *Sir Thomas Overbury* and other works. In 1727 he accidentally killed a Mr. Sinclair at a house of ill-fame, in a drunken quarrel. After enduring much privation, he died in a debtor's prison at Bristol.

ll. 6, 7. **through a veil,** *i.e.* in spite of the excuses that are made for them.

ll. 7, 8. **What a sycophant,** etc. Dryden pandered to the vicious taste of his day by writing licentious plays, though his life was pure. Hence he "sinned against his feelings" which were on the side of morality. Cf. Scott, *Marmion*, Introduction to Canto I. :—

"And Dryden, in immortal strain,
Had raised the Table Round again,
But that a ribald King and Court
Bade him toil on, to make them sport;
Demanded for their niggard pay,
Fit for souls, a looser lay,
Licentious satire, song, and play."

l. 9. **lewd in his writings,** etc. Similarly Ovid (*Tristia*, II. 353, 354) claimed that if his poetry was licentious, his life was chaste. *Conversation* means here 'conduct,' as frequently in the Bible.

l. 11. **with a candle,** etc. Cf. Bible, *Zephaniah* ("the prophet"), i. 12: "I (the Lord) will search Jerusalem with candles, and punish the men," etc. Cowper probably also had in his mind the story of Diogenes, who was found going about with a lighted candle, and, in answer to inquiries, said that he was "in search of a man."

a man, a true man, a man worthy of the name.

l. 12. **unless, perhaps, Arbuthnot.** See note to p. 37, l. 36. In another letter Cowper excepts Collins as the only poet "whose mind seems to have had the slightest tincture of religion." "But," he continues, "from the lives of all the rest there is but one inference to be drawn—that poets are a very worthless, wicked set of people."

l. 13. **Beattie.** See p. 50, l. 8, and note. James Beattie (b. 1735, d. 1803) is a Scottish poet, the author of *The Minstrel, or the Progress of Genius* (1771 and 1774), a poem designed to trace the progress of a poetical genius from the first dawning of fancy to complete poetical development.

ll. 15, 16. **a glimpse from Heaven,** some small amount of religious enlightenment.

l. 17. **evangelical light,** knowledge or appreciation of the truths of the Gospel.

faithful to, firm in his adherence to.

l. 20. **call him blind,** say that his belief was clouded by error.

l. 24. **indulge myself**, etc., allow myself the gratification of making notes in the margin of the book.

l. 26. **wantonly**, unnecessarily, without restraint.

l. 28. **Irish**, *i.e.* Irish linen cloth.

l. 32. **a round slouch**, a round, limp hat whose sides hang down.

l. 33. **well-cocked**, 'elegantly shaped'; 'with the sides neatly turned up.' The 'cocked hat' of the period was of triangular form, with the three sides or flaps turned up and fastened back. Johnson (*Dict.*) quotes: "You see many a smart rhetorician turning his hat in his hands, moulding it into several different cocks"; and *to cock*, "to mould the form of a hat." The poet seems to have been particular about his attire. Cf. p. 14, ll. 30-35.

l. 35. **chip**, a coarse kind of straw.

Page 47, l. 1. **his majesty's pleasure**, etc. Since franks were signed by Members of Parliament, a dissolution would for the time being deprive Cowper of the opportunity of using franks. See *Introduction*, p. xxxviii. The younger Pitt had at this time just become Prime Minister, and after a short struggle with the Opposition led by Fox and North, in which his majority dwindled to one, Parliament was dissolved by George III. on March 25th. The announcement of the dissolution was, however, delayed by the unexplained theft of the Great Seal, which explains why Cowper, writing on the 29th, had not yet heard of it.

l. 5. **an extraordinary gazette**, a special issue of the official newspaper, giving notice of some unusual event.

l. 10. **turbulent times**. They were times of great political excitement.

Orchard side. See note to p. 35, l. 27.

l. 11. **the political element**, 'political affairs,' the analogue of the watery element.

l. 14. **We were sitting**, etc. Another of Cowper's inimitably told incidents; see *Introduction*, p. xxxi.

l. 17. **one lady knitting**. Mrs. Unwin; see p. 77, l. 15, and note.

l. 18. **winding worsted**. See note to p. 28, l. 30.

ll. 20, 21. **Mr. Grenville**. William Wyndham Grenville, a partizan of Pitt.

l. 21. **Puss**. See note to p. 10, l. 16.

l. 23. **the grand entry**, the front door.

l. 32. **no vote**. Because he was not a freeholder. Cf. p. 51, l. 30.

for which, etc., a statement which he readily believed.

Page 48, l. 2. **Mr. Ashburner.** The "Herculean" Olney draper often appears in Cowper's letters; see p. 51, l. 34. *Drapier* is the French form; we now write *draper*.

l. 14. **nice**, delicate, requiring much discrimination.

a senator, a legislator, a member of Parliament.

l. 15. **which he wore**, etc., *i.e.* an eye-glass.

ll. 23, 24. **the dispute between the Crown and the Commons.** On Feb. 21, 1784, the Shelburne ministry had resigned in consequence of the coalition between Lord North and Fox, who succeeded in carrying amendments on the address to the Crown. For five weeks George III., who hated Fox, hunted in vain for a Prime Minister, and was obliged at last to accept the Coalition Ministry of Fox and North. But the defeat of Fox's India Bill in the House of Lords gave the King the much-desired opportunity of dismissing this Ministry on Dec. 18, and choosing Pitt as Premier (see note to p. 47, l. 1). The Coalition, however, held the majority in the Lower House, so that the dissolution was an appeal to the people on the part of the Crown against the existing House of Commons. The dispute ended in the complete triumph of the Crown and Pitt, who remained Premier for seventeen years. Cowper, who thought that "Stuartism had been the characteristic of the present reign" (*To Newton*, Feb., 1784), gives his view of the matter thus: "The Crown, no less than the India Company, quarrelled with Fox's India Bill: the Crown, for causes palpable enough, espoused the cause of Mr. Pitt. The Crown interfered by a whispered message to nullify the former, and by upholding the new minister in his place, in opposition to a majority of the House, in hopes to give effect to the latter; but finding itself unable to carry this favourite point in a Parliament so unfriendly to its designs, the Crown dissolved it; expecting, and I fear with too good reason, that a new one will be more propitious" (*To Newton*, March 11, 1784).

l. 25. **on the side of the former.** Mr. Grenville, being a Pittite (see note to p. 47, ll. 20, 21), was also on the side of the Crown.

l. 29. **gain his election.** He was elected at the head of the poll, along with another Pittite; the single Foxite candidate being defeated.

l. 35. **Mr. Scott.** See note to p. 20, l. 15.

Page 49, l. 2. **hurts him**, injures his reputation.

l. 3. **Paul**, the great apostle of the Gentiles.

l. 5. **but I hear it**, 'without my hearing it'; 'which I do not hear.' This *but* is really a preposition (= except) having for its object the clause "I hear it highly commended"; but it is generally parsed as a subordinative conjunction (= unless). Cf. p. 85, l. 11.

l. 7. **defeats the end.** The object of preaching being to win people over, not to disgust or anger them.

l. 13, **conclude ourselves**, subscribe ourselves in conclusion.

l. 15. **M. U.** stands, of course, for "Mary Unwin," as *M.* at the close of the next letter is for the same "Mary."

l. 24. **bleeding**. Bleeding was a common remedy in Cowper's day, but is now quite gone out of fashion.

ll. 24, 25. **an embrocation**, a lotion, a fomentation. The word is derived ultimately from Gk. *βρέχειν*, to wet. What with his weak eyes, his indigestion, and other ailments, Cowper consumed a good deal of medicine, and his name is found frequently occurring in the ledger and day books of Dr. George Grindon, the Olney surgeon. Cf. p. 39, l. 18.

l. 26. **fidgets about the world**, goes bustling about.

ll. 29, 30. **an Æsculapius**, a perfect doctor. See note to p. 28, l. 20.

Page 50, ll. 1, 2. **a practitioner upon**, etc., one who practises upon (*i.e.* applies medical treatment to) the constitutions of others.

l. 3. **runs**, 'has a run'; 'is successful.' The "book" is probably the same as that referred to above. See note to p. 36, l. 17.

l. 5. **the liberal**, those who are not blinded by party spirit.

l. 8. **Beattie.** Probably his *Dissertations, Moral and Political*, published in the previous year. See note to p. 46, l. 13.

ll. 8, 9. **Blair's Lectures**, *Lectures on Rhetoric and Belles Lettres*, also published in 1783. The Rev. Hugh Blair, D.D. (b. 1718, d. 1799), was a Scotch minister, and professor of rhetoric.

l. 16. **his air**, 'his manner,' 'mode of expression,' as distinguished from his style or language.

l. 24. **Aristotle**, the great Greek Peripatetic philosopher (b. B.C. 384, d. 322). His works include treatises on logic, rhetoric, politics, ethics, etc.

l. 28. **acumen**, 'penetration,' 'insight' (Lat. *acumen*, sharpness; *acuere*, to sharpen).

Page 51, l. 4. **having drawn their rules**, etc. Cf. Pope, *Essay on Criticism*, 88-91:—

"These rules of old discover'd, not devis'd,
Are Nature still, but Nature methodiz'd;
Nature, like liberty, is but restrain'd
By the same laws which first herself ordain'd."

And again, 92-99:—

> " Hear how learn'd Greece her useful rules indites,
>
> . . . .
>
> Just precepts thus from great examples given,
> She drew from them what they deriv'd from Heaven."

So also Cicero and Quintilian.

l. 8. **a map of the boundaries**, etc. They give us a general body of rules which a correct writer ought not to overstep.

l. 10. **pestered**, 'annoyed.' *Pester* is a shortened form of *impester*, Fr. *empêtrer*, Low Lat. *impastoriare*, to hobble a horse while at *pasture*.

l. 11. **vagaries**, literary freaks, solecisms.

l. 12. **them**, the "boundaries" of l. 8.

l. 16. **to open no houses.** It had previously been the custom for the candidates to throw open the public-houses to the people, and treat them with liquor.

l. 24. **hustings**, a platform used by the candidates from which to address their supporters. *Husting* is lit. *house-thing*, 'a house-meeting,' 'a council.'

The sheriff, a county officer, one of whose duties it is to superintend the elections.

l. 29. **fire the town.** The recent Gordon Riots (see *Introduction*, p. xv.) had shown what an English mob was capable of in those days.

ll. 29, 30. **the freeholders**, the possessors of freehold property (*i.e.* land or houses held free of duty or payment, and not on lease).

l. 31. **a merry andrew's jacket**, the fantastic dress worn by a buffoon or one who attends a mountebank or quack doctor in his rounds. For *Andrew*, cf. "a cheap *Jack*."

l. 32. **the best man**, the strongest, boldest man; their champion.

l. 33. **Olney sent**, etc., *i.e.* the hero was an inhabitant of Olney.

the field, the field of battle.

l. 34. **Mr. Ashburner.** See note to p. 48, l. 2.

l. 36. **the hollowness of his skull**, *i.e.* his hollow or empty skull.

Page 52, l. 4. **ragamuffins**, rough, ragged fellows.

l. 8. **four quires of verse.** The "verse" was *The Task*, commenced in the summer of 1783, at the suggestion of Lady Austen, and finished, revised, and transcribed in the autumn of this year.

ll. 11, 12. **to give the last hand to the points**, to give a final revision to the punctuation.

l. 15. **escape,** escape notice, remain uncorrected.

l. 18. **very satirical.** See *Task*, ii. 255-284, 351-371, 445-454. If Cowper was satirical from a sense of duty, there is no doubt that, with his love of humour and gentle persiflage, he thoroughly enjoyed writing in that vein. There is nothing forced in his satire, which is of that graceful and polished kind of which Horace's satire is the type. Where Cowper falls short is in knowledge of his subject, a deficiency which, combined with his religious asceticism, led him sometimes to denounce amusements which we now justly deem innocent. Cf. p. 56, l. 19 *et seq.*, and note.

l. 20. **it were beneath my years,** 'it would be unbecoming to me at my age.' Cowper was now fifty-three.

l. 22. **such abuses,** etc. In the second book Cowper attacks the clergy and the Universities, and the evils of profusion and profligacy. Cf. p. 60, l. 20 *et seq.*

ll. 22, 23. **is not to be expected,** etc. Cf. *Expostulation*, 724, 725:—

> "I know the warning song is sung in vain;
> That few will hear, and fewer heed the strain."

l. 24. **indifference,** 'disregard.' See note to p. 25, l. 20.

l. 26. **were to approve it,** would be equivalent to commending the world.

l. 27. **tacitly nor expressly,** by being silent about its faults, nor by approving its conduct.

ll. 30, 31. **so fair an occasion,** so good an opportunity.

l. 31. **I forget myself.** More emphatic than 'I forget.' Cf. 'to recollect oneself,' 'to overeat oneself,' 'to oversleep oneself,' etc.

there is another. Cf. *Task*, i. 262-265:—

> "Thanks to Benevolus—he spares me yet
> These chestnuts ranged in corresponding lines,
> And, though himself so polish'd, still reprieves
> The obsolete prolixity of shade."

"Benevolus" stands for Mr. John Throckmorton (for whom see *Introduction*, p. xlii.), in whose grounds stood this avenue of chestnuts.

Page 53, l. 2. to Mr. Smith. Cf. *Task*, iv. 424-428:—

> "Meanwhile ye (the honest poor) shall not want
> What, conscious of your virtues, we can spare,
> Nor what a wealthier than ourselves may send.
> I mean the man who, when the distant poor
> Need help, denies them nothing but his name."

And see note to p. 29, l. 6.

l. 3. **make the application**, understand to whom it refers.

l. 5. **delicacy**. See p. 29, l. 25, and note.

l. 6. **cast**. See p. 18, l. 30, and note.

l. 8. **revolt the reader**, disgust the ordinary, irreligious reader, and make him throw the book aside. Cf. p. 19, ll. 13-26; p. 60, ll. 15-17.

l. 10. **Lope de Vega**, a celebrated Spanish poet (b. 1562, d. 1635). He was so prolific a writer that scarcely a week passed without producing a drama from his pen.

l. 11. **Voltaire**, a distinguished French poet, historian, and deistical philosopher (b. 1694, d. 1778). His works fill 70 octavo volumes, and range over almost all subjects.

this tincture, this religious tinge.

l. 12. **so much the worse for them**, *i.e.* they are the losers. Cf. p. 32, l. 8, and note.

l. 15. **My descriptions are all from nature**, etc. It is to this that they owe their consummate truth and wonderful pictorial power. There is no vagueness in them, no loose and inaccurate generalities, such as marked the poetry of the Pope school.

l. 16. **second-handed**. We now say "second-hand," *i.e.* copied from other writers, and not taken direct from nature.

My delineations of the heart, etc., my sketches of human feelings and conduct are based upon what I have felt and observed myself.

l. 18. **numbers**, 'rhythm.' See note to p. 5, l. 11.

l. 19. **blank verse**, 'unrhymed verse.' Cf. p. 55, ll. 5-7; p. 61, ll. 20-23; p. 62, ll. 6-13.

ll. 20, 21. **bladder and string**, 'monotonous sound,' such as would be made by the bladder carried by the Fool or Jester, which had a few peas in it and was tied by a string to a short stick.

l. 21. **I have imitated nobody**. While it may be conceded that Cowper had too much independence of character to become a copyist of others, there is no doubt that in the *Task*, both as regards rhythm and phraseology, he is to some extent indebted to Milton, and that he owes still more to the influence of Thomson. Cf. p. 61, l. 29 *et seq.*

l. 25. **a regular plan**. Cf. p. 62, ll. 33, 34; p. 108, l. 29 *et seq.* Certainly the *Task* has no preconceived plan whatever; it rambles through a vast variety of subjects—moral, religious, political, social, philosophical, and rural. And this want of method doubtless contributed not a little to the great success of the poem. The medley of satire and description, humour and pathos, gentle irony and personal touches, delighted readers to whose taste the hard didacticism of the Moral Satires had failed to appeal. Cf. *Task*, iv. 232, 233:—

"Roving as I rove,
Where shall I find an end, or how proceed?"

And *ib.*, 241, 242, where he says that he paints

"Every idle thing
That Fancy finds in her excursive flights."

l. 27. **are naturally suggested.** Cf. p. 60, ll. 3-5.

l. 29. **a political aspect.** The fifth book of the *Task* dilates upon monarchy and its evils, liberty and patriotism, and the perishable nature of the best human political institutions.

l. 30. **to discountenance,** etc. Cf. p. 60, ll. 17-20; and *Task*, iii. 729-740, 811-834; iv. 587-592.

l. 32. **friendly to the cause,** etc. Cf. *Task*, i. 678-692; iii. 290-305.

l. 34. **an omen,** etc., a presage that it will be generally popular.

Page 54, l. 5. **poem.** The *Task* is again referred to.

l. 9. **five thousand lines.** The exact number of lines in the *Task* is 5235.

ll. 10, 11. **the last.** See note to p. 12, l. 21.

l. 12. **Johnson.** See *Introduction*, p. xlii.

l. 13. **a piece,** viz., *Tirocinium; or a Review of Schools;* see p. 58, ll. 21-28; p. 60, l. 28 *et seq.*

l. 17. **seven or eight hundred verses.** It actually comprises 922.

turns on, bears upon, has special reference to.

l. 21. **Stock.** See note to p. 44, l. 27.

l. 22. **to inscribe it to you.** The poem was dedicated "To the Rev. W. C. Unwin, the Tutor of his two sons, Nov. 6, 1784." Cf. p. 61, ll. 4, 5.

ll. 24, 25. **the tittle of an i,** *i.e.* the dot on an *i*. *Tittle* is a doublet of *title*, and meant originally a mark over a word or letter in writing, as the mark over the Spanish *ñ*; and so a small particle, a jot.

l. 27. **John Gilpin.** *The Diverting History of John Gilpin* was written in Oct. 1782, and first printed anonymously in the *Public Advertiser* of Nov. 14 of that year. Cowper's publisher at first objected to his design of appending it to his new volume, on the ground that it had been "hacknied in every magazine, in every newspaper, and in every street" (*To Unwin*, May 8, 1784). A fresh impulse was given to its popularity by its recitation by John Henderson, the actor, at Freemasons' Hall in 1785. Cf. p. 64, l. 13 *et seq.*

l. 30. **The Critical Reviewers**, the writers in the *Critical Review*, for which see note to p. 22, l. 30. The *Critical Review* (April, 1782) had severely condemned Cowper's first volume, and declared that he had not succeeded in his "attempt to be lively, facetious, and satirical, any more than in the serious and pathetic."

l. 31. **an attempt at humour.** The emphasis is on "attempt," implying that the attempt was unsuccessful. "John" is, of course, *John Gilpin*.

Page 55, l. 1. **in this article**, on this point or item (viz., whether *John Gilpin* should be included). Cf. p. 17, l. 3; p. 60, l. 33; p. 110, l. 9; p. 130, l. 25.

l. 2. **set down**, settled, guided.

l. 4. **the piece**, *i.e.* *Tirocinium*.

l. 5. **I do not intend**, etc. Cf. p. 61, l. 19.

l. 8. **stroke his chin**, etc., gestures implying hesitation.

l. 9. **anticipate him**, *i.e.* anticipate his expression of reluctance to accept the book.

ll. 14, 15. **that punctilio once satisfied**, when that point of etiquette (viz., the offer of the book to Johnson) has been complied with.

l. 15. **indifference**, unconcern. See note to p. 25, l. 20.

l. 16. **Longman**, the publisher.

l. 24. **a gentleman usher**, an official whose duty it is formally to introduce people at public functions, etc.

l. 25. **the Gentleman's Magazine**, a periodical started by Edward Cave in 1731. Dr. Johnson was among its early contributors.

l. 33. **banged**, attacked, blamed. Cf. *Tirocinium*, 401-403; 412-427; 823-826.

l. 34. **Alma Mater**, the University; lit. "benign or fostering mother," a term applied by students to their University.

banged her too. Cf. *Tirocinium*, 240-246.

Page 56, ll. 4, 5. **Knox's Essays.** Dr. Vicesimus Knox (b. 1752, d. 1821), eminent as an author and preacher, published in 1777 *Essays, Moral and Literary*. He was head master of Tunbridge School for thirty-three years.

l. 14. **to an Harveian tawdriness.** "Harveian" should probably be "Herveian," referring to James Hervey (b. 1713, d. 1758), an excellent divine but florid writer, and known in his day as the author of *Meditations among the Tombs*, and many other works.

l. 19. **he gives me information**, etc. This passage is interesting as showing that what Cowper knew or thought he knew of the gay world he satirizes was drawn mainly from newspapers and books. Society was to him for the most part an abstraction; he had, as Dr. Johnson remarks of Milton, "mingled little in the world, and was deficient in the knowledge which experience must confer" (*Life of Milton*).

l. 26. **at Johnson's**, in Johnson's (his publisher's) hands.

l. 28. **this time twelvemonth**, twelve months ago dating from the present time. Notice that in *twelvemonth*, with a numeral preceding, the sign of the plural is dispensed with; cf. 'fort (*i.e.* fourteen) *night*,' 'a three-*year* old' (of an animal), 'a two-*foot* rule.'

l. 30. **I mentioned it not sooner.** Newton felt hurt at this reticence; see p. 59, ll. 15-27.

Page 57, l. 2. **it spurred me to the work.** Because literary employment brought some relief to his mental sufferings.

l. 4. **as tardy as before.** See p. 13, ll. 17-31.

l. 6. **the crocuses**, flowers that appear in early spring.

l. 7. **to wait on you**, *i.e.* by sending you a copy of my book.

l. 8. **my Muse**, my book of poetry.

l. 9. **Mr. Bacon.** John Bacon, the eminent sculptor (b. 1740, d. 1799), a friend of Newton, had been delighted with the poet's first volume, and sent him a print of his monument to Lord Chatham in Westminster Abbey, which he was then executing. Cowper introduced him into the *Task* (i. 702-704):—

"Bacon there
Gives more than female beauty to a stone,
And Chatham's eloquence to marble lips."

He subsequently (in 1788) visited the poet at Weston. Cf. p. 61, ll. 24-27.

l. 13. **without a frank.** See *Introduction*, p. xxxviii.

l. 18. **proved**, turned out to be.

l. 24. **your heart fluttered**, you were full of trepidation.

l. 26. **the Thorntons.** Mr. John Thornton was a wealthy merchant, a friend of Newton. He had sent a copy of Cowper's first volume to Benjamin Franklin, who was delighted with it. Cowper wrote some verses in his memory in 1790.

l. 31. **perhaps not pleased.** See note to p. 56, l. 30.

Page 58, ll. 16, 17. **forced up the lid**, etc., *i.e.* strongly induced me to reveal my treasured secret.

l. 18. **closeness**, 'secrecy.' *Close* is common in Shakspere in this sense.

l. 22. **do I give**, etc., *i.e.* do I esteem any man more highly than I do you.

l. 24. **my new work.** See p. 54, l. 13, and note.

l. 26. **the Muse,** my poetical powers.

l. 28. **Mr. Smith.** See note to p. 29, l. 6.

l. 32. **lucubrations,** 'compositions,' 'productions composed in retirement.' From Lat. *lucubratio*, a working by lamp-light, night-work.

l. 36. **John Gilpin.** See note to p. 54, l. 27.

Page 59, l. 1. **nobody's child,** etc. The poem had been published anonymously, but was now to be included in his second volume. When Cowper consented to its publication in the *Public Advertiser*, it was with the proviso that the author's name should not appear.

l. 5. **given the finishing stroke,** etc., finally touched up the poem.

l. 8. **a little one of three words.** The motto is *Fit surculus arbor*, 'the twig becomes a tree,' in reference to the growth of the *Task* from small beginnings.

l. 10. **a stricture upon,** etc., a censure of the parade of learning shown by some authors in filling their title-pages with mottoes.

l. 12. **Knox.** See note to p. 56, ll. 4, 5.

l. 13. **half a dozen,** *i.e.* mottoes.

l. 17. **right to my confidence.** See p. 56, l. 30 *et seq.*; p. 57, l. 30 *et seq.*; p. 65, l. 14 *et seq.*

l. 20. **opposite claims,** viz., my claim to the option of secrecy, and your claim to my confidence.

l. 21. **done my best,** *i.e.* to adjust them; to explain matters.

l. 29. **advertisement to the reader.** Printed at the commencement of the *Task*, and explaining how Lady Austen gave him the *Sofa* for a subject.

Page 60, l. 1. **circumstantial,** particular, minute. Cf. p. 80, l. 6.

l. 3. **tenons and mortises,** 'joints,' 'links.' The *tenon* (Lat. *tenere*, to hold) is the end of a piece of wood which is inserted into the *mortise* or socket of another, to hold the two together.

l. 11. **numbers.** See note to p. 5, l. 11.

ll. 12, 13. **the subjects being so various.** See note to p. 53, l. 25.

l. 15. **to allure the reader.** See p. 19, l. 22, and note.

l. 18. **that predilection,** etc. See p. 53, l. 30, and note.

l. 20. **collaterally,** indirectly, obliquely.

ll. 22, 23. **I have not spared the Universities.** Cf. *Task*, ii. 699-770.

l. 26. **has all the appearance,** etc., quite seems to be a genuine production.

l. 30. **Tirocinium.** See note to p. 54, l. 13.

l. 33. **article,** item. Cf. p. 55, l. 1, and note.

Page 61, l. 4. **Mr. Unwin,** etc. See note to p. 54, l. 22. He afforded "an instance in point," because he was educating his two sons himself.

l. 6. **command your hunger,** etc., control your eagerness to see the book, and be satisfied with the specimen of it that I send, till the volume itself reaches you.

l. 8. **piecemeal perusal,** 'reading it by portions at a time.' The *meal* in "piecemeal" is the M. E. termination *mele* or *melum,* "by portions"; so that *piecemeal* is a cumulative word, meaning "by pieces-pieces."

l. 9. **disadvantageous to the work,** 'unfair to the poem.' It would not give you a proper idea of it.

l. 10. **waive,** 'give up,' 'not insist upon.' See note to p. 17, l. 14.

l. 13. **Tully's rule,** etc. The Latin proverb means "No day without a line (or stroke)," and is derived, Pliny says, from a habit of the famous artist Apelles, who made it his rule never to let a day pass without making at least one stroke with his brush. Hence the proverb means generally "No day without some work done." "Tully" is Marcus Tullius Cicero, the famous Roman orator and writer, who lived in the time of Julius Cæsar.

l. 15. **three lines.** See p. 78, l. 30.

l. 16. **to compass,** to attain, to compose.

ll. 16, 17. **finding ... a more fluent vein,** finding myself in the mood to write more freely.

l. 19. **write blank verse.** See p. 55, l. 5.

l. 21. **the pause,** the cæsura or break in the line which prevents monotony in the rhythm; cf. p. 53, ll. 19-21. The cadence is the modulation or rhythmical structure of the verse.

l. 24. **Mr. Bacon.** See note to p. 57, l. 9.

l. 26. **finest,** most refined, delicate.

l. 29. **Having imitated no man.** See p. 53, l. 21, and note.

Page 62, l. 1. **Thomson's.** James Thomson, the poet of the "Seasons" (b. 1700, d. 1748), helped, with Cowper, to usher in that revolution in popular taste and sentiment which substituted the "romantic" for the "classical" type in poetry—the return from conventionalism to nature. Cowper speaks of him as "admirable in description," and as "a true poet" (*To Mrs. King,* June 19, 1788).

l. 6. **is susceptible,** etc. Cf. p. 53, ll. 19, 20. *Manner* means rhythmical method, the plan of its structure.

l. 9. **cast their numbers alike,** 'give the same rhythmical structure to their lines.' For *numbers*, see note to p. 5, l. 11.

ll. 13, 14. **the reviewer of my former volume.** See note to p. 54, l. 30. He had pronounced Cowper to be "a poet *sui generis*," *i.e.* of a class by himself.

l. 26. **to accommodate the name,** etc., *i.e.* he gave it the title of the *Task*, as being a "task" imposed upon him by Lady Austen.

l. 28. **more than my task.** The "task" was a poem on the Sofa, a "trifle" which grew into a volume.

l. 32. **the Sunday newsmonger,** the seller of newspapers on a Sunday.

Olio, 'medley,' 'miscellany.' *Olio* is for *olia*, the Spanish *olla* or *olla podrida*, a dish of various meats and vegetables, hence a mixture, a medley (Lat. *olla*, a pot).

l. 33. **much variety.** See note to p. 53, l. 25.

l. 35. **the interior titles,** the titles of the separate books; the sub-titles.

Page 63, l. 5. gridiron, 'a frame-work of bars for baking flesh over the fire.' *Gridiron* is the M. E. *gredire*, probably a form of *gredil*, 'a griddle,' so that the *iron* would be a popular corruption.

l. 10. **in my account,** as I reckoned, in my opinion.

l. 13. **pretend,** 'lay claim to.' Cf. "The young *Pretender*," *i.e.* claimant to the Crown.

l. 14. **The Time-piece,** the title of Book ii.

l. 17. **to strike the hour,** etc., to announce that the time is near when God will punish the nations for their sins.

l. 21. **the word worm,** etc. Cf. *Task*, vi. 778-780:—

> "The mother sees,
> And smiles to see, her infant's playful hand
> Stretched forth to dally with the crested worm."

Milton gives the appellation to the serpent, the form that Satan assumed, in *Par. Lost*, 1068:—

> "O Eve, in evil hour thou didst give ear
> To that false worm."

Shakspere (*Antony and Cleopatra*, v. ii. 244, 245) makes Cleopatra say in reference to the asp:—

> "Hast thou the pretty worm of Nilus there,
> That kills and pains not?"

Cf. also Tennyson, *A Dream of Fair Women*, 155: "With a worm I (Cleopatra) balk'd his (Cæsar's) fame."

l. 26. **she thought fit**, etc. The story of Cleopatra's death by the bite of an asp is probably an invention. She poisoned herself after her defeat at Actium, in order to deprive Augustus Cæsar of the glory of carrying her as a captive in his triumphal procession.

l. 30. **an epithet significant**, etc. By the epithet "crested" Cowper shows that he alludes to the basilisk (Gk. βασιλίσκος, 'little king'), probably the Greek name for the cobra, and called basilisk because its hood was supposed to resemble a crest or crown. Tennyson (*Œnone*, 36) has "the cold crown'd snake."

l. 36. **it had like to have been**, 'it was very nearly.' In this phrase *like* is a noun; = likelihood.

Page 64, l. 1. **my greenhouse**. See note to page 20, l. 17.

l. 3. **the mercury**, in the thermometer.

l. 13. **warm with the intelligence**, full of affectionate pleasure at telling me the news.

John Gilpin. See note to p. 54, l. 27.

l. 14. **I little thought**, etc. Cf. *To Unwin*, Nov. 18, 1782: "I little thought when I was writing the history of John Gilpin, that he would appear in print. I intended to laugh and to make two or three others laugh, of whom you were one. But now all the world laughs."

mounted him upon my Pegasus, took him as my subject for a poem. Pegasus, the winged horse of Grecian fable, was the favourite of the Muses, and abode on Mount Helicon. Hence 'to mount Pegasus' means to 'write poetry' and 'my Pegasus' means 'my poetic faculty.'

ll. 17, 18. **a second part, on the subject**, etc. Possibly this incident suggested to Charles Lamb his short paper entitled *Mrs. Gilpin riding to Edmonton*, a *jeu d'esprit* which appeared in Hone's *Table Book* (1827-28) vol. ii., and in which three stanzas of a supposed episode or sequel to *John Gilpin* are fathered upon Cowper. He declined to write one; see note to p. 25, l. 11.

l. 20. **St. Paul's School**, a school in London founded by John Colet in 1512, near St. Paul's Cathedral. In 1884 the school was removed to West Kensington.

ll. 24, 25. **Tirocinium will spoil all**. Because *Tirocinium* inveighs against the public school system; see note to p. 54, l. 13.

ll. 25, 26. **knight of the stone-bottles**, a playful designation of Gilpin, who rode with "a bottle swinging at each side." Cowper hoped that the popularity of *John Gilpin* might help the sale of the volume.

l. 28. **Those events**, etc., *i.e.* trifling and seemingly unpromising events (such as my writing *John Gilpin*) often turn out to be an opening to great success.

l. 30. **The disappointment**, etc. Cf. Horace, *Ars Poetica*, 21, 22: *Amphora coepit Institui; currente rota cur urceus exit?* "When the design is to make a wine-jar, why does the revolving potter's-wheel turn out a water-jug?" The difference Horace intends is in *kind* rather than in *size*; whereas Cowper's point depends upon the differing sizes of the two receptacles.

Page 65, l. 3. **impression**, printed copy.

l. 6. **operated to admiration**, 'produced a most admirable effect.' See p. 27, l. 30, and note. Cowper had had to complain before of his publisher; see p. 13, l. 24 *et seq.*

l. 8. **We now draw**, etc., *i.e.* in printing the book.

l. 10. **budge**, 'stir'; from Fr. *bouger*, Ital. *bulicare*, 'to bubble up,' Lat. *bullire*, 'to boil.'

l. 21. **those reasons**. See p. 57, l. 30 *et seq.*

l. 28. **Bensley**. Cowper mentions the early death of the elder Bensley in one of his Huntingdon letters.

ll. 30, 31. **a club of seven Westminster men**. The club was the Nonsense Club, and the seven, with Cowper, were Bonnell Thornton, Colman, Lloyd, Joseph Hill, Bensley, and De Grey.

l. 32. **to perform**, etc., *i.e.* to gain distinction as a poet.

l. 34. **who have since treated me**, etc. Cowper no doubt had in his mind the treatment he had received from Thurlow and Colman, to whom he had presented copies of his first volume, but who had made him no acknowledgment. He branded these "false friends" in *The Valediction*, written in Nov. 1783. Subsequently Thurlow took occasion to correspond with the poet as to the propriety of using blank verse in a translation of Homer.

Page 66, l. 8. **Dr. Johnson**, etc. Cf. note to p. 4, l. 17. The passage referred to is in the Life of Young, who, in the latter part of his life (writes Johnson) "held himself out for a man retired from the world ... To the vessel which is sailing from the shore, it only appears that the shore also recedes; in life it is truly thus. He who retires from the world will find himself, in reality, deserted as fast, if not faster, by the world." Cf. Pope's line (*Eloisa to Abelard*, 207):—

"The world forgetting, by the world forgot."

l. 16. **the Wilderness**. This formed part of the grounds of Mr. Throckmorton at Weston Underwood, and was a favourite haunt of the poet. He celebrates it in the *Task*, i. 350-354:—

"And now, with nerves new braced and spirits cheered,
We tread the Wilderness, whose well-rolled walks,
With curvature of slow and easy sweep—
Deception innocent—give ample space
To narrow bounds."

l. 23. **brood and hatch**, etc., *i.e.* compose poetry, which in due time is published to the world.

ll. 29, 30. **Miss Cunningham's illness.** She was Newton's niece, of whose death subsequently he wrote a "Narrative."

Page 67, l. 1. habit, habit of body, constitution.

l. 3. **I remember Southampton**, etc. Southampton, to which Newton had made his "excursion," was visited by Cowper for several months in 1753 in the company of Sir Thomas Hesketh.

l. 6. **the assembly-room**, the public room at a watering-place, where the visitors and others assembled for card-playing and dancing. Cf. note to p. 1, l. 11.

l. 8. **Netley Abbey**, etc., places in the neighbourhood of Southampton.

l. 12. **pressed into the service**, induced to accompany the party on their sailing excursions.

l. 13. **gave myself an air**, affected a nautical demeanour.

wore trowsers. In Cowper's day gentlemen ordinarily wore knee-breeches, trowsers being the garb of sailors.

l. 15. **in great waters.** A Biblical expression; cf. *Psalms*, cvii. 23: "They that ... do business in great waters."

l. 18. **Hampton river.** The river is about twenty miles north-east of Portsmouth.

l. 19. **the confinement.** These remarks of Cowper remind us of Dr. Johnson's "A ship is worse than a gaol"; and "Being in a ship is being in a gaol, with the chance of being drowned" (Boswell's *Life*, ii. 438; v. 137).

l. 30. **tedium**, the Lat. word *tædium*, 'irksomeness.'

Page 68, l. 1. Noah. See note to p. 43, l. 13.

l. 2. **Jonah.** A prophet in the Bible, whose disobedience to God resulted in his being swallowed by a great fish, which after three days "vomited him upon the dry land."

l. 4. **the Harriet.** The sloop was named after Cowper's cousin Harriet, at that time engaged to be married to Sir (then Mr.) Thomas Hesketh.

l. 5. **Mr. Perry**, etc. His friends despaired of his recovery, and his physician said that he was sure to die. "A dead man" = so ill as to be as good as dead. Mr. Perry was one of the Olney folk.

l. 15. **Illness sanctified**, illness that works the spiritual good of the sufferer.

ll. 15, 16. **I know a man**, etc. Cowper alludes to himself.

l. 17. **almost these fourteen years.** He dates from his second derangement and religious despair of 1763.

l. 19. **Mr. Scott.** See note to p. 20, l. 15.

l. 20. **a Sunday school.** Five years before this, in 1780, Sunday schools had been organised by Robert Raikes, and the subject was now occupying the attention of the religious community.

raise a fund. In the early days of Sunday schools the teachers were paid.

l. 21. **Mr. Jones,** the Rev. J. Jones, the clergyman at Clifton Reynes, one mile from Olney. Cf. note to p. 17, l. 14.

l. 30. **principle,** rule of action, sense of duty.

l. 36. **Such urchins,** etc., children so young could not be so proficient in wickedness without being encouraged by their parents. *Urchin* means (1) a hedgehog; (2) a goblin, an imp; (3) a child (a playful use).

Page 69, l. 1. **connivance.** From Lat. *connivere,* to wink at (a fault), to overlook or tolerate it.

l. 4. **any other,** anything else; come to any other conclusion.

l. 6. **inveteracy,** 'long continuance'; from Lat. *in,* intensive, and *veter,* stem of *vetus,* old. Cf. *veteran.*

l. 7. **desperate,** hopeless, irremediable.

Mr. Teedon, Samuel Teedon, a poor schoolmaster at Olney. He was a singular character, and thought himself a special favourite of Heaven. He exercised an extraordinary influence over Cowper in his later years, who regarded him as a kind of religious oracle.

l. 27. **franked.** See *Introduction,* p. xxxviii.

my uncle, Mr. Ashley Cowper, his father's younger brother, and Lady Hesketh's father.

l. 28. **a letter from you.** Cowper had corresponded with Lady Hesketh from Huntingdon twenty years before this, but the religious tone of his letters had repelled her, and communication between them had ceased. The perusal of Cowper's new volume, and especially of *John Gilpin,* now led her to write to him, and their correspondence was renewed. See p. 72, l. 31.

Page 70, l. 11. **scenes, in which,** etc., *i.e.* old incidents, in which we were each other's sole companions.

ll. 14, 15. **the Arabian Nights' Entertainment,** presumably the famous book of Eastern tales, so named, is referred to.

l. 16. **forgot.** We now use the form *forgotten.*

l. 17. **Netley Abbey.** See p. 67, l. 8. It is doubtless to this Southampton visit that Cowper here refers.

l. 19. **upon the field,** etc., *i.e.* my memory has recalled these feats, and I have mentally re-enacted them with you.

l. 20. **these few years,** 'the last few years.' Similarly *this twelvemonth* (l. 21) = 'the last twelvemonth.' For *twelvemonth*, see note to p. 56, l. 28.

l. 25. **my poor friend.** Sir Thomas Hesketh died in April, 1778, and left Cowper a small legacy. *Poor*, as an expression of pity, is the conventional epithet applied to anyone who is dead. Cf. p. 114, l. 11.

Page 71, ll. 6, 7. **under Providence,** by God's care.

l. 11. **uncommonly supported,** had special strength given her by God to endure the trial.

l. 13. **to particularise,** to mention each detail.

l. 14. **a sable hue,** a gloomy colouring or character.

l. 19. **post-diluvian.** In the times before the Flood (see p. 43, l. 2) human life was so prolonged that men might well have "the vivacity of youth" at an advanced age.

l. 21. **apt to outlive,** etc., likely to lose, as they grow older, their love for their parents.

l. 24. **three female descendants.** These were Harriet (Lady Hesketh), Theodora, and Elizabeth (Lady Croft).

l. 27. **dejection of spirits,** etc. Cf. p. 57, l. 2, and note; p. 80, l. 27; and *To Unwin*, April 6, 1780: "Amusements are necessary in a retirement like mine, especially in such a state of mind as I labour under. The necessity of amusement makes me sometimes write verses." See also *To Lady Hesketh*, Dec. 15, 1785.

l. 32. **having tried many.** See p. 80, l. 33 *et seq.*; p. 110, l. 6 *et seq.*

l. 34. **I transcribe,** I make a fair copy of what I have composed.

Page 72, l. 5. **attended my brother.** Cowper's brother John died at Cambridge on 20th March, 1770, at which time Cowper attended him for about a month.

l. 12. **run in my head,** been constantly in my thoughts.

ll. 13, 14. **will serve me,** 'will take the letter for me.' The post left Olney only twice a week at this time. Cf. *Introduction*, p. xxxix.

l. 21. **such a scene of things as this,** such a sad place as this world.

ll. 26, 27. **I make certain allowances,** etc. I deduct something from the value of your favourable opinion, on the ground of your liking for me.

l. 29. **drawbacks,** deductions.

l. 30. **measure,** amount.

l. 31. **I honour "John Gilpin."** See note to p. 69, l. 28.

Page 73, ll. 6, 7. **when I was once asked**, etc. In his early financial difficulties Cowper had received an anonymous letter, "conceived in the kindest and most benevolent terms imaginable," and promising to supply his needs. The writer was doubtless his cousin Theodora Cowper.

l. 7. **delicately**, with tact and consideration for my feelings.

l. 8. **my occasions**, my requirements.

l. 10. **inconveniences**, money difficulties.

l. 17. **trespassing**, going beyond due limits; taking too great advantage of a kind offer.

l. 22. **let you a little into**, give you some information about.

l. 25. **have had but one purse**, have shared our income and expenditure.

l. 32. **well-being of life**, happiness.

l. 34. **as my connexions**, etc., in a style suited to my social position.

l. 36. **at this end of the kingdom.** It seems that, in and before Cowper's day, the north of England was regarded as a cheap place to live in, while the central and southern parts were dear. Cf. J. Reed's *The Register Office* (a Farce): "I shall not consent to allow her a shilling more as (*sic*) fifteen (pounds) a year—she may live very comfortably—very comfortably on it in the North."

Page 74, l. 2. **by the help of good management**, etc. This is said ironically. Cf. *To Hill*, July 3, 1765, where, after giving an account of his economical difficulties, he writes: "I never knew how to pity poor housekeepers before; but now I cease to wonder at the politic cast which their occupation usually gives to their countenance, for it is really a matter full of perplexity."

l. 5. **Strain no points**, etc., do not go beyond the proper limit (in assisting me), so as to cause yourself inconvenience. The metaphor is from the old meaning of *point* in the sense of a *lace* which fastened the hose to the doublet, the straining or stretching of which would cause the hose to fall. This might be done by any violent effort; hence to strain or stretch a point came to mean 'to exert oneself unduly.'

l. 7. **indulge yourself in**, etc., give yourself the pleasure of bestowing upon me anything that you can spare. Cf. p. 76, l. 1; p. 98, l. 8.

l. 11. **my next publication**, his translation of Homer; see l. 26 below.

ll. 18, 19. **by subscription**, by collecting, previous to publication, the names of subscribers or intending purchasers. See p. 79, l. 5 *et seq*.

l. 19. **Your vote and interest,** 'give me your influence in my favour'; a playful allusion to the common phrase used by candidates for Parliamentary election. Cf. p. 47, ll. 32, 33.

l. 21. **proposals,** invitations for subscriptions, giving particulars as to the price of the book, the number of copies published, etc. See p. 79, l. 10.

ll. 28, 29. **Herculean labour,** labour as hard as those of Hercules. See note to p. 29, l. 3.

l. 30. **effectually anticipated by Pope.** People might think that a new translation of Homer was unnecessary, on the ground that Pope had already produced a sufficiently good one. For Pope, see note to p. 21, l. 11.

ll. 30, 31. **he has not anticipated me.** Cf. *To Newton*, Dec. 3, 1785: "The literati are all agreed to a man that, although Pope has given us two pretty poems under Homer's titles, there is not to be found in them the least portion of Homer's spirit, nor the least resemblance of his manner. I will try, therefore, whether I cannot copy him somewhat more happily myself."

Page 75, l. 5. **smart youth of my years.** I am in a good state of preservation considering how old I am.

l. 7. **There was more hair,** etc., there is plenty of hair on other people's heads (which I can have made into a wig for my use).

l. 8. **having found,** etc., *i.e.* having had a wig made of hair long enough to curl, etc.

l. 13. **worn with a small bag.** This bag was a small silk pouch fastened to the back of the wig for ornament. A wig with this appendage was called a *bag-wig*. Cf. Addison: "I saw a young fellow riding towards us full gallop, with a bob-wig and black silken bag tied to it."

l. 20. **my desk,** the gift of his correspondent.

l. 21. **by the waggon.** For this mode of transit, in Cowper's day, for parcels, etc., see *Introduction*, p. xxxix., and cf. p. 44, l. 29; p. 138, l. 5.

l. 23. **Sherrington,** a village about two miles south of Olney.

l. 26. **you yourself have taught me.** You have told me about the desk, and so made me impatient to receive it.

l. 30. **to the inn,** *i.e.* the inn from which the waggon started.

Page 76, l. 7. **A fine day.** Said ironically.

l. 14. **at Troy.** Cowper means that he has been translating the account of the chariot-races in the 23rd book of the *Iliad.*

ll. 17, 18. **a kettle and a frying-pan.** Two of the prizes being τρίπους, 'a three-footed brass kettle,' and λέβης, 'a copper pan' or 'caldron.'

l. 24. **sagacity**, keenness of scent. The primary sense of *sagax* in Latin, is 'keen-scented,' being often applied to dogs. Cf. p. 104, l. 27; and *Task*, vi. 616, "that nice sagacity of smell"; and Milton, *Par. Lost*, x. 279-281:—

> "So scented the grim Feature, and upturn'd
> His nostril wide into the murky air,
> Sagacious of his quarry from afar."

l. 29. **the enclosures.** Between 1727 and 1844 some 7,000,000 acres of common land were enclosed and brought into cultivation by means of numerous private Acts of Parliament. Much opposition has since been raised to the enclosing of commons.

l. 30. **a scent in the fields.** Southey quotes a passage from Conde de Mora's History, which tells of a similar fragrance in the soil of a certain valley, hence called "the redolent."

Page 77, l. 3. **the Common-scene.** See *Task*, i. 526-533, where Cowper says:—

> "There the turf
> Smells sweet, and, rich in odoriferous herbs
> And fungous fruits of earth, regales the sense
> With luxury of unexpected sweets."

l. 8. **as good as my word.** I have kept my promise to you.

ll. 8, 9. **the doctor**, Mr. Grindon; see p. 49, l. 25 *et seq.*

l. 15. **knitting my stockings.** Lady Hesketh, after her visit to Olney, in June, 1786, wrote to her sister Theodora respecting Mrs. Unwin: "Her constant employment is knitting stockings ... Our cousin has not for many years worn any other than those of her manufacture. She knits silk, cotton, and worsted. She sits knitting on one side of the table, in her spectacles; and he on the other, reading to her (when he is not employed in writing) in his." And cf. *To Mary*, 9-12:—

> "Thy needles, once a shining store,
> For my sake restless heretofore,
> Now rust disused, and shine no more,
> My Mary!"

See also p. 47, l. 17; p. 130, l. 27.

l. 16. **Penelope**, the wife of Ulysses, the famous Greek hero. A model of domestic virtue, she sat among her maidens, industriously weaving during her husband's absence.

l. 25. **usher him in**, introduce him to your notice.

with the marrow-bones, etc., 'with noisy, vulgar demonstrations of praise.' A kind of rough music was made by striking cleavers or meat-choppers with marrow-bones. The cleaver was ground to give a particular note when struck with the bone. Cf. Arbuthnot: "You gentlemen keep a parcel of roaring bullies about me day and night, with huzzas and hunting-horns, and ringing the changes on butchers' cleavers."

l. 29. **making his praise**, etc., 'praising him beforehand to the person that he is to meet.' *Harbinger* is the M. E. *herbergeour*, one who went before to provide lodgings for an army or host of people; hence a 'forerunner.' *Harbour* means lit. 'host-shelter' (O. E. *here*, a host, and *beorgan*, to shelter).

Page 78, l. 4. **my volume**, his second volume.

l. 9. **inequalities**, *i.e.* some parts of the book are inferior to others.

l. 14. **Pope, I believe**, etc. Cf. Dr. Johnson's *Life of Pope:* "His (Pope's) declaration that his care for his works ceased at their publication, was not strictly true. His parental care never abandoned them; what he found amiss in the first edition, he silently corrected in those that followed."

l. 18. **level parts**, parts to which a lofty style is inappropriate.

l. 21. **But, again**, etc., *i.e.* the inequalities you object to are not to be excused on the ground that the inferior parts of the poem are "by nature humble."

l. 25. **served that office**, been made use of as an apology.

l. 27. **in what anguish of mind**, etc. See p. 106, ll. 32, 33.

l. 28. **perpetual interruptions**, etc. These "interruptions," together with the "anguish of mind," are explained in the next letter.

l. 30. **three lines.** Cf. p. 61, l. 15.

at a sitting, on each occasion when I sat down to compose; cf. p. 87, l. 10.

l. 32. **Grub Street**, 'a Grub Street production.' Grub Street (now Milton Street) in London was famous in Pope's time as the abode of literary hacks; so that a Grub Street writer meant an inferior writer. The *Dunciad* (i. 44) satirizes "all the Grub Street race."

ll. 33, 34. **the Magi**, *i.e.* learned critics and commentators. The reference is to the Persian Magi or Wise Men.

Page 79, l. 1. **line**, limit, verge.

l. 8. **free to levy**, etc., *i.e.* after the subscribers have received their copies, the book will be on sale to the public.

l. 11. **kiss your hands**, 'reach you'; one of Cowper's playful expressions. To "kiss hands" means to be presented to a sovereign on taking office, since the person presented kissed the royal hand.

l. 13. **Josephus** and "'Sephus" are often jocosely used by Cowper to indicate Joseph Hill.

l. 15. **Eton**, Eton College, near Windsor.

l. 18. **anguish of mind**, etc. See the previous letter.

l. 21. **delicacy**, tact, consideration for my feelings.

l. 24. **73**, *i.e.* 1773. In February of that year began Cowper's third derangement, which lasted till May, 1774.

Page 80, l. 6. **megrims**, 'fancies,' 'delusions'; properly, 'pains affecting one side of the head.' *Megrim* = *migrim* = *migrene* = *emigranea* = *hemigranea*, which is Gk. ἡμικράνιον, 'half the skull.'

l. 7. **circumstantial**, particular in giving all the circumstances or details. Cf. p. 60, l. 1.

l. 8. **Dr. Cotton.** He had a private lunatic asylum or "Collegium Insanorum" (as he called it) at St. Albans, and Cowper had been placed under his care during his second derangement.

l. 11. **attempt my life.** Cowper had made several such attempts during his previous derangement.

l. 20. **as I hinted.** See p. 71, l. 10.

l. 27. **I find writing**, etc. See p. 71, l. 27, and note; and below, p. 81, ll. 8, 9.

l. 28. **I had,** *i.e.* I should have.

l. 29. **lived upon fiddle-strings,** made use of music as my remedy.

l. 33. **this pit,** this abyss of despondency and melancholia. *Pit* is used in the Bible for Hell or Hades.

l. 34. **I commenced carpenter.** See note to p. 6, l. 27; and cf. p. 109, l. 26 *et seq.*

Page 81, l. 1. **gardening.** See note to p. 2, l. 1; p. 110, l. 21 *et seq.*

l. 2. **that of drawing.** See note to p. 8, l. 3.

ll. 4, 5. **in shorthand,** in small compass, in a few words.

l. 12. **pay double,** etc. He had filled one sheet, and saw that another would be required, involving double the ordinary rate of postage. See below, p. 84, ll. 12-15; and *Introduction*, p. xxxviii.

ll. 13, 14. **write myself out,** finish all that I have to write about.

l. 18. **her sister,** Mrs. Jones, at Clifton Reynes.

l. 28. **obtained,** prevailed, was established.

l. 34. **the rather expedient,** 'all the more useful.' This *the* represents *thi* or *thē*, the old instrumental case of *the* used as a Demonstrative, seen in '*The* sooner, *the* better.'

Page 82, l. 3. **devoirs,** 'respects.' The French word means lit. 'dues.'

l. 13. **a point of good manners,** a thing that politeness demanded.

l. 15. **the Muse.** Since poets were supposed to be inspired by the Muses, he gives this name to Lady Austen, as having suggested the subject that led to the composition of the *Task*.

l. 19. **the Bull**, a playful reference to the Rev. William Bull.

l. 27. **in your cover**, on the inside of your sheet; in your letter.

l. 28. **a certain author's work**, *i.e.* Cowper's second volume.

ll. 28, 29. **the Gentleman's Magazine.** See note to p. 55, l. 25.

Page 83, ll. 4, 5. **You must know**, I would have you know.

l. 12. **cursory**, 'hasty,' 'superficial'; lit. 'running'; Lat. *cursus*, from *currere*, to run.

l. 17. **the end of**, etc., the end of the sentence is placed before the beginning of it.

l. 20. **at Christmas.** Christmas Day is the 25th December, and the Magazine would be in printing about that date.

l. 21. **your printer.** For this *your*, see note to p. 40, l. 9.

l. 23. **Voltaire.** See note to p. 53, l. 11.

l. 28. **English Henriade**, 'the *Henriade* translated into English.' Voltaire's *La Henriade* is an epic poem, the subject of which is Henry IV. of France and his struggle with the "Holy Catholic League" (1576-1593).

l. 31. **bureau**, 'desk.' The French *bureau* (Lat. *burrus*, fiery-red) is first a thick russet cloth, then the table covered with it; and so, a writing-table, a desk.

l. 32. **in the Temple**, when he lived as a law-student in chambers in the Middle Temple.

at Westminster, at Westminster School.

Page 84, l. 5. **The mistake**, etc. The reference is to *Task*, iii. 112-116:—

> "There was I found by One who had himself
> Been hurt by the archers. In his side He bore,
> And in his hands and feet, the cruel scars.
> With gentle force soliciting the darts,
> He drew them forth, and healed, and bade me live."

It appears that the reviewer supposed that Cowper was alluding to his friend Unwin, whereas the reference is of course to Christ, who bore in His hands and feet the marks of the nails with which He was crucified, and in His side the scar made by the Roman spear. See Bible, *John*, xix. 34; xx. 25.

l. 13. **of these**, 'of these sheets.' See above, p. 81, ll. 12, 13.

l. 16. **your money burns in your pocket**, 'you are eager to spend your money.' In a previous (omitted) passage of this letter he had written: "How much I love you for the generosity of that offer which made the General observe that your money seemed to burn in your pocket."

ll. 26, 27. **this tormenting specimen.** The reference is to a previous letter to Lady Hesketh (Jan. 31, 1786): "On Wednesday last I received from Johnson the MS. copy of a specimen that I had sent to the General; and enclosed in the same cover, notes upon it by an unknown critic." The specimen of his translation that Cowper sent to be annexed to his proposals, consisted of 107 lines, taken from the interview between Priam and Achilles in the last book; and the unknown critic, the multitude of whose strictures at first sadly disquieted the poet, was Henry Fuseli, or Füssli (b. 1741, d. 1825), the painter and art-critic, a Swiss, who, after eight years' study in Italy, had lately come to settle in England. He was a great student of English literature, and had translated *Macbeth* into German.

l. 27. **the General,** General Cowper, the poet's cousin.

Page 85, l. 1. **me,** *i.e.* my translation.

l. 6. **my prospects,** the views that are to be seen here.

ll. 6, 7. **the hovel, the alcove,** etc. The "hovel" is the "Peasant's Nest," described in *Task*, i. 221-227. The "alcove" is described in the same book, ll. 278-283, and "the Ouse and its banks" in ll. 163-176.

l. 10. **Talk not of an inn,** do not speak of lodging at an inn instead of at our house.

for your life, 'as you value your life'—a playful threat.

l. 11. **but we could,** 'that we could not.' See note to p. 49, l. 5.

l. 15. **greenhouse.** See note to p. 20, l. 17.

l. 17. **When the plants,** etc. When the weather is warm enough for the plants to live in the open air, they are removed outside and make room for us inside.

l. 18. **you shall sit.** *Shall* here indicates, not compulsion, but a promise. So with "you shall find," "you shall see," below.

l. 23. **Imprimis,** in the first place.

ll. 26, 27. **my hares.** See note to p. 10, l. 16.

l. 28. **promises,** seems likely.

l. 33. **paralytic,** humorously used for 'rickety.'

l. 35. **superb vestibule,** 'magnificent entrance-hall.' Cowper writes ironically. *Vestibule* is lit. 'that which is separated from the abode' (Lat. *ve-*, apart from, *stabulum*, an abode), a part of the house cut off from the dwelling-rooms.

Page 86, l. 2. **as happy,** etc., happy throughout the whole day.

l. 3. **Order yourself ... to,** 'give orders that you are to be delivered at.' Cowper speaks playfully, as if Lady Hesketh were a parcel of goods. "The Swan" was the inn at Newport Pagnell where the coach stopped.

l. 5. **I have told Homer,** a playful way of saying that he has examined the works of Homer, and ascertained that the word *cask* (to represent the Greek πίθος), in his translation, is more correct than *urn.* Cf. p. 89, l. 8.

l. 10. **at his taste,** *i.e.* in preferring a cask to an urn.

l. 14. **a dispensation,** 'exemption.' In the Roman Catholic Church, a *dispensation* is a license to do what is forbidden, or to omit what is commanded.

l. 22. **beforehand with me,** etc. You wrote to me in praise of my letters before I wrote to you in praise of yours, and so you *seem* to have forestalled me; but it is not so *in fact,* since it has long, etc.

l. 26. **what comes uppermost,** the first thing that suggests itself.

Page 87, l. 4. **Signor Fuseli.** See note to p. 84, ll. 26, 27.

l. 7. **Mr. Burrows,** a friend of Lady Hesketh's to whom she had submitted parts of Cowper's Homer, of which he had expressed his "high approbation."

l. 10. **sittings.** See note to p. 78, l. 30.

l. 14. **Samuel,** Lady Hesketh's servant.

l. 15. **city-ward,** in the direction of the city, or business part of London.

l. 20. **elisions.** An "elision" is the cutting off or suppression of a letter, as in 'i' th' arm' for 'in the arm.'

l. 24. **pardonable.** In a previous letter to Lady Hesketh (March 6, 1786), Cowper writes in justification of the few elisions that he means to retain.

l. 30. **I am ... a very good boy,** playfully for 'I have been obedient to your wishes.'

l. 32. **hobbled,** *i.e.* were harsh in their rhythm. Cf. below, p. 88, l. 31.

l. 34. **a monotonous cadence.** Cf. p. 53, ll. 19-21; p. 61, ll. 20, 21.

Page 88, l. 1. **uneasiness,** unevenness, harshness.

l. 6. **rumbling,** heavy-sounding.

ll. 6, 7. **in my mind,** according to my opinion.

l. 7. **considering the subjects,** when we consider what the line is meant to describe.

l. 11. **Abominable**, etc. See *Par. Lost*, ii. 626-628. Milton wrote "inutterable," and "Than fables yet have feign'd." Quoting as he does from memory, Cowper often quotes incorrectly (cf. notes to p. 35, l. 35; p. 111, l. 29)—an additional proof, if one were needed, that he never contemplated the publication of his letters. The "Gorgons" were winged, scaly, snake-haired monsters, whose look turned men to stone. The "Hydra" was a water serpent destroyed by Hercules. The "Chimæra" was a fire-breathing animal, part lion, part goat, and part dragon.

l. 14. **the deformity**, *i.e.* the irregularity of its rhythm, with two extra syllables in the second and the fourth foot. Its scansion is:—

Ăbom̄ | ĭnăblĕ | ŭnūt | tĕrăblĕ | an̄d wor̄se.

l. 16. **uncouthness**, awkwardness, roughness. *Uncouth* (*un-*, not, *couth*, known) is lit. 'strange,' 'unfamiliar,' and so 'odd,' 'awkward.'

l. 20. **foils**, 'set-offs'; the irregular lines are introduced to enhance the attractiveness of the musical ones.

l. 21. **the tedium of**, etc. Cf. p. 119, l. 2 *et seq.*

l. 25. **numbers**. See note to p. 5, l. 11.

l. 29. **Half-strained**, lit. 'half-bred,' and so 'imperfect,' 'incompetent.' Cf. Dryden:—

"I find I'm but a half-strained villain yet,
But mungril-mischievous; for my blood boil'd
To view this brutal act."

strain = race, stock.

ll. 34, 35. **allow yourself to be of**, admit that you belong to.

Page 89, l. 5. **bespoke**, indicated, revealed.

ll. 7, 8. **the cask excepted**. See p. 86, l. 5 *et seq.*, and note. 'The *cask* (being) excepted' is an absolute clause.

l. 9. **the "gently away."** In a previous letter Lady Hesketh had objected to the rhythm of one of Cowper's lines:—

"Softly he placed his hand
On th' old man's hand, and push'd it gently away,"

whereupon the poet claimed that General Cowper had expressed himself as "particularly pleased" with this very passage. "Taste, my dear," he continued, "is various" (*To Lady Hesketh*, March 6, 1786).

l. 11. **Than the broad**, etc. Cowper had originally written:—

"Than th' whole broad Hellespont in all his parts."

In the letter of March 6 Cowper had defended the elision ("th' whole") because "W, though he rank as a consonant in the word *whole*, is not allowed to announce himself to the ear: and H is an aspirate."

l. 13. **stickled**, 'been persistent'; 'maintained that it ought to be inserted.' To *stickle* (M. E. *stightlen*, to arrange) meant originally 'to part combatants,' 'to act as umpire,' and then (as often devolved upon seconds) 'to maintain the quarrel of their principals.'

l. 18. **Mr. Hornby's note.** Mr. Hornby had written favourably of Cowper's first volume.

l. 21. **a clap on the back**, 'an encouragement.' Cf. *Friendship*, 169-171:—

"The man that hails you Tom or Jack,
And proves by thumps upon your back
How he esteems your merit," etc.

l. 22. **in my head**, *i.e.* my intellectual powers are stimulated by praise.

ll. 26, 27. **A true Whig.** See note to p. 6, l. 17; and cf. p. 136, ll. 10-16.

l. 32. **Au contraire**, French for 'on the contrary.' "Somebody else" is of course Cowper himself.

Page 90, l. 1. **to do**, 'to make us.' See note to p. 40, l. 16.

l. 3. **a cordial**, a strengthening medicine, that makes one strong and *hearty* (Lat. *cordi*, stem of *cor*, heart).

l. 7. **a village**, Weston Underwood.

ll. 7, 8. **of Mr. Throckmorton**, from Mr. Throckmorton.

l. 11. **as will.** *As* is a relative pronoun here. The true correlative of *such* (= so-like) was *which* (= what-like); cf. Pope, *Essay on Criticism*, 15:—

"Let such teach others *who* themselves excel."

Page 91, l. 1. **The house**, etc., Weston Lodge, a house belonging to Mr. Throckmorton.

l. 3. **more commodious.** Cf. p. 35, l. 27.

l. 7. **affords but indifferent**, etc., does not give much room for walking.

l. 9. **for eight months in the year.** Cf. *To Unwin*, July 3, 1786: "Here we are confined from September to March, and sometimes longer."

l. 11. **the Tower**, the Tower of London, formerly a state prison.

battlements, 'parapets.' *Battlement* is probably a corruption of *bastillement*, from Old Fr. *bastiller*, to fortify.

ll. 19, 20. **putrid fevers**, typhus fevers. Cf. p. 39, l. 13.

l. 21. **our respective maladies**, the different maladies that attack them and us.

l. 25. **the uplands**, the higher ground on which Weston stood.

l. 28. **frantic**, 'mad.' Cowper means that, having once known what it is to enjoy God's favour, he cannot be happy while he is estranged from Him.

l. 32. **a ballast-lighter**, a lighter or barge for conveying ballast (of broken stone or gravel) to or from ships. The work would be done by convicts.

Animal spirits, the exhilaration that comes from health of body.

Page 92, ll. 1, 2, **an experience**, etc. In 1782 Newton had drawn Cowper's attention to the case of Simon Browne, as resembling his own. Browne had fallen into a deep melancholy, which ended in a settled persuasion that God had caused his rational soul to perish, and left him only an animal life (cf. p. 32, ll. 14, 15, and note); hence, like Cowper, he thought it profane for him to pray. Cowper, however, considered his own case as essentially different from Browne's and far more deplorable (*To Newton*, March 14, 1782).

l. 3. **having walked**, etc. Cowper compares his period of melancholy to the passage of the Israelites through the Red Sea, and his hoped-for deliverance from it to their emerging on the opposite shore. See Bible, *Exodus*, xiv. 21, 22.

l. 6. **song of Moses**, the song of triumph sung by Moses and the Israelites after the passage. See *Exodus*, xv.

l. 8. **I could not be**, etc., even Satan himself could not delude me into doubting whether those hopes were sent me by God.

l. 14. **more comfortably**, with more comfort to myself.

l. 15. **scripturally**, in accordance with the teachings of Scripture.

l. 20. **despair excepted**, with the exception that she has not suffered from despair, as I have.

l. 24. **By her help**. She took them for drives in her carriage, enabling them to visit the Chesters and other neighbouring families.

Page 93, l. 2. **Mr. Greatheed**. See *Introduction*, p. xliii.

l. 2. **abroad**, 'out-of-doors.' We now generally use *abroad* in the sense of 'out of the British Isles.'

l. 5. **coz**, short and familiar for *cousin*.

ll. 14, 15. **the Swan**. See note to page 86, l. 3.

l. 19. **the Padre**, Dr. Gregson, Mr. Throckmorton's chaplain. Being a Roman Catholic priest, he would be styled "Father"; hence Cowper calls him *Padre*. Cf. p. 95, l. 28 *et. seq.*

ll. 20, 21. **Mrs. Marriot**, the landlady of the "Swan."

l. 22. **thou must write**. A playfully affectionate use of *thou*. Similarly with "child," p. 94, l. 3.

l. 26. **peepers**. Jocosely for "eyes."

Page 94, l. 2. **to a level**, *i.e.* in order to make them level.

ll. 16, 17. **a tea-waiter**, a tea-tray.

l. 18. **the Hall**, Weston Hall, the seat of the Throckmortons.

ll. 20, 21. **my worship**, 'my honourable self'; said jocosely. Cf. "my authorship," p. 25, l. 5.

l. 24. **my precious**, 'my dear one'; a familiar use.

l. 32. **embargoes**, 'prohibitions';—'do not forbid our sending you such small presents.' *Embargo* (Span. *em-*, in, *barra*, a bar) means lit. 'a putting of a bar in the way.'

Page 95, l. 2. **the every thing**. This *the* is the *the* of 'the bed,' 'the tea,' 'the chocolate,' 'the table,' above, repeated before 'every thing' to make it the more emphatic.

l. 6. **Giles Gingerbread**. The name of the hero of an old English nursery tale. Cowper adopts it in letters to Lady Hesketh (see the subscription to this letter) probably in allusion to some joke of his Temple days.

l. 10. **a peppercorn**, a "tiny acknowledgment," a "small matter." In the case of lands held rent-free, a "peppercorn rent" was charged, *i.e.* a mere nominal rent, as an acknowledgment of tenancy. Cf. *Table Talk*, 109, 110:—

"The courtly laureate pays
His quitrent ode, his peppercorn of praise."

l. 14. **the Welshman's letter**. The Welshman was Mr. Wm. Churchey, attorney-at-law, of Hay, Breconshire. Cf. *To Lady Hesketh*, Nov. 26, 1786: "Alas! (I am) in too much request with some people. The verses of Cadwallader have found me at last."

ll. 18, 19. **the weightier ... law**, 'his severer law studies';—a Biblical expression; cf. *Matthew*, xxiii. 23.

Page 96, l. 1. **Teedon**. See note to p. 69, l. 7.

l. 3. **the poor widow**, Mrs. William Unwin. Her husband died on Nov. 29 of this year.

l. 10. **by a sidewind**, indirectly; not from Mrs. Unwin herself.

l. 11. **Billy**, used familiarly for William Unwin.

l. 14. **Mrs. U.**, Mrs. Unwin, Senior.

jointured, etc. A jointure to be paid out of the estate or property of Mrs. Unwin, Senior, had been settled upon her. A jointure is property settled on a woman at marriage to be enjoyed after her husband's death.

ll. 16, 17. **from which circumstance**, etc., *i.e.* because her sister's income would thus be joined to her own.

ll. 23, 24. **recover the stroke**, get over her husband's death.

l. 25. **Henry C.**, Henry Cowper, cousin to the poet, who addressed a sonnet to him in 1788.

l. 26. **in kind**, 'in the same clever style.' *Kind* = 'nature,' hence 'an answer in kind' is an answer of the same nature as the letter. So 'payment in kind' means payment in natural produce, as distinguished from money.

l. 29. **So much the worse for you.** See p. 32, l. 8; p. 53, l. 12, and notes.

l. 35. **Gingerbread Giles.** See note above, p. 95, l. 6.

Page 97, l. 4. **your last favour**, your last kind letter.

l. 6. **interrupted.** In January, 1787, Cowper had been attacked by his fourth derangement, which lasted till the end of July; but for some three months longer he did not resume his pen, spending his time in reading and exercise.

l. 11. **since we parted**, since Rose's visit to him on Jan. 18 of this year.

l. 21. **A sensible mind**, etc., 'to part from even a familiar locality is very painful to a tender-hearted person.' See p. 35, l. 13, *et seq.*, and notes. *Sensible* = 'sensitive'; cf. below, p. 98, l. 2, where *sensible of* = 'sensitive to.'

l. 22. **my father died.** This was on August 3, 1756, Cowper being then twenty-five years old.

l. 25. **fee-simple in**, 'full legal possession of.' *Fee* is O. E. *feoh*, Lat. *pecus*, cattle, property; and land held in fee-simple is a freehold estate of inheritance absolute and unqualified. A rector retains the house and glebe (*i.e.* the land attached to the benefice) only during his term of office.

l. 32. **I sighed a long adieu**, 'I bade adieu for a long time, with a sigh.' Cf. *On the Receipt of my Mother's Picture*, 30, 31:—

"(I) drew
A long, long sigh, and wept a last adieu!"

Adieu is to be parsed as cognate object of *sighed*.

Page 98, l. 4. **the part of wisdom**, fitting conduct for a wise man.

ll. 4, 5. **to sit down ... under**, to yield to.

l. 10. **Causidice mi**, Latin for "My counsel," a jesting appellation which Sir Thomas (then Mr.) Hesketh had given the young law-student in the old Southampton days.

l. 17. **expatiate**, 'walk abroad,' 'range at large.' The meaning of the Latin verb *exspatiari* is 'to leave the proper course,' 'to go out of the beaten track.' Cf. *Task*, iv. 107, 108:—

> "He travels and expatiates, as the bee
> From flower to flower, so he from land to land"

And "Let us," writes Pope, *Essay on Man*, i. 5,

> "Expatiate free o'er all this scene of man."

The word is now confined to the metaphorical sense of 'to enlarge upon.'

l. 22. **you could not reach them.** Because the places were too rough for a lady's walking.

l. 23. **the flood**, the Deluge. Cf. notes to p. 43, ll. 2, 13.

Burnet. Thomas Burnet (b. 1635, d. 1715), Master of the Charterhouse, and author of *The Sacred Theory of the Earth*, a fanciful speculation, without any pretension to scientific truth.

l. 30. **Sam**, his servant, Sam Roberts, who had accompanied him to Olney from. St. Albans.

Page 99, l. 3. **All-Saints.** Many English churches are dedicated to "All Saints," *i.e.* the whole body of holy Christian men denominated *Saints*.

l. 4. **upholsterer**, one who supplies furniture, beds, etc. The original form of the word was *upholder* or *upholdster*, to which *-er* was needlessly added, as in the case of *fruiterer*, *poulterer*, *caterer*, *sorcerer*. The old "upholder" was a broker or auctioneer; so that the name may have arisen from his *holding up* wares for inspection while trying to sell them. A shop in the Brixton Road, London, has (or had a few years ago) the designation "upholder" (for "upholsterer") above its window.

l. 5. **a bill of mortality**, a register or statement of the deaths that had occurred within the parish.

l. 10. **statuary**, 'stone-cutter'; Lat. *statuarius*, from *statua*. a standing image (*stare*, *statum*, to stand).

l. 14. **of so much reading**, so learned.

l. 16. **the compliment.** Said ironically, since the speech implied that Cowper was less learned than Cox. Cf. "my mortified vanity" below, l. 21.

l. 19. **walked over**, etc. A distance of about twelve miles.

l. 25. **my effusions**, etc., 'my verses appropriate to the burial of the dead.' Besides these stanzas for 1787, the poet supplied stanzas "on a similar occasion" for the years 1788, 1789, 1790, 1792, and 1793.

ll. 32, 33. **a gentleman**, etc. Cowper playfully alludes to *viz.* (Lat. *videlicet*) in the sense of 'namely.'

Page 100, l. 1. **Addison's.** See note to p. 46, l. 3.

l. 3. **the Hall**, Weston Hall.

l. 4. **vermicelli**, small thread-like rolls made of dough; an Italian diminutive, from Lat. *vermis*, a worm. The man took the vermicelli for maggots.

l. 17. **our trim**, 'our position,' 'our views'; viz., that we did not care for balls. See p. 1, l. 14.

l. 18. **And why?** etc. *A Metrical Version of the Psalms* was produced in 1562, by "Sternhold, Hopkins, and others." It was the first version of the Psalms of David in English metre, and was commonly used in churches until superseded by Tate and Brady's version in 1696. The authors are fond of the rhetorical device "And why?" for introducing a statement, and Cowper humorously apportions the question and its answer between the two authors named.

l. 24. **other good things**, gifts of his correspondent.

l. 26. **furbished up**, etc., *i.e.* improved and amended it, so that its style is polished and elegant.

l. 30. **notable job**, important piece of business.

Page 101, l. 7. **The course of a rapid river.** Cf. *A Comparison*:—

> "The lapse of time and rivers is the same,
> Both speed their journey with a restless stream," etc.

ll. 8, 9. **our scene below**, the course of human life.

l. 9. **Shakespeare says**, etc. Cowper seems to have made a mistake in his reference here. Cf. Heracliti, *Epp. Reliq.* I., p. 16: ποταμᾶσι δὶς τοῖσι αυτοῖσι οὐκ ἂν ἐμβαίης, "you cannot go twice into the same rivers." See also Plato, *Cratylus*, 402a.

l. 15. **Deuce take**, 'may the devil take them for interrupting me!' *Deuce* (Germ. *Daus*, *Taus*) seems to represent the *Tuss* of Northern mythology, a huge, savage goblin (Wedgwood), rather than the Norman oath, *Deus*, 'O God,' corrupted (Skeat). The prevalence of profane swearing among all classes of society at this time could not be more strikingly illustrated than by the fact that a man such as Cowper allows himself to use this expression, which modern taste would condemn. Cf. *To Lady Hesketh*, Feb. 10, 1793: "How the deuce you came to be a Tory is best known to yourself."

l. 31. **ditto note**, the aforesaid note, the Bank note.

Page 102, l. 1. **fadge**, 'manage,' 'get on,' 'succeed' (M. E. *fegen*, to fit, suit). Cf. Shaks. *Twelfth Night*, ii. 2. 34: "How will this fadge" (*i.e.* turn out)?

is turned, is over, is past.

l. 2. **to draw upon you**, to ask you for a remittance.

l. 4. **Anonymous.** There are several references in Cowper's letters to this personage, who gave him an annuity of fifty pounds a year, with various other presents. In all probability this nameless friend was his cousin and first love, Theodora, Lady Hesketh's sister.

advice of, information of its despatch.

l. 7. **Drop of Ink.** See Cowper's poem entitled "Ode to Apollo. On an Inkglass almost dried in the sun." Stanza 3 runs—

"Why, stooping from the noon of day,
Too covetous of drink,
Apollo, hast thou stol'n away
A poet's drop of ink?"

l. 15. **chirurgical**, the older form of *surgical*, into which it was shortened (Low Lat. *chirurgus*, Greek, χειρουργός, 'working with the hand,' 'skilful').

l. 24. **meet**, find, produce.

l. 33. **son of ... Rowley.** See *Introduction*, p. xliii.; and cf. Letter, p. 125.

Page 103, l. 6. **another in Scotland**, Samuel Rose. See *Introduction*, p. xli.

ll. 6, 7. **a third in Wales.** See note to p. 95, l. 14.

l. 9. **My dog.** This was Beau, presented to the poet by the two Miss Gunnings, daughters of Sir Robert Gunning, one of his neighbours. Three of Cowper's poems relate to this dog, viz.: "The Dog and the Water-lily," and "On a Spaniel, called Beau, killing a young bird," with "Beau's Reply."

l. 18. **personal endowments**, good looks.

l. 24. **The Throcks**, 'the Throckmortons. Cowper also sometimes sportively calls them "Mr. and Mrs. Frog"; cf. p. 116, l. 4.

ll. 24, 25. **invited us to the measure**, proposed that we should take part in the proceeding.

l. 27. **stumping**, 'trudging.' Cf. the vulgar expression, 'to stir one's stumps' (*i.e.* feet); so that 'to stump' = to foot it, to walk. The man "stumped" to Newport Pagnell to fetch the letters to Olney, whence the Throckmortons' servant brought them to Weston.

l. 30. **closes**, enclosed spots, passages.

Page 104, l. 2. **half-boots.** 'Boots,' in Cowper's time, meant boots that came up to the knee, as riding-boots or fishermen's boots; so that 'half-boots' were the same as our modern boots.

ll. 9, 10. **the wilderness.** See note to p. 66, l. 16.

l. 11. **the cry of hounds**, 'the barking of dogs engaged in hunting'; cf. the phrase 'in full cry,' of hounds. Shakspere (*Coriolanus*, III. iii. 120: "You common cry of curs!") and Milton (*Par. Lost*, ii. 654: "A cry of Hell-hounds") use *cry* for *pack*.

l. 15. **a terrier.** *Terrier* is short for 'terrier-dog,' *i.e.* 'burrow-dog,' a dog that pursues rabbits, etc., into their burrows (Low Lat. *terrarium*, a hillock, burrow; *terra*, earth).

l. 23. **cavalcade**, body of horsemen; the hunters.

· **The huntsman**, a man whose business it is to take charge of the pack of hounds.

l. 27. **a sagacity.** See p. 76, l. 24, and note.

Page 105, l. 1. **reynard** is the name of the fox in the famous Teutonic epic, *Reincke Fuchs*, "The History of Reynard the Fox." The word means 'strong in counsel.'

l. 11. **not less expressive**, etc., expressing the same intelligent pleasure that the hunters showed.

l. 14. **a bolus.** See note to p. 7, l. 22.

l. 17. **to open a lane**, to stand back on either side, so as to leave a long, open space.

l. 22. **as Virgil says.** Cf. *Æneid*, ix. 6. 7: *Turne, quod optanti divûm promittere nemo Auderet, volvenda dies en attulit ultro*, "Turnus, what none of the gods could have ventured to promise to our wishes, lo! time in its course has brought of its own accord."

l. 25. **in at the death.** This is the usual sporting term; it means 'present at the capture and killing.'

Page 106, l. 5. **from above**, *i.e.* from God.

l. 11. **sanctified**, consecrated to God's service.

l. 16. **at your hands**, 'from you.' See the first three lines of the letter.

ll. 28, 29. **day-spring from on high**, 'celestial sun-rising.' Cf. Bible, *Luke*, i. 78: "Through the tender mercy of our God; whereby the dayspring from on high hath visited us" (*i.e.* by the coming of Christ). Cowper means that he, like Mrs. King, was blest with a sense of God's forgiveness and favour.

l. 32. **In the depths**, etc. Cf. p. 78, l. 27.

Page 107, l. 7. **Mr. Unwin**, *i.e.* Mr. Unwin, Senior.

l. 8. **cure**, the district under his spiritual charge as clergyman.

l. 9. **he died.** He was thrown from his horse on June 28, 1767, and died four days afterwards.

the same views, etc. They both belonged to the Evangelical party in the Church of England.

l. 10. **of attending**, etc. They wished to be under an Evangelical minister of the Gospel.

l. 18. **threatening to fall**, etc. Of Orchard Side, Cowper, writing to Newton (Dec. 16, 1786), says that its ceilings were cracked and its walls crumbling, and that its fall is prophesied, "unless it be well propped." The house, however, is still standing and likely to continue to stand.

ll. 24, 25. **singularity of the matter**, special interest or importance of the subject-matter of my letter.

Page 108, l. 5. **by way of map**, to take the place of a map.

l. 7. **your paradise**, 'your beautiful neighbourhood.' *Paradise* is of Persian origin; cf. Persian *firdaus* (plur. *farádís*), a garden.

l. 11. **the lime walk**, the avenue of lime trees in Mr. Throckmorton's grounds, celebrated in *Task*, i. 338-349.

l. 12. **woodbill**, a kind of hatchet for cutting wood.

l. 14. **intercepted the arch**, prevented the arch formed by the boughs from being clearly defined.

l. 15. **no cathedral**, etc. Cf. *Task*, i. 341-343 :—

> "How airy and how light the graceful arch,
> Yet awful as the consecrated roof
> Re-echoing pious anthems!"

And Warburton, *Itinerarium Curiosum*: "The cloisters in this Cathedral (at Gloucester) are beautiful beyond anything I ever saw. ... The idea of it is taken from a walk (*i.e.* avenue) of trees, whose branching heads are curiously imitated by the roof." And Tennyson, *Palace of Art*, 26: "Cloisters, branch'd like mighty woods." See Ruskin (*Stones of Venice*, ii. 6. 70) on Naturalism in Gothic architecture.

ll. 18, 19. **an object of taste**, a beautiful sight.

l. 19. **the refreshment**, etc. Cf. *Task*, i. 335-337 :—

> "Refreshing change! where now the blazing sun?
> By short transition we have lost his glare,
> And stepped at once into a cooler clime."

l. 22. **rectilinear**, 'in a straight line.' The taste of the day in landscape gardening demanded curves.

l. 25. **the account**, etc. The title of the book is—*Characters of 500 Authors of Great Britain now living.* By W. Marshall. *London, 1788.* 8vo.

l. 27. **the high crime and misdemeanor**, 'serious crime and offence.' The phrase is common in bills of indictment for conspiracy or sedition.

ll. 27, 28. **neglecting method**. See p. 53, l. 25 *et seq.*, and note; p. 62, ll. 33, 34.

Page 109, l. 2. **a logical precision**, an exact arrangement according to the rules of logic.

l. 6. **for aught I know**, as far as I am aware.

l. 11. **the fee simple**. See note to p. 97, l. 25.

l. 12. **for poets**. Because poets are or were regarded as proverbially poor. See below, l. 18 *et seq.*; p. 115, l. 31.

ll. 14, 15. **Strawberry Hill**, the part of London where Lady Hesketh was living. For "thee," see note to p. 93, l. 22.

l. 22. **I commenced writer**. See note to p. 6, l. 27.

l. 26. **the chisel and the saw**. Cf. p. 80, l. 33 *et seq.*

l. 29. **joint-stools**, *i.e.* 'joined stools,' stools of which the parts were inserted in each other. Cf. *Task*, i. 19-21:—

> "Joint-stools were then created; on three legs
> Upborne they stood—three legs upholding firm
> A massy slab, in fashion square or round."

l. 30. **Pertenhall**, the village in Bedfordshire of which Mrs. King's husband was rector. In his verses *To Mrs. King*, Cowper calls her "The gentle fair of Pertenhall."

Page 110, l. 6. **'squire**, short for "esquire" (Low Lat. *scutarius*, a shield-bearer, from *scutum*, a shield). Usually written *squire*, without the apostrophe.

l. 9. **the article**, 'the item.' Cf. p. 55, l. 1, and note.

cabbage-nets, nets for covering and protecting cabbages.

l. 10. **hardiness**, 'boldness.' *Hardihood* is the more common form.

the pencil. Cf. note to p. 8, l. 3.

l. 13. **unparalleled**, etc. They bore no resemblance to anything produced by an artist or to anything seen in nature.

l. 17. **three landscapes**, etc. An engraving from one of these drawings may be seen in *The Gentleman's Magazine* for June, 1804. The three landscapes still exist. The "lady" was Lady Austen.

l. 18. **I then judged**, etc. Said jocosely. On p. 81 Cowper tells us that he gave up drawing because it injured his eyesight.

l. 21. **gardening**. See note to p. 2, l. 1.

ll. 24, 25. **cucumbers**. Cowper devotes some hundred lines of the *Task* (iii. 446-543) to a description of the raising of the cucumber.

ll. 25, 26. **an orange-tree . . myrtles**. Cf. *Task*, iii. 570 *et seq.*:—

> "The spiry myrtle with unwithering leaf
> Shines there (in the greenhouse) and flourishes. The golden boast
> Of Portugal and Western India there,
> The ruddier orange," etc.

l. 36. **a greenhouse.** See note to p. 20, l. 17.

Page 111, l. 4. **I left Olney for Weston.** See p. 91, l. 1 *et seq.*

l. 19. **evening reading.** See note to p. 1, l. 23.

ll. 19, 20. **Mrs. Piozzi's Travels.** This lady (b. 1739, d. 1821) married Mr. Thrale in 1763, and soon after her friendship with Dr. Johnson commenced, of whom she published "Anecdotes" in 1786. In 1781 she married Piozzi, an Italian music-master, and subsequently published "A Journey through France, Italy, and Germany."

l. 27. **the Dunciad.** See p, 21, l. 11, and note.

l. 29. **The mercy,** etc. See Pope's *Universal Prayer*, ll. 39, 40. "The mercy" should be "That mercy"; cf. note to p. 88, l. 11. The lines are a paraphrase of a petition in *The Lord's Prayer*: "Forgive us our trespasses, as we forgive them that trespass against us."

Page 112, l. 1. **Alas! for Pope,** etc., Pope's condition would be a bad one, if God were to treat him as he treated his brother-poets in the *Dunciad.*

l. 6. **noddle,** a ludicrous word for *head.* It means properly the projecting part at the back of the head, and stands for *knoddel*, dim. of *knod*, which is another form of *knot.*

l. 11. **withered,** etc. In allusion to the name, *Rose*, which Cowper gave her. Her real name was Ann.

l. 15. **jot,** 'a tittle, a bit.' The word is Englished from Lat. *iota*, Greek, *ἰῶτα* (*i*), Heb. *yód* (*y*), the smallest letter in the Hebrew alphabet.

l. 18. **remove,** 'generation.' Similarly we speak of a person's 'first cousin once *removed*,' *i.e.* the son or the daughter of his first cousin.

l. 21. **the picture,** the portrait of his mother, which Mrs. Bodham had sent him. It is a miniature in oils by Heines, now in the possession of the Rev. C. E. Donne, vicar of Faversham, Kent. See Cowper's poem, *On the Receipt of my Mother's Picture out of Norfolk.*

l. 29. **fidelity of the copy,** resemblance of the portrait to the original.

l. 30. **maternal tendernesses.** See *On the Receipt* etc., ll. 58-81.

Page 113, l. 1. **more of the Donne,** etc., I inherit my natural disposition from my mother rather than from my father. See *Introduction*, p. xi.

l. 4. **to your side,** *i.e.* to your, or the Donne, side of the family.

l. 13. **our venerable ancestor,** Dr. John Donne (b. 1573, d. 1631). He wrote some poems of much originality, and has been called "the greatest preacher of the 17th century."

l. 16. **the dear boy**, John Johnson. See *Introduction*, p. xli.

l. 25. **answer to us**, etc., *i.e.* your visiting us will be as gratifying as our visiting you.

l. 29. **crazed**, *i.e.* much troubled.

l. 32. **Hewitt**, etc. The poet's uncle, the Rev. Roger Donne, had four daughters and one son; viz., Elizabeth (Mrs. Hewitt), Catherine (Mrs. John Johnson), Harriet (Mrs. Balls), Ann (Mrs. Bodham), and Castres (vicar of Ludham).

Page 114, l. 1. **Catfield**, the residence, in Norfolk, of his uncle Roger, where Cowper, as a boy, would sometimes spend his holidays.

l. 11. **Castres.** See note to l. 32 above. For this use of *poor*, see note to p. 70, l. 25.

l. 20. **sister.** See note to p. 123, l. 18.

l. 23. **in New Norfolk Street**, *i.e.* at Lady Hesketh's, whose residence was in this street.

l. 24. **your labours**, *i.e.* in copying the manuscripts (of his Homer) referred to in the previous line.

l. 27. **amanuensis**, 'copyist'; properly, 'one who writes to dictation' (Lat. *a manu*, 'by hand,' with suffix *-ensis*, 'belonging to').

ll. 27, 28. **Mr. George Throckmorton**, the brother of John.

l. 29. **who have never read**, etc., *i.e.* since you have still that pleasure in prospect.

Page 115, l. 3. **Longinus**, a celebrated Greek critic and philosopher of the third century, noted for his commentaries on ancient authors.

l. 4. **His comparison**, etc. He denoted the superiority of the *Iliad* to the *Odyssey* by comparing the former to the noon-day sun and the latter to the setting-sun.

l. 6. **just**, true, correct.

l. 7. **seduced him**, *i.e.* he was so pleased with the neatness of the comparison that he employed it without sufficient consideration.

l. 15. **snarling generation**, carping body of persons.

l. 16. **thee.** See note to p. 93, l. 22.

l. 19. **a shred**, etc., *i.e.* you belong to my mother's side of the family.

l. 20. **fall into**, etc., be in the same position as I am, *i.e.* love you as I do.

l. 22. **your own personal right**, etc. We attribute our affection for you to other grounds than any lovable qualities that you may possess.

l. 23. **There is nothing**, etc. Knowing how easily a young man's vanity is flattered, I am very careful not to spoil him by such flattery.

l. 27. **a coxcomb.** See note to p. 9, l. 28.

l. 31. **valued**, 'esteemed.' Cowper frequently, in his letters, uses "valuable" where we should say "estimable."

a poor poet. Cf. p. 109, l. 12, and note.

Page 116, l. 4. **Mrs. Frog.** See note to p. 103, l. 24.

l. 5. **desired**, requested.

l. 7. **urchin** means (1) a hedgehog; (2) a goblin, imp; (3) a small child (Old Fr. *ireçon*, Lat. *ericius*, a hedgehog).

l. 8. **in old times.** As in Shaks. *Titus*, II. iii. 101:—

"A thousand hissing snakes,
Ten thousand swelling toads, as many urchins."

l. 9. **Bucklands**, the family seat of the Throckmorton family, in Berkshire.

l. 11. **divers**, 'various.' This is the Biblical spelling of the word, rather than *diverse*.

l. 26. **wilderness.** See note to p. 66, l. 16.

Page 117, l. 2. **mastiff**, 'a large dog'; probably from Venetian *mastino*, 'large-limbed, strong'; originally 'well-fed,' from Germ. *masten*, to feed.

l. 4. **an attorney**, a lawyer, to threaten him with legal proceedings.

l. 5. **Don Quixote**, the hero of a celebrated Spanish romance of the same name, by Cervantes. Don Quixote is represented as a country gentleman crazed by reading books of chivalry, and sallying forth as a knight-errant to fight with giants and rescue the oppressed.

l. 8. **foxhunters.** Cf. his satiric sketches of the hunting squire and the hunting parson (*Progress of Error*, 82-123); and *Task*, vi. 425-438, and 577-580; *The Needless Alarm*, 24-28.

universities. See notes to p. 55, l. 34; p. 60, ll. 22, 23.

ll. 9, 10. **the Turnpike Bill.** A *turn-pike* is a toll-gate, or gate set across a road to stop those liable to pay toll for the use of the road. The name was given to the toll-gate, because it took the place of the old turnstile, which was made with four horizontal *pikes* or arms, which *turned* or revolved on the top of a post. Toll-gates were first set up in 1663, and from time to time Acts of Parliament were passed abolishing them.

l. 10. **alive or dead**, *i.e.* still being proceeded with or dropt.

ll. 10, 11. **ignoramuses**, 'ignorant persons.' *Ignoramus* (Lat. for "we are ignorant") was formerly a law term, written on bills of indictment when the evidence was considered too weak to make them good.

l. 16. **on this occasion.** By the death of Thomas Warton, in this year, the poet-laureateship had become vacant, and Lady Hesketh wished to obtain the post for Cowper, and with that view had persuaded him to write loyal verses on the recovery of George III. After being declined by Hayley, it was conferred upon Pye.

l. 17. **the wreath,** 'the wreath of laurel.' *Laureate* means 'crowned with laurel,' the classical insignia of the poet, the laurel being sacred to Apollo, the patron-god of poetry.

whatever wreath, etc., whatever other honours I may win.

Page 118, l. 1. **a scatter-brain,** 'a heedless fellow'; lit. one whose *brain scatters* instead of orderly arranging things, so as to remember them. Cf. *hare-brained.*

l. 5. **shyness.** See *Introduction*, p. xx.

l. 12. **as a dream,** etc. The quotation is made up of two passages in the Bible; see *Psalms*, lxxiii. 20; and xc. 4.

l. 14. **It,** *i.e.* our human life.

l. 20. **Donne's poems.** See note to p. 113, l. 13.

l. 24. **music.** Johnson played on the fiddle.

l. 28. **tampered with,** 'meddled with.' *Tamper* is a doublet of *temper*, but always used in a bad sense. Cf. p. 14, l. 7 *et seq.*

l. 32. **delicate,** 'fastidious.' Cf. p. 29, l. 25, and note; and cf. *Table-talk*, 510-513 :—

"Modern taste
Is so refined, and delicate, and chaste,
That verse, whatever fire the fancy warms,
Without a creamy smoothness has no charms."

Page 119, l. 6. **Pope.** Cf. p. 23, l. 6 *et seq.*

l. 10. **Give me,** etc. Cf. *Table-talk*, 522, 523 :—

"Give me the line that ploughs its stately course
Like a proud swan, conquering the stream by force."

l. 13. **oily smoothness.** Cf. "creamy smoothness" in note to l. 32 above.

l. 16. **our common friend,** more correct than the modern 'our mutual friend.' The friend was Lady Hesketh. The poem is the *Iliad.*

l. 18. **nice,** fastidious.

l. 27. **sacrifice the spirit,** etc. Cf. *Table-talk*, 514-517 :—

"Thus, all success depending on an ear,
And thinking I might purchase it too dear,

If sentiment were sacrificed to sound,
And truth cut short to make a period round," etc.

l. 29. **a beautiful poem.** Mr. Buchanan had suggested to Cowper that the four divisions of human life—infancy, youth, manhood, old age—was a suitable subject for a poem, and at the poet's request, furnished him with a sketch of the topic.

Page 120, l. 1. **I will.** Cowper began the poem (*The Four Ages*), but only thirty-eight lines were written.

l. 18. **jot.** See note to p. 112, l. 15. Few readers will agree with Cowper's estimate of the comparative merits of his first and second volumes.

Page 121, l. 2. **attachment to animals.** See *Introduction*, p. xxi.

l. 7. **laying,** etc. See the following note.

l. 8. **little ewe lamb.** When King David had compassed the death of Uriah for the sake of obtaining his wife, God sent Nathan to David, who convicted him of his wrong-doing by a parable. There were two men, he said, in one city: the one, rich in flocks and herds; the other, with only a little ewe lamb which "did eat of his own meat, and drank of his own cup, and lay in his bosom, and was unto him as a daughter." On the arrival of a traveller, the rich man spared to take of his own flock, but took the poor man's lamb and dressed it for his guest. See Bible, 2 *Samuel*, xii. 1-4.

ll. 16, 17. **assembly rooms.** See note to p. 1, l. 11.

l. 25. **wants not a fiddle,** etc., who is kind and good-humoured in the ordinary circumstances of life, away from a dancing party. "A fiddle" means the music played at a ball.

l. 31. **sages.** Said ironically;—'I do not expect, as some wiseacres do, to find the staidness and sobriety of age in young men.'

Page 122, l. 1. **draft,** order for the payment of money. To "negotiate" a draft is to sell it or exchange it for money.

l. 4. **draw,** obtain a draft from you.

l. 5. **a purse,** *i.e.* money due to me from Johnson (his publisher).

l. 9. **loose cash,** money available for spending.

l. 12. **my copy,** 'my publication,' 'my manuscript.' Johnson proposed to recoup himself for the cost of publishing the Homer by taking all the proceeds of the sales—the terms on which he published Cowper's first volume; see p. 13, ll. 11, 12.

l. 17. **below par,** 'below their ordinary level.' A stock is "at par" (Lat. for *equal*) when its market value corresponds with the sum at which it was issued. Cf. p. 124, l. 18, "I felt my spirits sink ten degrees," where the metaphor is drawn from the thermometer.

ll. 19, 20. **copyright**, the exclusive right of an author, lasting for a term of years, to publish his work.

l. 21. **clench**, 'ratify.' *Clench* or *clinch* is the causal of *clink*, and means 'to make to clink' by striking smartly, and so 'to rivet.'

l. 22. **Josephus**. See note to p. 79, l. 13.

l. 30. **signing**, etc. The plan was for Cowper to attach his signature to each of the copies, so as to prevent Johnson from publishing more and selling them without accounting for them to the author.

l. 33. **It would be**, etc., such a procedure would imply that Johnson was a dishonest man, who could not be trusted.

Page 123, ll. 9, 10. **the King and Queen of France.** The French Revolution of 1789 made King Louis XVI. a puppet in the hands of the National Assembly; and on June 21, 1891, while attempting to escape from France, the king, queen, and royal family, were arrested at Varennes, and brought back prisoners to Paris.

l. 11. **melancholy circumstances.** In October, 1788, King George III. had been seized with a violent illness with symptoms of lunacy, and a struggle arose between Pitt and Fox regarding the Regency, Fox supporting the "inherent right" of the Prince of Wales (who was on bad terms with his parents) to be Regent.

l. 16. **scurvily**, 'badly,' 'meanly.' *Scurvy* is the same word as *scurfy*.

l. 18. **the establishment**, 'the establishing,' 'the settling.' In June of this year John Johnson, his sister Catherine, and their aunt Mrs. Balls, had paid Cowper a visit, and it had been arranged that they should settle at Weston, "if Aunt Bodham, who is most affectionately attached to them all, can be persuaded not to break her heart about it" (*To Lady Hesketh*, June 23, 1791).

l. 26. **the Mediterranean hint**, the suggestion that he should take the Mediterranean Sea as the subject of a poem.

l. 27. **there would be**, etc., *i.e.* the subject would be beyond my ability.

Page 124, l. 1. **Catherine**. See note to p. 123, l. 18.

l. 2. **Dr. Kerr**, a Northampton physician. His prescription, probably a cathartic, had made her feel ill.

l. 3. **pettitoes**, used playfully for *feet*. The word ordinarily means the toes or feet of a pig when cooked for food.

ll. 4, 5. **for my own peculiar**, 'as regards myself particularly' (Lat. *peculiaris*, 'one's own,' from *peculium*, 'property').

l. 17. **lady of quality**, 'lady of rank,' 'great lady.' Similarly 'the quality' is used for 'the nobility.'

l. 18. **I felt**, etc. See note to p. 122, l. 17.

l. 23. **Lady Spencer.** She had called upon Cowper at Weston in 1790,' and subsequently presented him with a set of the engravings of Flaxman's illustrations of the *Odyssey*.

I am a shy animal. Cf. p. 118, l. 5, and see *Introduction*, p. xx.

ll. 26, 27. **by the by**, lit. 'near the near' (time); *i.e.* in passing, by the way. Cf. p. 19, l. 5, and note.

l. 28. **Ranger's observation**, Ranger is the leading character in Dr. Benjamin Hoadley's (b. 1706, d. 1757) comedy of *The Suspicious Husband*, produced in 1747.

l. 30. **assurance**, self-confidence, excessive boldness.

Page 125, l. 1. **'em**, *i.e.* the two great volumes. *'Em* is an elided form of *hem* (the old plural dative of *he*), for which *them* was afterwards substituted.

l. 6. **the late alarming occasion.** Dr. Joseph Priestley, eminent as a chemist and natural philosopher (b. 1733, d. 1804), was a Nonconformist minister at Birmingham, where his support of the claims of the Nonconformists, and especially his warm sympathy with the French Revolution, excited so much popular indignation, that riots took place in July, 1791, in which his house, library, and apparatus were burnt by the mob.

l. 15. **immeasurable distance.** Rowley lived at Dublin.

l. 26. **an editor.** Cowper had been offered by Johnson, his publisher, the editorship of a splendid edition of Milton that was in contemplation. He accepted the offer, and translated Milton's Latin and Italian poems, but annotated only two books of the *Paradise Lost*.

Page 126, l. 4. **studied Milton.** Cowper's fondness for Milton is illustrated in the *Task*, where there are many reminiscences of his style and manner. Cf. p. 5, l. 15 *et seq.*; p. 134, l. 31 *et seq.*

l. 9. **Fuseli.** See note to p. 84, ll. 26, 27.

l. 14. **le jeu**, etc., French for "the game would not be worth the candles," *i.e.* not worth even the cost of the candles that light the players. Cowper means that his poems are not worth the cost of their carriage to Ireland.

l. 18. **my subscription.** See p. 74, ll. 18, 19, and note.

l. 22. **to disappoint myself**, *i.e.* by putting off your visit.

Page 127, l. 1. **vertigo**, giddiness (Lat. *vertere*, to turn).

l. 12. **Truditur**, etc., "Day follows hard upon day, and new moons go on to their waning"; quoted from Horace, *Odes*, II. xviii. 15, 16.

l. 17. **the electrician.** In May of this year Mrs. Unwin had a second paralytic seizure, and was now slowly recovering "by the use of the electrical machine and other aids" (*To Mrs. King*, June 12, 1792), and able to move about with a little support. Cf. p. 132, l. 31 *et seq.*

l. 27. **assignation**, 'appointment,' 'arrangement.' The word is used chiefly of lovers' meetings.

l. 31. **hunted**, pressed, hurried.

Page 128, l. 5. **interception**, interruption.

l. 12. **arrival at Eartham.** See *Introduction*, p. xiii.

l. 13. **mansion**, Hayley's house.

l. 18. **in Buckinghamshire.** The country there being comparatively flat.

l. 26. **Barnet.** The party, consisting of Cowper, Mrs. Unwin, John Johnson, Sam, and his dog Beau, started from Olney on August 1st in a four-horse coach, reaching Barnet in Hertfordshire, the same evening. The second day they dined at Kingston, and passed the night at Ripley, six miles from Guildford in Surrey, and on the third evening arrived at Eartham—a journey of 120 miles, and, to the secluded poet, a "tremendous exploit."

Page 129, l. 6. **some terrors.** In a letter to Teedon, Cowper writes: "I indeed myself was a little daunted by the tremendous height of the Sussex hills, in comparison of which all that I had seen elsewhere are dwarfs."

l. 10. **a Paradise.** Hayley had enlarged and beautified his house at Eartham, and embellished the grounds, making the place so charming that his friend Gibbon, the historian, frequently a visitor there, called it the little Paradise of Eartham. See note to p. 108, l. 7.

l. 20. **so uncourteous a knight.** Cf. p. 12, l. 8, and note.

l. 21. **the last**, etc. Because he expected soon to return and see her.

l. 25. **laudanum**, a preparation of opium. *Laudanum*, a name transferred from one drug to another, is Lat. *ladanum*, the resinous substance exuding from the shrub *lada* (Pers. *ládan*). Cf. note to p. 39, l. 18.

l. 28. **Lethean vapours**, 'mists of oblivion,' 'a cloud of dulness.' *Lethe* (Greek, λήθη, 'forgetfulness') was a river in the Greek Hades, the waters of which the dead were made to drink that they might forget all that had happened in their lives. Shakspere forms the adjective *Lethe'd*—"a Lethe'd dulness," *Ant. and Cleo.* ii. 1. 26. Milton (*Par. Lost*, ii. 604) has *Lethean*.

Page 130, l. 2. 10th of August, the date of the attack made by the French Revolutionists upon the Tuileries, when the royal Swiss guards were cut to pieces and 5000 persons were massacred. See *Introduction*, p. xv.

l. 8. **the cause.** Their watchword was "Liberty, Equality, Fraternity."

l. 14. **My daily toast,** *i.e.* my daily wish in their behalf. At formal dinners it is sometimes customary to drink to the health or success of some person or persons named. Hence a *toast* = a health, or any good wish in some one's behalf. The term arose from its being formerly usual to put toasted bread in liquor.

l. 15. **Sobriety,** etc., *i.e.* may the French have Sobriety and Freedom.

l. 25. **articles,** 'items,' 'particulars'; cf. p. 55, l. 1, and note.

l. 27. **use her needles.** See note to p. 77, l. 15.

l. 28. **Doctor,** probably Dr. Grindon.

l. 31. **Epitaph.** See his poem entitled "Epitaph on Fop, a Dog belonging to Lady Throckmorton."

ll. 32, 33. **by the chisel.** The epitaph was inscribed on the basement of a monumental urn erected in the Wilderness (see note to p. 66, l. 16), where it may still be read.

ll. 34, 35. **requited Romney.** This Cowper did, on his return to Weston, in his "Sonnet to George Romney, Esq., on his Picture of me in crayons, drawn at Eartham in the 61st year of my age, and in the months of August and September, 1792." Cf. note to p. 18, l. 20. Romney, the great rival of Sir Joshua Reynolds, was a friend of Hayley, and was one of the guests invited to meet Cowper at Eartham. The artist considered this portrait as the nearest approach he had ever made to a perfect representation of life and character. It has, however, an "air of wildness in it expressive of a disordered mind."

Page 131, l. 1. the man in the fable. The reference is to an old Greek story of a Rhodian, who, when on his travels, boasted of his jumping powers. Asked to give a specimen of them, he evaded the test by saying that he could leap only at Rhodes.

l. 5. **tardiness of Andrews.** Before Cowper's visit to Eartham, John Johnson had presented him with a stone bust of Homer, for which Andrews (see note to p. 8, l. 3) had been commissioned to make a pedestal. The order was not completed till after nearly a year's delay.

ll. 7, 8. **Mr. Buchanan.** See *Introduction*, p. xlii.

l. 9. **enow** is the old plural form of *enough*, and is so used by Shakspere. Even Byron has "Have I not cares enow and pangs enow?" Tennyson employs it, as being antique, throughout the *Idylls*. It is now used only vulgarly or provincially.

l. 20. **double your debt**, write you two letters in return for your one.

Page 132, l. 7. **James's powder.** Cf. note to p. 39, l. 18.

l. 8. **laudanum.** See note to p. 129, l. 25.

l. 12. **the enemy's**, Satan's, the Devil's. *Satan* in Hebrew means "enemy" or "adversary." Cf. Milton, *Par. Lost*, i. 81:—

"th' Arch-enemy,
And thence in Heaven call'd Satan."

l. 22. **cast.** See note to p. 18, l. 30.

l. 23. **suits my frame of mind.** See *Introduction*, p. xxiv.

l. 24. **wild hills.** Cf. p. 129, l. 6, and note.

l. 34. **use her needles.** Cf. p. 130, l. 27, and note.

Page 133, l. 8. **Homer.** Cowper was now revising his Homer with a view to bringing out a second edition, which was to be annotated (see l. 10 below). Cf. p. 134, l. 24 *et seq.*

l. 13. **Poetry Professor.** Hurdis was at this time candidate for the Professorship of Poetry at Oxford, a post which he subsequently obtained. Cowper writes to him on Nov. 24th, congratulating him on his "victory."

l. 17. **string to my bow**, 'means to exert in your behalf.' The meaning is: 'I have but one way of helping you, and that I will not fail to employ.' The usual phrase is "to have two strings to one's bow," *i.e.* to have a second resource, should one fail.

l. 20. **in the natural way**, relating to Natural History.

l. 28. **somewhat**, something. *Somewhat* is not now used as a pronoun, but only as an adverb.

l. 30. **minnows**, small fishes. The base of *minnow* is *min*, small; cf. Lat. *minutus*, minute.

Page 134, l. 2. **half blown**, half in bloom, half opened.

l. 9. **flower borders**, 'rows of flowers forming the border of a path,' or perhaps merely 'flower-beds.'

l. 11. **Considering**, etc., on looking at it more closely.

l. 12. **spontaneity**, power to move itself as it liked.

l. 13. **distinction of parts.** Its body seemed to have no separate parts or organs.

l. 19. **inflamed eyes.** See note to p. 28, ll. 19, 20; and cf. below, p. 135, l. 29.

l. 22. **speedy.** Used here playfully in the sense of 'quickly written.'

l. 29. **Tom's remarks.** Cowper was so pleased with the talents and sweet disposition of Hayley's son, Tom, that he invited the boy to criticize his Homer. His "remarks" were sent to the poet on March 4th, who altered several of his lines in deference to them.

Page 135, l. 15. **affected me.** See note to p. 5, l. 15.

l. 23. **air**, manner, behaviour.

l. 25. **an apparition**, a ghostly manifestation.

l. 27. **dreams of Pindus**, dreams that come to poets. *Pindus* is a range of mountains in northern Greece, classically celebrated as being sacred to the Muses and Apollo.

l. 29. **Lippus**, Latin for "blear-eyed," "half-blind," in allusion to p. 134, l. 19.

Page 136, ll. 7, 8. **a Tory.** In a previous letter (Feb. 10) Cowper, after calling Lady Hesketh "loyal in the extreme," had said: "I am a Whig, and you, my dear are a Tory, and all the Tories nowadays call all the Whigs Republicans." For Cowper's politics, see notes to p. 6, l. 17; p. 48, ll. 23, 24; and cf. p. 89, ll. 26, 27.

l. 12. **tripartite**, shared between three parties.

ll. 18, 19. **by favour of.** She brought him the book.

ll. 19, 20. **Chapman's translation.** George Chapman (b. 1557, d. 1634), poet and dramatist, published his Translation of the Iliad in 1610-11. It is written in old English ballad metre, and is vigorous and expressive, though frequently marked by carelessness and unfaithfulness. Keats praised it in a well-known sonnet.

l. 26. **information**, *i.e.* his classical knowledge.

Page 137, l. 3. **Hobbes.** Thomas Hobbes (b. 1588, d. 1679), famous as a philosopher and writer on government, published in 1675 a translation of Homer into English verse, which did not add to his reputation.

l. 11. **12mo**, 'a duodecimo,' a book of which the sheets are folded so as to make twelve (Lat. *duodecim*) leaves.

ll. 17, 18. **of course**, naturally, as a natural consequence.

l. 25. **your MSS.** Park had sent Cowper a poem written by himself when he was twenty years of age, with the request that the poet would criticize it.

l. 26. **a poem of my own.** Probably *The Four Ages*; see notes to p. 119, l. 29; p. 120, l. 1.

l. 31. **present.** Her poem of *The Emigrants*, which she had dedicated to Cowper.

Page 138, l. 5. **the waggon.** Cf. p. 44, l. 29; p. 75, l. 21.

l. 6. **that I could ill afford**, that much disappointed me.

l. 12. **whimsical**, 'fanciful.' The adjective is formed from *whimsey*, a derivative of *whim*.

l. 25. **sonnets.** Her *Elegiac Sonnets*, published in 1784.

l. 26. **Monimia and Orlando.** The heroine and the hero of Charlotte Smith's novel of *The Old Manor House*, published in 1793, of which she had sent Cowper a copy. He says "old friends," because she was visiting at Hayley's house when the poet was there, and was then writing this novel, which she would read aloud to the guests.

l. 27. **to interpose**, etc. Quoted from Milton's *Lycidas*, 153, 154, *our* being altered into *my*. The introduction of the extract is explained by the next sentence.

Page 139, l. 18. **Mr. Gregson.** See note to p. 93, l. 19.

l. 19. **the Courtenays.** See *Introduction*, xliii.

l. 20. **my poor birds.** Cf. p. 38, l. 17 *et seq.*; and see *Introduction*, p. xxi.

l. 29. **The country**, etc. Cf. p. 108, l. 7.

Page 140, l. 1. **even under**, etc., even though the view of her that he sees has the drawback of possessing no particular beauty.

l. 4. **an universal blank.** Cf. Milton, *Par. Lost*, iii. 48, 49:—

> "Presented with a universal blank
> Of nature's works, to me expunged and rased."

ll. 4, 5. **different cause**, *i.e.* a cause different from blindness.

l. 13. **It neighbours**, etc., it is situated close to Catfield, and as closely resembles it in its scenery. See note to p. 114, l. 1.

l. 17. **Paradise.** See note to p. 108, l. 7.

l. 21. **We shall meet no more.** They did not meet. Lady Hesketh was now an invalid at Clifton and unable to travel.

l 22. **Johnson**, *i.e.* John Johnson.

INDEX TO THE NOTES.

[The references are to the pages of the book.]

GLASGOW: PRINTED AT THE UNIVERSITY PRESS BY ROBERT MACLEHOSE AND CO.

www.ingramcontent.com/pod-product-compliance
Lightning Source LLC
Chambersburg PA
CBHW030341270326
41926CB00009B/920

* 9 7 8 3 7 4 4 7 1 0 8 9 3 *